Baja California

A guide to points of interest, tourist facilities and recreational opportunities along major highways and side routes in Baja California, plus detailed information on lodging, restaurants, and campgrounds and trailer parks.

Automobile Club of Southern California

D1534528

Cover Photo:
Cañon San Pablo in the rugged northeastern corner of Baja California Sur,
by Chuck O'Rear/West Light

Writers	R. Clark Hunter and George Yago III
Graphic Artist	Barbara Stanfield
Cartographer	Edward F. Davis
Editor	Kristine Miller

ISBN: 1-56413-261-7
Printed in the United States of America
Copyright © 1995 by Automobile Club of Southern California
Travel Publications Department
2601 South Figueroa Street, Los Angeles, California 90007

Table of Contents

Baja California Norte

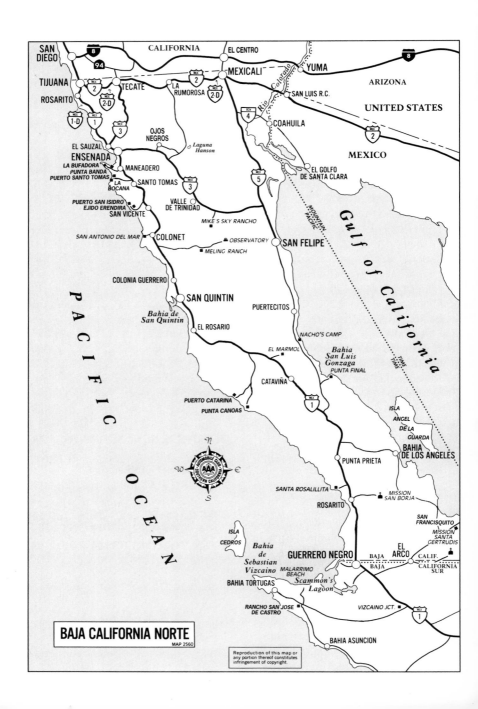

Baja California Sur

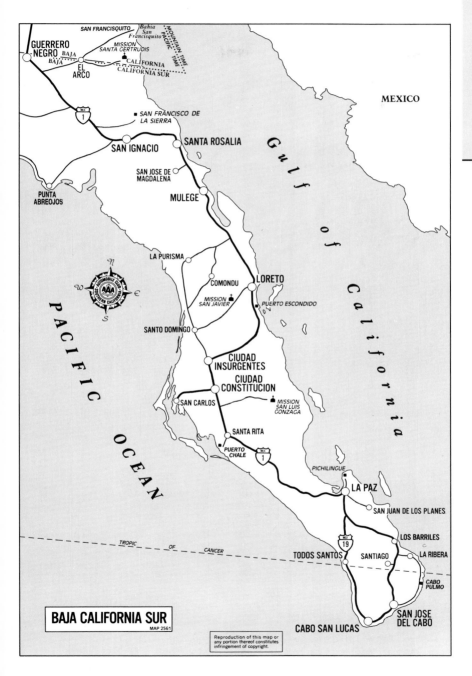

Bill Cory

Mexico Highway 1 crosses the path of the old highway in the Sierra de la Giganta just south of Puerto Escondido. In the background is the Gulf of California.

Introduction

Baja California! To many people, its very name carries an exotic connotation of ruggedness and adventure. Despite the long-standing popularity of its border towns and the fly-in fishing resorts near its southern tip, this 800-mile-long arid peninsula remained virtually unknown until recently. Geographically separated from the Mexican mainland and an insurmountable barrier to all but the hardiest overland travelers, the interior of Baja California resisted the large-scale intrusions of man for centuries.

But the peninsula's days of isolation are over. The completion of the paved Transpeninsular Highway (Mexico Highway 1) in late 1973 marked the beginning of a new era for Baja California. Once-remote regions are now being drawn into the mainstream of Mexico's rapid economic development, and population is increasing steadily. A ferry network and a microwave telephone system, along with the paved highway extending the entire length of the peninsula, have established new and effective lines of communication. An increasing number of tourists have been wandering past the border towns, discovering for themselves the distinctive charms of Baja California: rugged desert and mountain landscapes, the deep blue waters of the Pacific and the Gulf of California, unique vegetation, Spanish missions, winter sunshine, lush palm oases, unspoiled beaches, remarkably good sportfishing and friendly people.

With the completion of Highway 1, regular airline service, and the accompanying proliferation of new hotels, trailer parks and other tourist facilities, Baja California has become an accessible vacation destination for the average traveling family. At the same time, most of the peninsula has retained its essentially wild character, making it a continuing challenge for the avid off-road adventurer.

The key to an enjoyable, rewarding Baja California vacation is careful preparation. Baja California is a comprehensive guidebook designed to acquaint you with the peninsula's many attractions, as well as its major highways and interesting side routes. It includes important information on travel conditions and regulations for tourists, where to stay and eat, and a variety of other pertinent subjects. You will find it to be both a valuable trip-planning aid and a helpful day-to-day companion during your visit to Baja California. In addition, the Automobile Club of Southern California publishes a companion publication—the large, colorful *Baja California* map. Both should be used by those planning to visit the peninsula.

ROUTE DESCRIPTIONS

Detailed descriptions of Baja California's major highways are covered in several chapters in this book. The first and longest of these concentrates on *Mexico Highway 1,* a paved route extending from the U.S. border at Tijuana to Cabo San Lucas at the tip of the peninsula. The second chapter covers *Mexico Highway 5,* which runs along the Gulf of California coast from Mexicali to Bahía San Luis Gonzaga; it is paved beyond San Felipe to Puertecitos. The third chapter, entitled *Connecting Routes,* includes Mexico Highways 2 and 3—both of which connect Highway 1 with Highway 5 in northern Baja California—and Mexico Highway 19, the paved route along the Pacific coast in the extreme southern portion of the peninsula. A fourth chapter examines many of the most interesting and popular *Side Routes* branching off major highways. This chapter does not contain mileage logs, but important junctions and other intermediate mileages are noted within the text of each side route description. While some of these side trips can be made in a passenger car, many are bona fide off-road adventures best suited to experienced travelers in special-duty vehicles.

These route descriptions are divided into convenient sections, each of which is treated individually. Each begins with a paragraph outlining the terrain, the route and general driving conditions, followed by a detailed mileage log that lists important landmarks and junctions, roadside facilities and points of interest. Although the mileages were compiled with highly accurate survey odometers, you should keep in mind that instruments can vary, and the mileages you experience may not agree exactly with those contained in the logs. Driving times were computed under average driving conditions and are rounded off to the nearest quarter hour. The route descriptions also feature maps and special sections on Baja California's major cities and towns.

In the route descriptions, towns that contain stores and facilities useful to the traveler are shown in heavy black print.

For quick reference, key places and roads connecting them are shown on the maps on pages 6 and 7. Heavy lines indicate Mexico Highways 1, 2, 3, 5 and 19; lighter lines denote side routes. A detailed index of all place names begins on page 219.

GEOGRAPHY

Baja California is a very elongated, irregularly shaped peninsula that extends about 800 miles south-eastward from the Mexico-United States border. (Traveling the irregular path of Highway 1, which dodges the rugged mountains, is a trip of about 1000 miles.) Varying in width from 30 to 145 miles, it is separated from the Mexican mainland to the east by the Colorado River and the Gulf of California (also known as the Sea of Cortez), while on the west it is bounded by the Pacific Ocean. Both coastlines are indented by numerous bays and coves, and many barren islands lie offshore. The backbone of the peninsula comprises a series of mountain ranges—notably the Sierra de Juárez, just below the U.S. border; the Sierra San Pedro Mártir, farther south; the Sierra de la Giganta, along the southern gulf coast; and the Sierra de la Laguna, in the extreme south. The highest point is 10,154-foot Picacho del Diablo, located in the rugged

Sierra San Pedro Mártir between Meling Ranch and San Felipe.

The topography of northern Baja California is similar to that of nearby Southern California. Most of Baja is classified as desert, but sharp regional differences exist. Chaparral-covered hills rise abruptly from the seashore; they are dissected by numerous canyons and valleys. The northern mountains resemble California's Sierra Nevada in that they have gradual progressions of foothills on the west and steep eastern escarpments. The Mexicali Valley is part of a great rift that is a continuation of the Imperial Valley. South of the Colorado River Delta, this depression is submerged beneath the Gulf of California.

East of the mountains is an arid desert with scant plant life; some areas are almost devoid of vegetation. In contrast is the Mexicali Valley, where irrigated farmlands flourish on the rich alluvial soil deposited over the centuries by the Colorado River.

Central Baja California, which extends from El Rosario to La Paz, is a true desert. The topography of the central desert is characterized by barren mountains separated by rocky valleys and sandy plains. Abrupt slopes rise from the shore of the Gulf of California, while the Pacific side of the peninsula is less rugged. Two major lowlands, both near the Pacific coast, contrast with the sharply contoured landscape of much of the central desert. The Vizcaíno Desert near Guerrero Negro is a vast, sandy plain with little natural vegetation except saltbrush and scattered yucca válida. The Santo Domingo Valley (Magdalena Plain), farther south, is an important agricultural region, of which Ciudad Constitución is the center. Beginning near San Ignacio and spreading southward for more than 100 miles are extensive lava flows, which indicate fairly recent volcanic activity. Las Tres Vírgenes, three impressive volcanoes, sit side by side along Highway 1 near San Ignacio, and the

Tom Dell

Forest-rimmed Laguna Hansen is in the Sierra de Juárez (see Side Routes).

Sierra de la Giganta, a jagged range extending from Santa Rosalía almost to La Paz, is also of volcanic origin.

The southern portion of the peninsula, from La Paz to Cabo San Lucas, lies within the tropics. It is part desert and part semiarid. The region south of La Paz is dominated by the Sierra de la Laguna, which slopes downward from its 7000-foot crown toward both coasts.

CLIMATE

The climate of northern Baja California is similar to Southern California. The semiarid coastal zone, from Tijuana to San Quintín, is mild, with summer highs in the 70s and 80s (Fahrenheit); temperatures rise a short distance inland. Winter temperatures are in the 60s during the day and the 40s at night. Fog is common during late spring and early summer. Most rainfall occurs during the winter and the total rainfall varies greatly from year to year. The average winter has more sunny days than cloudy days.

Depending on their elevation and the direction they face, the inland hills and mountains receive sporadically heavy rains and occasional snow. In the rain shadow east of the mountains, including the Mexicali Valley and the Gulf of California coast, is an arid landscape, often called the Sonoran Desert. It is characterized by mild, sunny winters and intensely hot summers, whose high temperatures may reach 110 to 120 degrees. Average rainfall is scant, about 3 inches.

The Central Desert of Baja California extends from about El Rosario in the north to Ciudad Constitución in the south; it merges with the Sonoran Desert along the gulf. Rainfall is very irregular, as violent thunderstorms may bring several inches, or a year may pass with hardly a drop of moisture. Winter temperatures are mild and pleasant; the air is clear and the sunshine is brilliant. The Pacific coast section remains mild in summer as far south as the Vizcaíno Peninsula, but the rest of the Central Desert has oppressive summer heat. The hot, dry air of interior places like San Ignacio is easier to bear than the often humid air of coastal locations such as Loreto.

The southern portion of the peninsula, from Bahía Magdalena to Cabo San Lucas, lies within the tropics. It is part tropical desert and part tropical semiarid, but it receives occasionally heavy rainfall as a result of tropical storms between August and early November. Every several years, southern Baja California is ravaged by a hurricane (on rare occasions hurricanes move to the northern coast of the gulf). Occurring more frequently are severe squalls, called chubascos. Rainfall in La Paz averages 6 inches per year, San Antonio 16 inches. The most pleasant weather occurs from November to May, with highs in the 80s and lows in the 50s. Rain is rare during these months. Summers are quite hot, with highs from 100 to 110 degrees, except on the Pacific coast, which is a little cooler.

VEGETATION

The unusual vegetation types of Baja California are directly related to its climates. The semiarid northwest corner, including the Pacific Coast, has wild grasses, chaparral brush and scattered oaks, as in neighboring Southern California. In the towns, palms and other subtropical trees have been planted. Wildflowers are visible along the rural roads in the springtime. Unlike most of the peninsula, the northern mountains have forests of pine and fir blanketing the upper slopes.

BAJA CALIFORNIA CLIMATE CHART

	January Temp.*	January Rainfall	February Temp.	February Rainfall	March Temp.	March Rainfall	April Temp.	April Rainfall	May Temp.	May Rainfall	June Temp.	June Rainfall	July Temp.	July Rainfall	August Temp.	August Rainfall	September Temp.	September Rainfall	October Temp.	October Rainfall	November Temp.	November Rainfall	December Temp.	December Rainfall	Total Annual Rainfall
Cabo San Lucas . . .	64	—	66	—	68	—	70	—	73	—	79	—	81	0.4	82	1.6	81	2.5	79	1.2	72	1.2	68	0.8	7.7
Ciudad Constitution.	59	0.5	61	0.1	63	—	66	—	70	—	73	—	80	0.5	82	1.4	80	1.2	75	0.3	70	0.2	63	0.6	4.8
Colonia Guerrero . .	54	1.5	55	1.6	57	2.0	58	0.5	59	0.2	63	—	66	—	68	0.4	68	0.4	63	0.8	57	1.2	55	1.4	10.0
El Rosario	57	1.0	61	1.0	63	0.8	63	0.2	64	—	70	—	75	—	75	1.0	73	0.2	70	0.8	64	0.8	61	1.1	6.1
Ensenada	54	2.3	55	2.3	59	1.9	59	0.6	63	0.2	64	—	68	—	70	—	68	—	63	0.2	61	0.6	57	2.1	10.2
La Paz	63	0.4	63	—	64	—	70	—	73	—	81	—	82	0.2	84	1.2	82	2.4	77	0.8	70	0.8	63	0.4	6.2
Loreto	61	0.4	63	—	66	—	68	—	73	—	81	—	86	0.4	88	1.6	84	2.4	81	0.4	70	—	63	0.4	5.6
Mexicali	54	0.4	59	0.4	63	0.4	68	0.2	75	—	86	—	91	—	90	0.3	81	0.3	73	0.5	61	0.2	54	0.4	3.1
San Felipe	55	0.4	57	—	61	—	66	—	73	0.4	79	—	81	—	82	0.4	79	0.6	70	0.6	63	—	57	0.4	2.8
San Ignacio	57	0.4	61	0.4	63	0.4	64	—	72	—	75	0.4	81	0.4	82	0.4	79	0.8	73	0.4	64	0.4	57	0.4	4.4
San Vicente	54	2.4	55	2.4	55	1.9	57	0.2	63	—	68	—	72	—	73	—	70	0.1	64	0.1	59	0.7	57	2.1	9.9
Tecate	50	2.4	52	2	53	2	55	0.4	59	0.3	66	—	72	—	72	—	70	—	64	0.2	57	1	52	1.9	10.2
Tijuana	55	2	57	2.4	59	2	61	0.4	66	—	68	—	73	—	73	—	72	—	66	0.4	63	1.2	57	1.8	10.2

*Temperatures are expressed in degrees Fahrenheit · Rainfall in inches. Figures represent official monthly averages.

Plants of Baja California

Yucca válida

Cirios

Cholla cactus

Cardón cactus

Photos by Tom Dell

In sharp contrast is the very arid Sonoran Desert east of the mountains. The natural vegetation generally consists of various low shrubs, along with smatterings of cardón cacti, ocotillo and mesquite; some areas are almost devoid of vegetation. A different landscape is found in the Mexicali Valley, where irrigated farmlands of cotton and grains flourish on the rich alluvial soil deposited by the Colorado River.

The Central Desert of Baja California has unique vegetation well adapted for survival in its harsh environment. Because of its geographical isolation, the Central Desert is home to many plant varieties that grow naturally nowhere else on earth. They include the giant cardón cactus, which resembles the saguaro of Arizona and Sonora; and the yucca válida, a smaller cousin of California's Joshua tree. The strange cirio, a tall, columnar botanical oddity, grows only in Baja California and Sonora. Other species, such as agave, cholla and barrel cactus, fan palm, ocotillo, palo verde, pitahaya (organ pipe) cactus and elephant tree, with its short, fat trunk, also have relatives in the southwestern United States. Date palms are found in scattered cases, but they are not native to the peninsula; most were planted by Jesuit missionaries during Baja California's colonial era. Along both coasts are dense thickets of mangrove—a common plant of the tropics.

Two major lowlands of the central desert, both near the Pacific coast, offer contrasting vegetation. The Vizcaíno Desert near Guerrero Negro is a vast, sandy plain with little natural vegetation except saltbrush and scattered yucca válida. The Santo Domingo Valley, farther south, is an important agricultural region, growing wheat, garbanzo and sorghum.

The vegetation of the southern portion of the peninsula reflect somewhat higher rainfall. Botanists classify the natural vegetation here as tropical desert and tropical thorn forest, consisting of thick stands of cardón, pitahaya, cholla and other cacti, along with numerous small trees and thorny shrubs. Higher elevations in the Sierra de la Laguna contain some subtropical forest. Cultivated plants in and near the towns are various tropical fruit trees, stately palms and bougainvillea with brilliant blooms of red or purple.

Most of Baja's desert lands produce a rich variety of flora, considering the low precipitation. This is due to good soils, lack of frost and the occurrence of rainfall at different seasons of the year. Plants bloom at irregular times, following the occasional rains. On the average, however, wildflowers in the northern desert appear in the spring, and in the southern desert in the autumn.

FAUNA

Baja California's wildlife is as diverse as the terrain. Each animal seeks out its preferred environment, be it chaparral, desert, mountains, canyons, valleys, seashore, or any combination of these. The land mammals include mountain lions, big horn sheep, deer, wild boar (peccary), and many other smaller animals. Also seen on the Baja peninsula are a wide assortment of birds and reptiles. These include eagles, hawks and vultures in the bird family, and rattlesnakes, sidewinders and lizards in the reptile family.

Many of the world's larger marine mammals may also be seen visiting the coastline of Baja California. These include harbor seals, sea lions, porpoises, Minke whales, humpback whales and gray whales. The gray whale makes a yearly migration from northern waters, along the North American coastline to the area around Guerrero Negro, in order to bear their young in the warm waters of the region. They can be viewed from January through March.

ECONOMY

For many years Baja California's economic base reflected its population centers, which were in the extreme northern and the southern sections of the peninsula.

Because of their proximity to the United States, the cities of Tijuana, Ensenada and Mexicali are the hubs of economic development in northern Baja California. Tijuana produces a variety of goods, including electronic components, clothing and auto parts. Mexicali is in the peninsula's most important agricultural region and has light manufacturing. Ensenada is a busy seaport known for its fish canneries. In addition, Tecate produces beer.

INTRODUCTION

In the south, La Paz processes and ships farm products, and Ciudad Constitución has become a farm processing center. The most important industry of central Baja California is the salt-producing operation at Guerrero Negro. Tourism, however, remains Baja California's leading money maker.

Millions of tourists each year flock to the border towns and coastal resorts. While the Pacific coast is the focus of resort activity and tourism in the far north, the Gulf of California coast contains the most popular travel destinations south of Ensenada. La Paz and Los Cabos boast the plushest, best-known resorts, but San Felipe, Bahía de los Angeles, Mulegé and Loreto also draw thousands of visitors every year. Fishing is the number one lure here, but beautiful beaches and abundant year-round sunshine are also responsible for attracting tourists to the shores of the gulf.

Most of the central desert was sparsely inhabited until the 1960s, when agricultural development and tourism started to bring rapid growth to parts of this area.

Mexico's economic fluctuations have had relatively little impact on Baja California's economy, which has grown steadily over the past couple of decades.

SHOPPING

All of Baja is a duty-free zone, so shopping is popular with tourists. Stores offer substantial savings under U.S. prices on such imported merchandise as perfumes, jewelry, art objects, cosmetics and textiles. Careful shoppers can also find good buys on Mexican-made articles. Besides the inexpensive souvenirs manufactured locally for the tourist trade, shops offer high-quality pottery, ceramics, guitars, blown glass, wrought-iron furniture, baskets, silver and leather goods, sweaters, blankets, jewelry and works of Mexican art.

Cities most oriented to foreign shoppers include Cabo San Lucas, Ensenada, La Paz, Loreto, Mexicali, Rosarito, San José del Cabo and Tijuana. Shops in other communities cater primarily to the local population.

U.S. residents may bring back, duty-free, articles not exceeding $400 in retail value, providing they are for personal use and accompany the individual. For more information, refer to the *Tourist Regulations and Travel Tips* chapter, U.S. Customs Regulations section. U.S. Customs offices at border crossings have a number of pamphlets detailing regulations regarding the import of items purchased in Mexico.■

Tourist Regulations and Travel Tips

A safe and enjoyable journey through Baja California will be greatly enhanced by knowing some of the basics of Mexican law and by understanding the day-to-day culture of Mexico. This knowledge will make it easier to interact with the Mexican people and authorities, as well as help to plan your trip to Baja California. The information in this chapter is designed to help make you a veteran Baja traveler.

Motorists can enter or leave Mexico at any of five points along the California-Baja California border: Tijuana (two places), Tecate, Algodones and Mexicali. There are two ports of entry at Tijuana. The one opposite San Ysidro, California, is open 24 hours. The other Tijuana crossing is at Otay Mesa, 5½ miles to the east, and it is open 6 a.m. to 10 p.m. Tecate is open daily from 6 a.m. to midnight. Algodones is open daily from 6 a.m. to 8 p.m. The crossing at Mexicali is open 24 hours.

TOURIST REGULATIONS
Entering Mexico
Mexican Tourist Cards

U.S. and Canadian citizens who visit the immediate border zone or the city of Ensenada can do so without having to obtain a tourist card, provided the length of the stay does not exceed 72 hours. For travel beyond Maneadero on the Pacific coast or south of Mexicali on Highway 5, a tourist card is officially required for each individual visitor, regardless of age. It is advisable to carry proof of citizenship even when traveling where tourist cards are not required.

Mexico issues two types of tourist cards (tourist entry forms); both are free. The single-entry card is valid for up to 180 days; the exact length of its term is determined by the Mexican immigration official who validates the card. The second kind of tourist card, the multiple-entry card, permits unlimited entry into Mexico for a 180-day period; two front-view photographs are required. If a tourist card is not used within 90 days of its issue date, it becomes void. A tourist who overstays the time limit is subject to a fine. **Note:** It is important to have tourist cards validated at the point of entry because opportunities to do so elsewhere in Baja California are limited.

Tourist cards can be obtained in the United States from Mexican consulates or the Mexican Government Tourism Office. In California,

Mexican consulates are located in Calexico, Fresno, Los Angeles, Oxnard, Sacramento, San Bernardino, San Diego, San Francisco, San Jose and Santa Ana. The Mexican Government Tourism Office is in Century City, phone (310) 203-8191. Sometimes, offices of the Automobile Club of Southern California and the California State Automobile Association receive supplies of tourist cards from the Mexican government (these offices also distribute a detailed brochure about tourist cards and car permits). Airlines and travel agencies often provide tourist cards for their clients as well. They can also be obtained at the border from Mexican immigration authorities, but it is recommended that travelers acquire their tourist cards prior to leaving the United States.

Travelers obtaining a tourist card must fill in the necessary information and must have either a valid (current) passport or a birth certificate. Birth certificates must be certified and issued by the federal, state, county or city government where the person was born. Naturalized U.S. citizens must present a valid passport, a Certificate of Naturalization, or a Certificate of Citizenship issued by the U.S. Immigration and Naturalization Service; wallet-sized naturalization cards (form I-179) or other documents cannot be accepted. Citizens of Canada are required to have a valid passport or birth certificate. U.S. residents who are citizens of other nations must have a resident alien card and a passport. The original document presented as proof of citizenship must be carried into Mexico with the tourist card. Photocopies are not acceptable.

The tourist card must be certified by a Mexican immigration/customs official at the port of entry. Due to congestion at the Tijuana border crossing, it is easier to have the card certified at the Ensenada Immigration office, located at the entrance to the city on Boulevard Azueta, just before the corner of Boulevard Lázaro Cárdenas. The office bears the sign Servicios Migratorios.

Minors—In addition to a tourist card, any minor (under 18 years) who plans to enter Mexico without both parents must also have a completed and notarized copy of the form "Permission for a Minor to Travel in Mexico," available at the Mexican Government Tourist Office. Sample forms can be obtained at any office of the Automobile Club of Southern California. According to Mexican officials, this is the only document that will be honored, and it should be presented when applying for a tourist card. If a child's parents are divorced or separated, the signed form must be accompanied by the divorce or separation papers. If one parent is deceased, the death certificate must accompany the form in lieu of the deceased's signature; the surviving parent must still sign the form. If a child is under legal guardianship, the guardian(s) must sign the form and provide guardianship papers and, when applicable, death certificates for both parents.

Business Trips—U.S. citizens who desire to transact business of any kind in Mexico must obtain a business form by applying personally at a Mexican consulate. A 30-day form is free. For a one-year form the business traveler needs to show a passport and pay a fee that ranges from $73 to $119. Any person traveling on business with only a tourist card is subject to a fine.

Automobile Requirements

The Mexican Government Tourism Office, phone (310) 203-8191, distributes a free bilingual booklet, *Traveling to Mexico by Car,* with detailed explanations about car permits and tourist cards. Another source of information is the Mexican Treasury Department, phone (800) 446-8277.

It is illegal for a foreign citizen to sell a motor vehicle in Mexico.

Car Permits—Car permits, or Temporary Vehicle Import Permits, are not required in Baja California **except** for vehicles being shipped to mainland Mexico aboard Baja California ferries. Motorists must, however, carry acceptable proof of vehicle ownership and a valid driver's license. In mainland Mexico a car permit and tourist card are required for the principal driver; passengers and alternate drivers need only the standard tourist card. (In Sonora, these documents are not necessary in San Luis and El Golfo de Santa Clara; they are needed when traveling on Mexico Highway 2 beyond Sonoíta.)

Car permits are issued at all points of entry into mainland Mexico. Both tourist cards and car permits are available in the same building or in nearby buildings. (Because of congestion at the Tijuana crossing, it is easier to obtain these documents at another point of entry.) Car permits are also available at Baja California ferry ports. The permits are free and valid for up to 180 days. Information sheets and application forms for car permits are available at any office of the Automobile Club of Southern California or the California State Automobile Association.

To acquire a car permit, motorists are required to have proof of U.S. citizenship (see the Mexican Tourist Cards section for acceptable documents), as well as the **original** current registration or a notarized bill of sale for each vehicle, including motorcycles. Although it is not officially recognized as proof of ownership, the vehicle's ownership certificate (also called vehi-

cle title or, in California, pink slip) should be carried. Motorists whose vehicles are being purchased under finance contracts must obtain written notarized permission from the lien holder (bank, finance company, credit union, etc.) authorizing the applicant to take the vehicle into Mexico. No person may drive a vehicle owned by another person into mainland Mexico **unless the owner is present.** Individuals driving a vehicle registered in the name of the company for which they work must carry a **notarized affidavit of authorization.** Offenders are subject to confiscation of the vehicle or a heavy fine. The original and two photocopies of the driver's license and vehicle registration must be presented.

Only one car permit can be issued per person. For example, one person may not enter mainland Mexico or board a ferry in Baja California with both a motorhome and a motorcycle, even if he or she owns both vehicles. One of the vehicles must be registered to another person in the party, or a second person could obtain a car permit for the extra vehicle by using a notarized affidavit of permission from the owner. Under no circumstances can more permits be obtained than there are qualified drivers (18 years or older) in the party.

Crossing into the Mainland—A recent Mexican regulation, established in order to prevent theft or smuggling, calls for an additional procedure for visiting motorists who enter the mainland of Mexico or cross by ferry from Baja California to the mainland. The visitor must present a credit card—American Express, Diners Club, MasterCard, or VISA—along with a non-refundable fee of $11. The fee is paid to Banco del Ejercito, which has offices at all border crossings (at the Mexicali crossing, customs and the bank offices are open 24 hours). The motorist signs a declaration promising to return the vehicle to the United States. Failure to pay the fee with a credit card necessitates posting a bond (*fianza*), a more costly procedure with much paperwork.

Upon returning to the border the motorist gives back all documents to Mexican Customs. It is imperative to surrender all Mexican Government travel documents. Motorists failing to do so must return with them to the border. Otherwise, a large fine will be charged upon the next entry into Mexico.

Insurance—Mexican authorities recognize only insurance policies issued by companies licensed to transact insurance in the Republic of Mexico. Accordingly, motorists preparing to enter Mexico are strongly advised to purchase a separate policy issued through a Mexican-licensed company.

Mexican law differs from that in the United States. Persons involved in traffic accidents who cannot produce an acceptable policy may be held by the authorities regardless of the seriousness or type of accident, pending investigation. *Therefore, to be adequately protected, buy Mexican automobile insurance before crossing the border into Mexico.* **Note:** *in the event of an accident, a report should be filed with your Mexican insurance company before returning to the United States.*

AAA members may obtain this coverage at any office of the Automobile Club of Southern California. Policies are written by the day, with a discount for more than 30 days' coverage, and are issued immediately upon application. The member should call a touring representative in an Automobile Club district office to determine what specifications (vehicle ID number, accessories included on the vehicle, etc.) are needed so that the insurance policy may be accurately written. Low-cost automobile insurance providing one-day coverage within the city limits of Tijuana or Mexicali may be offered for sale in these border cities. Because such policies do not provide coverage for medical payments or for the driver's person and property, the Auto Club recommends that motorists purchase Mexican automobile insurance which provides more comprehensive protection.

The Auto Club also provides information on other travel insurance. A comprehensive travel plan is available which affords medical coverage, includes non-refundable travel expenses in the event of delay or cancellation, and insures baggage and personal possessions. Also included is air-passenger insurance, which covers scheduled or charter flights.

Other Requirements

If you plan to take a lot of expensive foreign-made items such as cameras, binoculars, etc., into Mexico, it is wise to register these articles with U.S. Customs before crossing the border, unless you possess the original purchase receipts. This will avoid any question that they were purchased in Mexico, in which case duties would be assessed. Only articles having manufacturers' serial numbers may be registered.

Baggage—Occasionally, baggage is inspected in Baja California at police or military roadblocks (see Highway Travel section in this chapter).

Cameras—Tourists may take one still camera and one motion picture camera (8 mm or 16 mm) or video recording camera and a total of 12 rolls of

Grupo Nacional Provincial S.A.

FOR COMPLETE ONE DAY TO ONE YEAR COVERAGES IN MEXICO

CAR ... BOAT ... TRAILER ...

Serving AAA Members or over 46 years.

Grupo Nacional Provincial has a country-wide network of service offices and adjusters, meaning prompt service and quick claim adjustments.

Grupo Nacional Provincial

film or videocassettes. Photography must not, however, be for commercial purposes. Tripods are allowed in most areas, but a special permit is required for their use in historic sites.

Citizens Band Radios—Mexico has legalized the use of citizens-band radios by tourists, and three channels— 9, 10 and 11—have been designated for visitors' use. Channel 9 is for emergencies; Channel 10 can be used for communications among tourists; Channel 11 is reserved for localization (directions and information). Permits are no longer required for CB radios. Any linear amplifier or other device that increases the transmission power to over five watts is prohibited.

Firearms—Guns are not permitted in Mexico except when brought into the country during hunting season for the express purpose of hunting and when accompanied by the appropriate documents (see Hunting in *Recreation*).

Pets—It is advisable to leave dogs and other pets at home because of special inspections, health certificates and the possible refusal of hotel operators to allow pets in their establishments. If an animal is taken into Mexico, it must have both a veterinarian's vaccination certificate for rabies and the Official Interstate and International Health Certificate for Dogs and Cats (form 77-043). If the pet is out of the United States for over 30 days, its owner must present the rabies certificate when returning to the United States.

Trailers—A trailer measuring more than 8 feet in width and 40 feet in length requires a special permit, obtainable only in Tijuana at the Federal Highway Police Road Office. Permits are issued at the discretion of the officials, since road conditions in much of

Baja California make trailer travel prohibitive.

RETURNING TO THE UNITED STATES

The proof of citizenship presented to obtain a tourist card should be carried along on the trip. It may be necessary to show this document to U.S. officials upon reentering the United States.

U.S. Customs Regulations

Each returning U.S. resident may bring back, duty-free, articles not exceeding $400 in retail value, providing they are for personal use and accompany the individual. This $400 exemption may be used only once in a 30-day period. Tourists returning from Mexico need not be absent from the United States for any minimum time to qualify for this exemption. U.S. Customs offices at border crossings have a number of pamphlets detailing these regulations. They also have information for the business traveler and persons returning with specialized products.

While away, tourists may send gifts not exceeding $50 in fair retail value to persons in the United States without payment of duty and taxes. As many gifts may be sent as desired, provided the total value of gift packages or shipments received by one person in one day does not exceed $50. The words "Unsolicited Gifts" and the value in large letters should be written on the outside of the package. Alcoholic beverages and tobacco products are not included in the privilege, nor are perfumes valued at more than $5. These bona fide gifts need not be included on the customs declaration nor within the customs exemption of returning travelers. Gifts accompanying a resident at the time of his or her return must be declared and included within an exemption.

Bringing certain agricultural products across the border is prohibited, including fresh fruits and vegetables, meats and poultry. One liter of liquor per adult (21 years and older) is allowed.

An increasing number of Americans are purchasing medications in Mexico for personal use. They may be brought in legally if the following regulations are observed. The medications must be declared to the U.S. Customs agent at the border. They have to be approved by the Food and Drug Administration for use in the United States. A written prescription from the physician must accompany the medication. The quantity is limited to a three-month personal supply.

TRAVEL TIPS
Currency

In 1993, Mexico adopted a new system of currency, sometimes known as *nuevos pesos*. The former currency, due to years of inflation, had denominations that numbered 1000 times the present coins and bills. Astronomical prices resulted. Under the new system, 100 centavos equal 1 peso. Coins come in denominations of 5, 10, 20 and 50 centavos and 1, 2, 5 and 10 pesos. Bills also come in 10 pesos and run in denominations of 20, 50, 100, 200 pesos, etc.

At the time of publication the exchange rate between Mexican and American currency was about 5.9 pesos to the dollar, an individual peso worth about 17¢, but the exact value of the peso fluctuates slightly from week to week. In any case, travelers should expect rates to deviate depending on the time and place of a transaction. *Mexico uses the same symbol*

($) to denote pesos as the United States uses for dollars.

Although most Mexican Government agencies and many business establishments quote prices in pesos, U.S. dollars are readily accepted in tourist areas of Baja California. **Prices contained in this publication are listed in dollar equivalents as they were quoted at press time.** In the border cities, prices in Mexican money frequently carry the abbreviation "m.n." (*moneda nacional*) and prices in American money, "dlls." (*dollars*).

Members traveling beyond the immediate border zone are strongly urged to convert at least some of their funds into Mexican pesos. While U.S. dollars have become commonly used at tourist-oriented businesses and in resort areas, they are frequently not accepted in locations distant from the border or away from major tourist destinations. Since travelers usually lose money each time they exchange currencies, a good rule to follow is this: if you pay in pesos, try to receive change in pesos; if you pay in dollars, attempt to receive your change in dollars.

With exchange rates in flux it is especially important to obtain a clear understanding about prices, whether in dollars or pesos, before making a purchase or agreeing to a service. Sales tax in Baja California (both states) is 10 percent. Usually included in the base price of goods and services, it occasionally appears added to the bill. In Mexico, U.S. currency can be converted into pesos at some banks, which usually give the best exchange rates. Certain currency exchange firms on both sides of the border also offer good rates. All large towns in Baja California have banks, but business hours are slightly different from those of their U.S. counterparts: Monday through Friday most open at about 9 a.m., close between noon and 2 p.m. and reopen from 4 to 6 p.m.; they are closed on all Mexican holidays. Some banks will send and accept wired funds. Arrangements should be made through the bank and the local telegraph office.

Traveler's checks are accepted at most hotels and large tourist restaurants and can be cashed at Mexican banks, but they are not accepted at gasoline stations and most stores and restaurants. American credit cards—American Express, MasterCard, VISA and occasionally Diners Club—are accepted at some tourist establishments in Tijuana, Ensenada, Mexicali, La Paz and Los Cabos. They are not accepted in most of Baja California. Since business establishments in Baja California's more remote areas frequently keep very little cash on hand, smaller denomination traveler's checks and currency are more readily accepted. It is wise to have enough cash to cover several days' needs.

Facilities and Services

While it is generally advisable for travelers to bring everything they need into Mexico from the United States, Baja California does have facilities for those who need to obtain or replenish supplies. Most communities have small markets or general stores offering a limited selection of merchandise. Only in major cities and towns can travelers expect to find such items as clothing, pharmaceuticals, sporting goods, hardware and fuel for camp stoves. U.S.-style supermarkets are located in Tijuana, Rosarito, Mexicali, Tecate, Ensenada, Loreto, Ciudad Constitución, La Paz and Cabo San Lucas; prices average about the same as those in the United States.

Although the large cities and popular resorts in Baja California offer fine accommodations and many tourist facilities, smaller Mexican communities are distinctly different from their U.S. counterparts. Some have very few retail businesses and lack accommodations, restaurants, public restrooms, telephones and auto repair facilities. In emergencies, however, townspeople are usually pleased to help travelers in any way they can.

Postal service extends throughout Baja California, but letters can take two or three weeks in transit—even when mailed from a town with scheduled air service. Telephone and telegraph terminals are now located in all towns on the peninsula; microwave telephone service is operational between San Ignacio and Cabo San Lucas, and northern Baja California has telephone lines that connect with those of the United States. In cases of emergency, travelers can send messages via government radio, which has terminals in most of the peninsula's communities.

Telephone numbers printed in this book include the international code 01152, the city code of two or three digits (shown in parentheses), and the local number of five or six digits. For local calls in Baja California you need to use only the five or six digits; these shortened numbers appear in all local advertisements and telephone directories. For example, the state tourism office in Ensenada has the local number 2-3000, which you use in that vicinity. To call from the United States, dial 01152 (617) 2-3000 (do not dial "1" before 01152).

Public telephones in Mexico are few in number, except in the larger cities, but they are low-priced, requiring only one small coin.

Time Zones

The northern state of Baja California observes Pacific Standard Time from the last Sunday in October to the first Sunday in April and Pacific Daylight Time during the rest of the year; in other words, it is always on the same time as the state of California. Baja California Sur—the southern state—observes Mountain Standard Time all year. Its clocks are one hour ahead of California's during the winter season but identical during the summer.

Holidays

A number of major holidays are observed in Mexico. In addition, smaller communities may observe some church feast days.

January 1	New Year's Day
February 24	Flag Day
March 21	Benito Juarez' Birthday
March-April	Palm Sunday Easter Sunday
May 1	Labor Day
May 5	Cinco de Mayo
September 15-16	Independence Day
October 12	Dia de la Raza
November 1	Presidential State of the Nation Address
November 20	Revolution Day
December 12	Feast of the Virgin of Guadalupe
December 25	Navidad

Language

Many Baja Californians speak at least some English—especially in the areas most frequented by tourists. Outside these areas, however, the number of bilingual residents decreases significantly. Very few gasoline stations beyond Ensenada have English-speaking employees; neither do most shops, stores, cafes, or even some hotels, trailer parks and government agencies. Some knowledge of Spanish is certainly helpful to the traveler. The tourist armed with a good English-Spanish dictionary, a basic Spanish phrase book and a little patience will do quite well in Baja California. Included in this guidebook's *Appendix* is a section entitled "Speaking of Spanish," which contains useful Spanish words, phrases and sentences, as well as a simple pronunciation guide. Don't be bashful about trying out your Spanish—the Mexican people are usually very patient and helpful with visitors who make an attempt to speak their language.

The Metric System

Mexico uses the metric system of weights and measurements. Speed limits are posted in kilometers and gasoline is sold by the liter. Knowledge of simple conversion factors for kilometers/miles and liters/gallons is essential, and may keep you from getting a speeding ticket or being overcharged at the gas pump.

Health Conditions and Medical Emergencies

Health conditions in Baja California are good, but tourists anywhere may react unfavorably to any change in their environment—particularly in their drinking water. Probably the best way to avoid the intestinal disturbance known as the *turistas* or "Montezuma's revenge" is to avoid overindulgence in food, beverages and exercise, and to get plenty of rest. Travelers should avoid tap water; fresh bottled water and good beer, soft drinks and juices are readily available. Choose carefully when selecting dairy products and fresh fruits and vegetables. It is interesting to note that Mexicans often contract a malady similar to the *turistas* when they visit the United States. Smallpox and other vaccina-

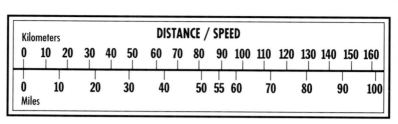

DISTANCE / SPEED

Kilometers
0 10 20 30 40 50 60 70 80 90 100 110 120 130 140 150 160

0 10 20 30 40 50 55 60 70 80 90 100
Miles

METRIC CONVERSION

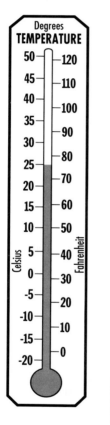

Degrees
TEMPERATURE

Celsius / Fahrenheit

50 — 120
45 — 110
40 — 100
35 — 90
30 — 80
25 — 70
20 — 60
15 — 50
10 — 40
5 — 30
0 — 20
-5 — 10
-10 — 0
-15
-20

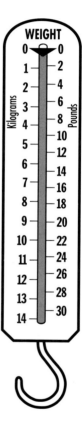

WEIGHT

Kilograms / Pounds

0 — 0
1 — 2
2 — 4
3 — 6
4 — 8
5 — 10
6 — 12
7 — 14
8 — 16
9 — 18
10 — 20
11 — 22
12 — 24
13 — 26
14 — 28
— 30

CUSTOMARY		METRIC
One inch	=	2.54 centimeters
One foot	=	0.30 meters
One mile	=	1.61 kilometers
One quart	=	0.95 liters
One gallon	=	3.79 liters
One pound	=	0.45 kilometers
One psi*	=	6.89 kilopascals

METRIC		CUSTOMARY
One centimeter	=	0.39 inches
One meter	=	3.28 feet
One kilometer	=	0.62 miles
One liter	=	1.06 quarts
One kilogram	=	2.21 pounds
One kilopascal	=	0.145 psi*

*Pounds of force per square inch.

TEMPERATURE

To convert Fahrenheit to Celsius, subtract 32 from the Fahrenheit temperature, multiply by 5 and divide by 9; to convert Celsius to Fahrenheit, multiply by 9, divide by 5 and add 32.

LIQUID MEASURE

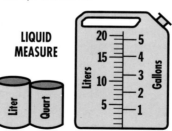

Liter Quart

Liters / Gallons
20 — 5
15 — 4
10 — 3
— 2
5 — 1

AIR PRESSURE

551	482	413	345	276	207	138	69	kPa
80	70	60	50	40	30	20	10	psi

tions are no longer necessary for entry into Mexico or re-entry into the United States.

Baja California has good physicians and dentists, along with well-equipped hospitals, clinics and pharmacies, but they are found only in the largest cities and towns. Small towns have clinics with limited facilities. The local Red Cross (*Cruz Roja*) can also be helpful. Since medical facilities are scarce elsewhere on the peninsula, travelers should carry first-aid kits and know how to use them. In case of emergency, help can be summoned via a government radio network, which is available for public use in most communities.

Travelers having emergencies anywhere in Baja California may contact the Binational Emergency Medical Committee, located in Chula Vista, (619) 425-5080 (available 24 hours). This voluntary organization works with both Mexican and American authorities to help travelers stranded due to accident, illness, legal difficulty or lack of money.

In addition, emergency critical-care air transport service operates throughout Baja California with in-flight physicians and nurses. The following companies offer 24-hour emergency air service. Air-Evac International, located in San Diego, can be reached at (619) 278-3822, or from outside California at (800) 854-2569. Critical Air Medicine, also in San Diego, may be contacted at (619) 571-0482, or toll-free within Mexico at 95 (800) 010-0268. Transmedic, in Ensenada, has phone numbers 01152 (617) 8-1400 and 8-2891.

Highway Travel

Baja California's paved highways are generally well signed and well main-

tained, although they are quite narrow by U.S. standards; the widths of Highways 1, 2, 3, 5 and 19 range from about 19 to 25 feet. Shoulders are nonexistent along many stretches, and turnouts are rare. In some areas the pavement has a rounded crown and rests on a raised roadbed; this makes careful steering important, because vehicles tend to drift to the right. High winds can also create driving difficulties, especially for operators of recreational vehicles, trucks and vehicles pulling trailers. Large, oncoming trucks and buses pose a real danger on hills and curves, because some drivers like to straddle the center line. Safe speeds for all vehicles are less than on most U.S. highways: 40 to 50 m.p.h. on level terrain, 20 to 30 m.p.h. in hilly or mountainous areas. Driving at night should be strictly avoided. Cattle and other livestock commonly wander onto the asphalt at night for warmth, and have caused many serious nighttime accidents. If you must drive at night, reduce your speed drastically.

Be alert for occasional roadblocks of armed police or military personnel at which vehicles are searched for arms or drugs. You should cooperate fully with the police, but afterward report any unfair treatment to the U.S. Consulate in Tijuana and the tourist assistance offices located in several cities. Visitors who encounter trouble or require emergency services while in Mexico should immediately contact the office of the State Tourism Department or, if there is no office nearby, notify local police. In Tijuana, Rosarito, Ensenada, Tecate, Mexicali and San Felipe, the following three-digit telephone numbers are operating: police 134, fire 136, Red Cross (medical) 132. Outside major cities, Mexican government authority rests with the *delegado,* an elected official who oversees all emergencies and civil or legal

Road Signs

Mexico has officially adopted a uniform traffic sign system in which many signs are pictorially self-explanatory. Some of the most common appear below with Spanish-English definitions.

STOP

ESCUELA
School

PUENTE ANGOSTO
Narrow Bridge

GANADO
Cattle

CRUCE F.C.
Railroad Crossing

Yield Right of Way

CURVA PELIGROSA
Dangerous Curve

CAMINO SINUOSO
Winding Road

HOMBRES TRABAJANDO
Men Working

VADO
Dip
(across arroyo)

VADO
Dip
(across arroyo)

ZONA DE DERRUMBES
Slide Area

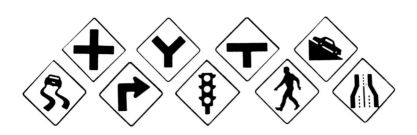

One Way

Two Way

Left Turn Only

Speed Limit

Keep to the Right

No Passing

NO VOLTEAR EN U
No U Turn

No Parking
8 a.m. to 9 p.m.

PROHIBIDO ESTACIONARSE
No Parking

One Hour Parking

DESVIACION

Detour

NO HAY PASO

Road Closed

DESPACIO

Slow

AIRPORT

TRAILER PARK

TELEPHONE

MEDICAL SERVICES

FERRY

RESTAURANT-BAR

GAS & MECHANICAL SERVICE

disputes; he can be found at the *delegación municipal* or *subdelegación*. In more isolated places, authority is usually vested in an appointed citizen who reports to the nearest *delegado*. Although crime is less a problem in Baja California than in the United States, travelers should take the usual common-sense precautions against theft:

1. **Lock your car at all times.**
2. **Avoid driving at night whenever possible. If you do drive after dark, park only in well-lighted areas.**
3. **Carry as much cash as necessary, but use travelers checks whenever possible.**
4. **Avoid carrying all your money in one wallet or purse.**
5. **Keep a list of all your travelers checks and credit card numbers.**
6. **Never leave valuables in your car or hotel room.**

Gasoline

Gasoline is usually available along Baja California's major highways, but because local shortages sometimes occur, travelers are advised to keep their fuel tanks at least half full. This is especially important during long holiday weekends, when resort areas sometimes experience shortages. All gasoline sold in Mexico is distributed by *Pemex (Petróleos Mexicanos)*—the government-controlled oil monopoly. Pemex stations can be found in all cities and towns on the peninsula; the longest stretch of any paved highway without gasoline is the 84-mile section of Highway 1 between Mulegé and Loreto. In this book, very small towns and villages selling unleaded fuel at their gasoline stations have the words *magna sin* in their description. Diesel fuel is easier to find in Baja California than in the United States; the longest paved stretch between diesel outlets is the 96-mile stretch along Highway 19 from La Paz to Cabo San Lucas.

The method used to establish octane ratings in Mexico differs from that used in the U.S. Consequently, higher ratings may appear on Pemex pumps. Premium grade unleaded fuel, called *magna sin,* has an octane rating of 92 and is dispensed from green pumps. Widely available from the border south to Ensenada and San Felipe and in the

Typical of Highway 1 is this section between Ciudad Constitución and La Paz. Note the narrow roadbed and the lack of shoulders.

TOURIST REGULATIONS AND TRAVEL TIPS

vicinity of La Paz and Los Cabos, it is rather scarce in the central part of the peninsula. Regular grade leaded fuel, called *nova*, is sold at all gasoline stations. It has an octane rating of 80 and comes from blue pumps. (Continued use of leaded gasoline in all but very old U.S.-made automobiles may damage the vehicles' catalytic converters.) Diesel fuel is sold from red pumps plainly marked *diesel*, and is available at most stations that carry *magna sin*.

Some vehicles do not run well on Mexican gasoline, especially older ones that require high-octane leaded fuel. The use of low-octane fuel commonly causes pinging and preignition, conditions that can result in engine damage. If pinging or loss of power should occur, a gasoline additive may alleviate the problem. Mexican gasoline may occasionally contain water or other impurities. To prevent clogged fuel lines and carburetor jets, motorists should be prepared to clean or replace their in-line fuel filters if necessary while in Baja California. When gasoline is obtained in out-of-the-way locations (especially when it's pumped from drums), travelers occasionally filter the fuel through a chamois cloth.

At press time, fuel prices in pesos per liter were 1.31 for *nova*, 1.37 for *magna sin* and 1.06 for *diesel*. Converted into dollars and gallons, these figures equal about $0.87 for *nova*, $0.94 for *magna sin* and $0.72 for *diesel*. Some stations have been known to overcharge. It is a good idea to have a calculator handy to check the price charged. Be sure that the pump registers zeros when the attendant starts filling the tank.

The service provided at Pemex stations varies from one facility to the next. Generally, however, travelers should be prepared to check their vehicle's oil, water and air. Pemex attendants do not usually clean windshields, but if they do a small tip is expected. Motorists will find it convenient to carry paper towels and glass-cleaning fluid, as these products are not usually provided.

Emergency Road Service and Auto Repairs

The Green Angels, a government-sponsored group whose sole purpose is to provide free emergency assistance to tourists, regularly patrol Baja California's major highways, supposedly passing any given point at least twice a day. Their staff are mechanics (some bilingual) who carry limited spare parts and gasoline (provided at cost) and who can radio for assistance.

Before traveling in Mexico, your vehicle should be in top mechanical condition. Tires, including spares, should be inspected for tread wear and proper inflation, and all fluid levels should be checked. Brakes, batteries, shock absorbers, filters, pumps and radiators all warrant special attention. The wise traveler will carry extra belts and hoses, as well as the tools needed to install them.

There are automobile dealerships in Tijuana, Mexicali, Ensenada, Ciudad Constitución and La Paz, and skilled mechanics can be found in most larger towns on the peninsula. But although competent mechanical help is relatively easy to find in Baja California, parts are not. The most prevalent makes of automobiles in Baja are Ford, Chevrolet, Dodge, Volkswagen and Nissan—parts for other makes are extremely scarce. Even in major cities, a breakdown can sometimes result in a considerable wait for parts. And in rural areas, while local mechanics are wizards at salvaging parts from junk cars and are adept at repairing vehicles of less-than-recent vintage, many are bewildered by the complexities of fuel injection, air conditioning, anti-smog devices and electronic ignition.

Backcountry Travel

When the paved Transpeninsular Highway was completed in 1973, Baja California became an accessible destination for virtually anyone with a car and a tourist card. Many off-road "purists" bemoaned the loss of what they regarded as their special domain. Their worries were unwarranted, however, because the "old" Baja California still exists, as any traveler who leaves the security of the pavement soon discovers. Despite the peninsula's rapid growth and development, most of its territory remains a wild, rugged frontier—a timeless land of vast, empty spaces, unspoiled beaches, lonely ranchos and roads that by and large are little better than mule trails. Baja California's backcountry is difficult to traverse and is definitely not for those seeking comfort and amenities. But for travelers with the proper vehicles and equipment, it offers beauty, solitude and adventure. To enter this fascinating realm is to leave the jet age behind and experience a region little touched by the works of man.

A journey into the remote reaches of the peninsula requires careful planning and preparation. Before leaving the pavement, let someone know where you are going and when you plan to return. Consider traveling under the buddy system—with two or more vehicles in a caravan. And plan to be as self-sufficient as possible as facilities are extremely scarce. Take enough extra gasoline to extend your vehicle's range by at least 50 miles, and if possible store this fuel outside the vehicle. Five gallons of water per person should be carried, along with ample nonperishable food for two weeks' sustenance. A good first-aid kit is essential. To protect cameras and other valuable items from the everpresent Baja California dust, take along a supply of plastic bags. For a complete list of recommended equipment, see the "Suggested Supply Lists" section in the *Appendix*.

Although some of Baja's dirt roads are occasionally maintained and regularly traveled, others are seldom-used tracks that are downright grueling. Even the "good" roads have bad stretches, and any unpaved route is only as good as its worst spot. Along many of the peninsula's back roads, the traveler can expect to encounter jarring, washboard sections, deep sand, hazardous arroyo crossings, precarious curves, rocks jutting upward from the surface and grades reminiscent of rollercoasters. These roads can damage any vehicle. As a result, backcountry travel in Baja California calls for a specially prepared heavy-duty rig, preferably one with four-wheel drive. It should be equipped for high clearance, with oversize tires, extra low gears, and protective steel pans beneath the engine, transmission and gasoline tank. Dual rear tires are not advisable because they do not easily fall into existing road tracks. As important as the proper vehicle is the driver who proceeds slowly and cautiously; to attempt to go too fast is to invite disaster.

There are few road signs in Baja California's backcountry—probably because local residents assume that anyone driving the back roads knows where to go. As a result, numerous unsigned junctions confront the motorist. In many cases, however, both branches leaving a fork soon rejoin one another. If you reach a junction and are unsure of the proper route, a good rule to follow is to choose the most heavily traveled fork; it will either be the correct route or will often lead

Bill Cory

Backcountry driving in Baja California takes careful preparation, specialized vehicles and constant attention to the road conditions. Here, Auto Club vehicles on the 1973 mapping expedition cross an old wooden bridge on the road to Punta Canoas (see Side Routes*).*

you to a ranch where you can obtain directions. Be sure to take along the Automobile Club of Southern California's *Baja California* map and check all junctions against those indicated. Remember, however, that odometers vary, and the mileages you experience may disagree somewhat with those on the map.

Extensive off-pavement travel in Baja California involves camping out. When selecting your camping equipment, keep in mind that high winds often whistle across the desert, and temperatures can be quite cool at night. You can camp almost anywhere, but avoid the bottoms of arroyos, where flash floods sometimes occur. All trash that cannot be burned should be packed out. Wood for campfires is not abundant in the desert, but cactus skeletons make suitable fuel.

The prospective off-pavement explorer has a wide variety of routes and destinations from which to choose. Some

of the most rewarding are described in the chapter entitled *Side Routes*. If you are inexperienced in traveling the backcountry of Baja California, it is recommended that you begin with one of the trips outlined in this book.

Tourist Assistance

Tourist Assistance/Protección al Turista provides assistance to visitors who experience legal difficulties with local businessmen or police. Offices throughout the peninsula are listed below. Tourist Assistance recommends the following steps to tourists who believe they have received inappropriate treatment by Mexican police: (1) Observe or ask for as many of the following as possible—the officer's name (most police wear nameplates), badge number, department (municipal, state, federal) and car number. (2) If there is a fine, go to the nearest police station to pay it and ask for a receipt. Traffic tickets received in Tijuana may be paid by mail from the United

States. (3) Write out the complaint and mail it to the attorney general.

Ensenada
State Tourism Office on Boulevard Lázaro Cárdenas (Costero) at Calle las Rocas
01152 (617) 2-3000

La Paz
State Tourism Office, Paseo Alvaro Obregón at 16 de Septiembre
01152 (112) 4-0100 or 4-0103

Mexicali
State Tourism Office on Calle Calafia at Calzada Independencia
01152 (65) 56-1172

Rosarito
Boulevard Juárez and Calle Acacias
01152 (661) 2-0200

San Felipe
State Tourism building at Avenida Mar de Cortez and Calle Manzanillo
01152 (657) 7-1155

Tecate
State Tourism Office on the south side of the plaza
01152 (665) 4-1095

Tijuana
State Tourism Office in Plaza Patria on Boulevard Díaz Ordaz
01152 (66) 81-9492

The U.S. Consulate, in Tijuana on Calle Tapachula near Agua Caliente Racetrack, offers assistance to U.S. citizens traveling in northern Baja California. Travelers should report to the consulate any inappropriate treatment they receive by Mexican police. Questionnaires concerning police mistreatment are available at the consulate. The consulate is open Monday through Friday 8 a.m. to 4:30 p.m.; call 01152 (66) 81-7400 during these hours. For after-hours emergencies call (619) 585-2000, or write to P.O. Box 439039, San Ysidro, CA 92143. In Baja California Sur, U.S. citizens can obtain help in Cabo San Lucas from the U.S. consular agent, located at Boulevard Marina y Pedregal No. 3. The phone is 01152 (114) 3-3566.■

History

Before the arrival of the Europeans, Baja California was inhabited by numerous tribes of Indians. The main linguistic groups from north to south were the Yumans, Guaicura, Huchiti, and the Pericu. While most of the tribes are now extinct, archeological evidence and the written histories of the early Europeans have shown that these Indians were hunter-gatherers. Their most enduring legacy has been the fantastic cave paintings and rock art that can be found along the length of the peninsula.

Following the conquest of central Mexico, rumors of great wealth to the west attracted the conquistador Hernán Cortés, who in 1535 sailed from the west coast of Mexico into present-day Bahía de La Paz. There he established a small colony, naming the bay and land Santa Cruz (modern La Paz). Due to supply shortages, the colony was abandoned in 1537.

Exploration of the peninsula's coastline was continued in 1539 by Francisco de Ulloa and in 1542 by Juan Rodríguez Cabrillo. In 1596 Sebastián Vizcaíno re-established a colony at the site of Cortés' settlement and renamed the bay La Paz. This colony also failed due to a shortage of supplies. In 1602 Vizcaíno explored the Pacific Coast of the Californias, produced the first detailed maps of the area and established place names, most of which are still in use.

Continued rumors of great wealth in pearls attracted more Spaniards to the Gulf of California in the 17th century, although their efforts were rewarded with only moderate quantities of the semi-precious gems. Francisco de Ortega in 1628, Alonzo Gonzales in 1644, and Bernardo Bernal de Pinadero in 1663 were among those who came to the Gulf of California, but they added little in exploration and knowledge of Baja California.

In 1683, Isidro de Atondo y Antillón attempted to set up a colony at La Paz, but conflict with the Indians forced him to relocate to the site of modern San Bruno. An 18-month drought exhausted the provisions and he disbanded the colony in 1685. Along with him on this journey was Padre Eusebio Kino, whose urging resulted in renewed efforts 12 years later under the Jesuit religious order to convert the Indians to the Roman church.

On October 15, 1697, Padre Juan María Salvatierra landed on the east coast of the peninsula with six soldiers. He founded a mission at Loreto, which became the first permanent Spanish settlement in California, and for the next 70 years the Jesuits controlled Lower California. The Jesuits financed their own venture, with the Spanish government supplying only the soldiers.

The padres were brave, undiscouraged by the wild surroundings. They charted and explored the east and west coasts of the peninsula; they developed pioneer agricultural settlements. The mission fathers taught the Indians to cultivate the land. Grapes were grown and wine pressed to be exchanged for goods from Mexico. They founded 23 missions, 14 of which were successful; they instructed the Indians in religious matters and taught them useful arts; they made a network of trails connecting the missions, took scientific and geographical notes, and prepared ethnological reports on the native peoples.

But they were unable to conquer disease, and epidemics plagued the population. With thousands of Indians dying and many killed in revolts, the elaborate political and economic structure established by the Jesuits began to weaken. Then, just as the priests were preparing to move north, enemies of the Jesuit order spread tales in Spain that the mission fathers were accumulating great wealth and power. Acting with dispatch, the Spanish government expelled the Jesuits from California in 1768.

Later that same year, 13 padres of the Franciscan Brotherhood, under the leadership of the small, energetic Padre Junípero Serra, landed at Loreto. A quick appraisal convinced them that their work lay in Alta (Upper) California near what is now San Diego, although they founded one mission on their way northward. In 1773 the Franciscans were succeeded on the peninsula by the Dominicans, who successfully carried on the establishment of the missions until the system was attacked by the Mexican government. In 1829 a newly independent Mexico expelled all Spaniards; in 1832 the Mexican government ordered the secularization of all missions and their conversion to parish churches. The Dominican missions in the north, however, were considered the only vestiges of civilization there and were retained until 1846. Some of the mission churches are still in use, while the ruins of others can be seen along the back roads of Baja California. A government-sponsored program of mission restoration is currently in progress.

Far from the seat of government in Mexico City, Baja California soon became the forgotten peninsula—a haven for criminals, smugglers and soldiers of fortune. Lower California was a land torn by internal strife and poverty.

The Mexican-American War (1846-48)—which finally separated the Californias—created further turbulence, and there were hard feelings toward the new neighbor to the north. Moreover, investment of American capital in land and mines kept Mexico suspicious of U.S. intentions. The notorious filibuster William Walker only confirmed these suspicions when he invaded Lower California in a surprise attack and proclaimed himself president. Though he was soon relieved of his position, other rebels were quick to step into the gap. In 1911, in activity peripheral to the Mexican Revolution, Mexican Ricardo Flores Magón led the rebellion known as the Tijuana Revolution. Tijuana was successfully taken by the rebels, but Flores' inability to implement his theories caused the rebellion to fail. Thereafter, a succession of politically appointed governors maintained precarious rule over this troubled area.

Prohibition in the United States brought uncertain prosperity to the border towns. Americans entered Mexico in droves, seeking the pleasures of a more liberal rule. It was not until 1938 that Mexican President Cárdenas declared a "deep preoccupation" with the future of Lower California. Gamblers and undesirables were routed, and intense agrarian and educational reforms were instituted. In 1952, under the leadership of President Alemán, the northern part of Baja California officially became a state of Mexico, with an elected government in the state capital, Mexicali. The official name of this northern state is Baja California, although it is often referred to as Baja California Norte. The southern half of the peninsula (below the 28th parallel) officially became Mexico's 30th state,

Baja California Sur, in 1974 with La Paz as its capital.

Each state is divided into *municipios* (municipalities), roughly equivalent to American counties. The state of Baja California, population about 2,200,000, is divided into municipios bearing the same names as its cities: Tijuana, Ensenada, Tecate and Mexicali. Baja California Sur, with a population of about 340,000, contains the municipios of Mulegé, Loreto, Comondú, La Paz and Los Cabos.

The last 20 years have seen great progress for Baja California. Surrounded by a huge supply of fish, lobster and shrimp, the arid peninsula is gradually yielding to man's efforts to make it a productive land. Through government assistance, farming cooperatives have sprouted. And with the completion of Mexico Highway 1, Baja California entered the modern era, growing and prospering as a mechanized land and a prime tourist objective.∎

Auto Club Historical Photo

Since 1926 the Auto Club has sponsored numerous research expeditions to Baja California, most recently in September 1994. This photo shows trucks negotiating the road to La Purísima during the 1949 expedition.

Mexico Highway 1

Until 1973, the only way to reach the tip of Baja California by passenger car involved driving to Topolobampo or Mazatlán on the Mexican mainland, then crossing the Gulf of California by ferry to La Paz. Paved roads probed into the interior from the border and from La Paz, but they were separated by a vast, sparsely populated desert traversed by a rough, meandering track that could break even the sturdiest of off-road vehicles.

In late 1973, however, road crews working north and south at a feverish pace met near Rancho Santa Inés, completing the paving of a modern highway extending the entire length of the peninsula. Mexico Highway 1, Baja California's new lifeline, was named *La Carretera Transpeninsular Benito Juárez* (Benito Juárez Transpeninsular Highway) after one of Mexico's most revered heroes. The official dedication was made in December by then-President Luis Echeverría Alvarez in ceremonies held at the 28th parallel, near Guerrero Negro.

Designed to promote the peninsula's economic development, the paved highway allows for the movement of Baja California's internal commerce, and it has been an important stimulus for the peninsula's recent growth. It is no coincidence that in October 1974, less than a year after the completion of Highway 1, the territory of Baja California Sur became a full-fledged Mexican state.

To the tourist, the Transpeninsular Highway brings within reach the mountains and valleys of the north, the fascinating central desert and the beaches of southern Baja California. Convenient overland access to fine hunting and some of the world's best sportfishing is now available. Tourism has been further encouraged by the completion of government-financed hotels and gasoline stations along the highway. Automobile touring in Baja California, once a dream, is now a reality.

CROSSING THE BORDER

The San Ysidro-Tijuana border crossing, open 24 hours, is the world's busiest international gateway. While Mexico-bound tourists are normally waved through the border station without formality, travelers returning to the United States must stop for inspection. This can result in congestion, es-

Bill Cory

Mexico Highway 1—Baja California's lifeline—south of La Paz

pecially on weekends and holidays, when delays of more than two hours can occur. On weekdays carpool lanes (for four or more persons) are open into San Ysidro.

Interstates 5 and 805 lead from San Diego directly to the international border. When approaching or returning from the border, particularly after dark, please be alert for persons (undocumented immigrants) crossing the freeways. Visitors who wish to walk across the border will find ample pay parking on the U.S. side. Before driving into Mexico, be sure to read the *Tourist Regulations and Travel Tips* chapter, and make sure you are protected by Mexico automobile insurance.

Tourists wishing to drive to the border, then cross into Tijuana on foot can find a number of parking lots on the U.S. side in San Ysidro. They are located near the border on Camiones Way (west of I-5) and at the end of San Ysidro Boulevard (east of I-5). Parking rates run $2 for a half-hour, but only $6-$8 for 24 hours. Some provide security, others do not; inquire before parking. On the Mexico side, taxis and buses are available, or the

visitor may continue walking a half mile to downtown Tijuana via a pedestrian bridge over the Río Tijuana.

The Otay Mesa crossing is located just east of the Tijuana International Airport and just south of SR 905/Otay Mesa Road. It is open daily from 6 a.m. to 10 p.m. This border crossing is particularly useful for travelers returning from Mexico on weekends. Delays are not nearly as long as at San Ysidro, but on weekends and holidays motorists may have to wait an hour in line.

From San Diego, the Otay Mesa crossing can be reached by taking SR 905 east from either I-5 or I-805 to Otay Mesa Road. Continue east for about four miles, following signs to the border.

From the south, the crossing is reached by a bypass which loops around southern and eastern Tijuana to Otay Mesa (both sides of the border are called "Otay Mesa"). Motorists approaching Tijuana from the south via Highway 1D (the toll road) should exit onto Highway 1 at the Rosarito Norte interchange. Follow the highway,

MEXICO HIGHWAY 1

Distance Table

This table gives distances between major points in Baja California both in miles and in kilometers; the italicized (upper) figures indicate miles, while the figures in regular type (lower) denote kilometers. All figures have been rounded off to the nearest whole mile or kilometer. To find the distance between two points, first find the northern point and read down the column below the name. Second, find the southern point and read across the column to the left of the name. The intersection of the two columns shows the distance. Note: Figures are based on the use of Mexico Highway 1D (Toll Road) between Tijuana and Ensenada.

Distances are given as **miles / kilometers**.

	Ensenada	Colonet	San Quintín	El Rosario	Cataviña	Bahía de los Angeles Jct.	Guerrero Negro	San Ignacio	Santa Rosalía	Mulegé	Loreto	Ciudad Constitución	La Paz	Cabo San Lucas
Tijuana	68 / 109	144 / 232	187 / 301	223 / 359	299 / 481	364 / 586	444 / 714	532 / 856	577 / 928	615 / 990	699 / 1125	788 / 1268	922 / 1483	1059 / 1704
Ensenada		76 / 123	119 / 191	155 / 249	231 / 372	296 / 476	376 / 605	464 / 747	509 / 819	547 / 880	631 / 1015	720 / 1158	854 / 1374	991 / 1594
Colonet			43 / 69	79 / 127	155 / 249	220 / 354	300 / 483	388 / 624	433 / 697	471 / 758	555 / 893	644 / 1036	778 / 1252	915 / 1472
San Quintín				36 / 58	112 / 180	177 / 285	257 / 414	345 / 555	390 / 628	428 / 689	512 / 824	601 / 967	735 / 1183	872 / 1403
El Rosario					76 / 122	141 / 227	221 / 356	309 / 497	354 / 570	392 / 631	476 / 766	565 / 909	699 / 1125	836 / 1345
Cataviña						65 / 105	145 / 234	233 / 376	278 / 449	316 / 510	400 / 646	489 / 789	623 / 1005	760 / 1226
Bahía de los Angeles Jct.							80 / 129	168 / 271	213 / 344	251 / 405	335 / 541	424 / 684	558 / 900	695 / 1121
Guerrero Negro								88 / 142	133 / 215	171 / 276	255 / 412	344 / 555	478 / 771	615 / 992
San Ignacio									45 / 73	83 / 134	167 / 270	256 / 413	390 / 629	527 / 850
Santa Rosalía										38 / 61	122 / 197	211 / 340	345 / 556	482 / 777
Mulegé											84 / 136	173 / 279	307 / 495	444 / 716
Loreto												89 / 143	223 / 359	360 / 580
Ciudad Constitución													134 / 216	271* / 437*
La Paz														137* / 221*

* Distance via Mexico Highway 19 is only 96 miles, 154 km.

42

which is four-lane divided, 7½ miles to the bypass, named *Libramiento*. Watch for "La Mesa-Tecate-Mexicali" signs. Bear right onto the bypass and follow signs marked "Aeropuerto."

Although the bypass route is continuous in nature, it changes names several times between Highway 1D and the Otay Mesa crossing. As the airport area is approached, signs in Spanish indicate the Otay Mesa border crossing (*Garita de Otay*) and separate lanes for heavy vehicles (*Vehículos Pesados*) and for light vehicles (*Vehículos Ligeros*), which include automobiles and recreational vehicles.

Tijuana

(See also *Lodging & Restaurants*)

Colorful gateway to Baja California, Tijuana extends from the coastline for more than a dozen miles along the international border. The heart of the city is about six miles inland from the coast, near the point where the intermittent-flowing Rio Tijuana emerges from a narrow valley onto a broad lowland. The river swings northwest at this point, crosses the U.S. frontier and empties into the Pacific Ocean. Downtown Tijuana is just south of the river and less than a mile from the border crossing. The traditional tourist zone is a seven-block stretch of Avenida Revolución—a busy thoroughfare lined with cafes, nightclubs and curio shops. About a mile to the southeast rise modern business buildings and shopping centers. Farther up the valley to the southeast are many of Tijuana's factories and warehouses, while residential areas sprawl across hills and mesas to the east, south and west.

Tijuana—today the farthest point in Mexico from the national capi-

tal—was settled late in Mexico's history, in the 1860s, as a center for ranching. In the 1870s customs offices were established, and a rough, rickety border town came into being.

Tourism, given spice by gambling and horse racing, grew into a big business in the early 1900s. It waned when border crossings were restricted during World War I, then boomed during Prohibition, when Hollywood celebrities helped make Tijuana a fashionable destination for thirsty tourists. In the United States the repeal of Prohibition and the Depression brought hard times to Tijuana, but the Mexican government responded by designating all of Baja California as a free port, and shoppers flocked to Tijuana in search

R. Clark Hunter

Aztec hero Cuauhtémoc stands above a glorieta, or traffic circle, on Tijuana's Paseo de los Héroes.

Take note . . . in Tijuana

Tourist Information and Assistance

The **State Tourism Department's** main office is on the third level of the Plaza Patria on Boulevard Díaz Ordaz (see *Tijuana Area* map). The office is open Monday through Saturday, 9 a.m. to 7 p.m., Sunday 10 a.m. to 5 p.m.; phone 01152 (66) 81-9492 or 81-9493; FAX 81-9579. State Tourism also has an office on Calle 1 at Avenida Revolución, open 9 a.m. to 7 p.m.; phone 01152 (66) 88-0555. The **Chamber of Commerce**, located at Calle 1 and Avenida Revolución, also gives tourist assistance. There are additional tourist information facilities at the international border and beyond the toll gate at the beginning of the expressway to Ensenada.

The Tijuana Convention and Tourism Bureau may be reached by calling (800) 252-5363. Another information source for Tijuana and Baja California is **International Marketing/Baja California Tourism** at (619) 298-4105 or (800) 522-1516.

An additional service for visitors is the **Protección al Turista/Tourist Assistance,** which provides legal assistance to tourists who encounter problems while in Tijuana. It is located in the state tourism offices, with their same hours and phone numbers. The **U.S. Consulate** is on Calle Tapachula near the Agua Caliente Racetrack, phone 01152 (66) 81-7400 (see *Tourist Regulations and Travel Tips,* Emergency Road Service and Auto Repairs section, and the *Tijuana* map).

Newspapers

Several English-language tourist newspapers, including the *Baja Shopper,* are distributed free at tourist information centers, hotels and certain stores. In addition to advertisements, they contain information about tourist attractions in Tijuana and other parts of Baja California. The *San Diego Union* and the *Los Angeles Times* are sold at some newsstands and hotels. Tijuana has several Spanish-language dailies; *El Heraldo* and *Baja California* are two important ones. Newspapers from Mexico City are sold here and in other large cities of Baja California.

Radio and Television Stations

Many California radio stations are received in Tijuana and northern Baja California. Tijuana's radio stations feature a variety of Mexican music. Several San Diego TV stations are received, along with the Tijuana and Mexico City stations.

Driving in Tijuana

Many visitors find their car to be the most convenient means of transportation, but the traffic in Tijuana can be a bit daunting. (Be sure to have Mexican auto insurance before driving across the border—see Automobile Requirements in the *Tourist Regulations and Travel Tips* chapter.) Many wide through streets facilitate traffic flow. Outside of the main business districts, however, side streets are often unpaved and contain ruts and potholes. Speed bumps are common. The old downtown, referred to as *Centro,* including avenidas Revolución and Constitución and calles 2 and 3, is very congested; watch for the many one-way street signs. Traffic circles, or *glorietas,* found along Paseo de los Héroes and Paseo de Tijuana, often pose a challenge for visitors. When entering a traffic circle, bear right, then follow the flow of traffic counterclockwise. Traffic lights in Baja California often resemble old-fashioned American signals and are not readily visible from any distance.

Most parts of the city have street parking, and most shopping centers have free parking lots. The congested downtown area has a number of pay lots. Some visitors prefer to park on the San Ysidro (California) side of the border, crossing on foot via the elevated pedestrian promenade into Tijuana. Some continue into downtown by foot; others prefer to take a taxi.

Local Transportation

A typical taxi ride within town or from the border area costs about $6, although sometimes bargaining can lower the fare. A price should be agreed upon before getting into the cab. Many small bus lines provide service to all parts of Tijuana, running frequently in the downtown area and on major thoroughfares. The basic fare is only about 25¢. It is useful to know at least a little Spanish, have an idea of the layout of the city and be willing to ride in old vehicles, which do not offer the best in comfort. For travel on large, modern buses between Tijuana and other parts of Baja California, see Bus Service in the Transportation section of the *Appendix.*

of bargains. In the mid-1930s, a series of reform laws helped curb some of the city's undesirable elements, but not until the 1960s did progressive leadership establish Tijuana as a tourist center of wide appeal.

If you haven't seen Tijuana since the early 1970s, or if you know the city only by its once-tawdry reputation, you will likely be surprised when you pass beyond the San Ysidro border crossing. Although it retains touches of gaudiness, intrigue and sidewalk color, Tijuana is no longer the ramshackle border town that existed for the sole purpose of separating fun-seeking tourists from their dollars. In its stead is a bustling, modern metropolis that combines a diversified economy spurred by manufacturing and commerce with a tourism industry that places Tijuana among the top visitor attractions on the West Coast, lessen-

ing the city's economic dependence on the United States. At the same time, vast numbers of immigrants from the Mexican mainland—lured by the top minimum wage in the republic, one of Mexico's highest standards of living and the proximity of the U.S. border—have swelled the population to approximately 1,300,000, making Tijuana the fourth-largest city in Mexico and one of the fastest-growing cities on the North American continent. It is also the seat of government for the *municipio* (county) of Tijuana. Civic pride shows itself everywhere. A new, ultramodern business and industrial complex has risen in the formerly depressed riverbed area. Streets are cleaner and smoother than in past years. Entertainment caters to a broad range of interests, and the city in general exudes a warm welcome to visitors. As a result, more and more

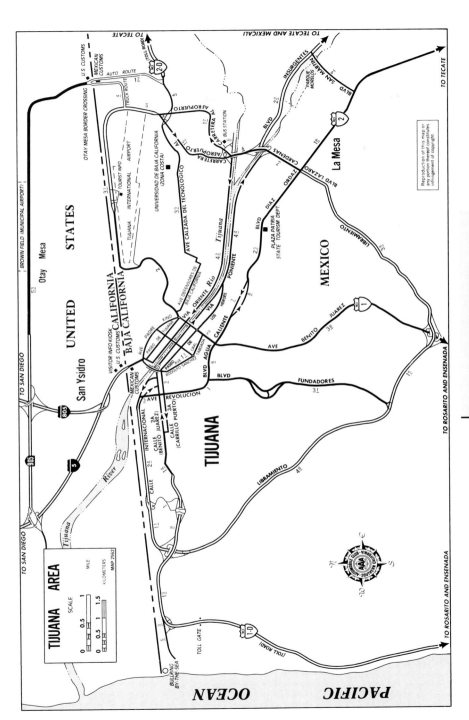

MEXICO HIGHWAY 1

46

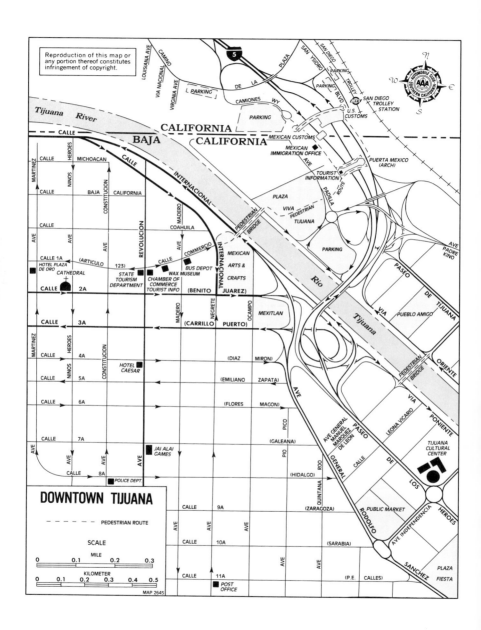

DOWNTOWN TIJUANA

– – – – – PEDESTRIAN ROUTE

SCALE

MILE

KILOMETER

MAP 2645

families are finding Tijuana to be an appealing destination.

Shopping

Probably the most popular tourist objective in Tijuana is shopping, partially due to the town's status as a duty-free port. U.S. currency is accepted virtually everywhere and some stores even accept U.S. credit cards. While English is spoken at most shops in the downtown area and at principal shopping centers, some knowledge of Spanish is helpful in other parts of the city.

The oldest tourist shopping is downtown (*Centro*) on **Avenida Revolución,** where rows of shops line the sidewalks and occupy numerous arcades. Virtually every type of merchandise sold in the city can be found along this street. **Avenida Constitución,** one block west of Revolución, is popular with local shoppers. **The Mercado de Artesanías/Mexican Arts and Crafts,** on Calle 2 between avenidas Negrete and Ocampo, contains a large number of booths selling a variety of crafts and clothing.

Also downtown, a district specializing in **automobile services,** bordered by Calle 3, avenidas Ocampo and Pío Pico, and Calle 8, offers bargains on seat covers, painting and body work. Most auto shops have an experienced English-speaking manager.

Plaza Río Tijuana Shopping Center, located on Paseo de los Héroes in the new Río Tijuana development, contains Dorian's, Sears and Comercial Mexicana, numerous specialty shops, bakeries, several restaurants and a movie theater. Directly across Héroes is the attractive new **Plaza Fiesta.** Built in traditional colonial style, it features a series of small shops and eating places. Next door shoppers find **Plaza del Zapato,** a mall specializing

in all types of shoes. Nearby, at Héroes and Avenida Independencia across from the cultural center, is the colorful **Public Market (Mercado M. Hidalgo).** It has fresh produce stalls, arts and crafts shops and liquor stores. **Pueblo Amigo** is on Vía Oriente a half mile southeast of the border crossing. Built in modified traditional Mexican style, it has a variety of restaurants and shops.

Boulevard Agua Caliente is lined for several miles with stores and other businesses. Plaza Patria is a modern three-level mall on Boulevard Díaz Ordaz, the extension of Boulevard Agua Caliente in La Mesa district.

Dining

With a long and varied list of eating places, Tijuana has fare to please all tastes. The following are some of the better-known restaurants throughout the city. Some of the restaurants listed here are AAA approved; more information about these can be found in the *Lodging & Restaurants* chapter. Non-AAA-approved restaurants are also listed here as a service to visitors.

In the Downtown (*Centro*) area, **Bol Corona,** Avenida Revolución at Avenida 2, in the Plaza Revolución (Mexican food and varied menu); **Pedrins,** on Avenida Revolución across from the Frontón Palacio (seafood); **Sanborn's,** at Avenida Revolución and Calle 8 (varied menu).

In the Rio Tijuana district is **Las Espuelas,** in Plaza Río Tijuana shopping center (ranch atmosphere, varied menu); **Rívoli,** in the Hotel Lucerna, Paseo de los Héroes and Avenida Rodríguez (varied menu); **Guadalajara Grill,** Paseo de los Héroes and Avenida Diego Rivera (Mexican cuisine, steaks and seafood); **La Taberna de Infante** (Mediterranean cuisine), on Avenida Diego Rivera between Paseo de los Héroes and Via Poniente; **Ochoa's Restaurant,** on Paseo de los Héroes 61, three blocks west of Hotel Lucerna (varied menu).

In the Agua Caliente district, **Bocaccio's,** near the Tijuana Country Club on Boulevard Agua Caliente 2500 (continental cuisine); **La Escondida de Tijuana,** Calle Santa Mónica 1, about ¼ mile east of the racetrack (seafood, steaks and international cuisine); **Grand Bistrot Restaurante,** in the Hotel Fiesta Americana, on Boulevard Agua Caliente, ¼ mile east of Avenida Rodríguez (French cuisine).

Nightclubs

After-dark entertainment in Tijuana includes such diverse activities as floor shows, dancing and mariachis. A few of the city's many popular night spots include **Tijuana Charlie's** in the Pueblo Amigo entertainment center on Paseo de Tijuana, ⅗ mile southeast of the border; **Tia Juana Tilly's,** by the Frontón Palacio on Avenida Revolución at Calle 7; **Oh!,** on Paseo de los Héroes, just east of Avenida Cuauhtemoc; and the lobby bar of the hotel **Plaza las Glorias.**

Points of Interest

Boundary Monument (Monumento de la Frontera) *Near the Pacific Ocean in Playas de Tijuana north of the bullring.* At the fence separating Tijuana from Imperial Beach, California, lies the monument marking the western terminus of the Mexico-United States boundary. Bilingual plaques here tell the history of the border.

Casa de la Cultura *Calles Paris and Lisboa.* A classic old schoolhouse, Casa de la Cultura is now a multi-arts cultural center for local children. Approached via Calle 4 or by a high stairway west of Parque Guerrero (see

description), it affords a panoramic view of Tijuana and the California side of the border.

Mexitlan *Calle 2 and Avenida Ocampo. 01152 (66) 38-4101; (619) 685-3628.* Open all year, Wednesday through Sunday: May through October, Wednesday through Friday from 10 a.m. to 6 p.m., Saturday and Sunday 9 a.m. to 9 p.m. November through April, 10 a.m. to 5 p.m. Adults $3; children under 12 free. A splendid introduction to Mexico, this attraction contains an outdoor display covering a city block, featuring some 150 scale models of the nation's greatest monuments, churches, buildings, plazas, stadiums and other architectural treasures. Focusing mostly on Mexico's heartland, the south-central plateau region, the display spans four centuries of history. Mexitlan also has a souvenir shop and several snack bars. On Saturday and Sunday evenings the model structures light up and give out music. Pedro Ramírez Vásquez, noted Mexican architect, designed Mexitlan.

Nuestra Señora de Guadalupe Cathedral *Calle 2 and Avenida Niños Héroes.* The twin towers of this classic example of Mexican church architecture rise majestically above the old downtown district.

Otay Mesa Industrial District *Southeast of the Otay Mesa border crossing; follow signs for Ciudad Industrial.* Of growing importance to American business people, this bustling new district contains *maquiladoras,* plants which are owned by Americans and other foreigners attracted to Mexican border areas because of low production costs.

Parque Teniente Vicente Guerrero *Calle 3 at Avenida F.* This pleasant park is named in honor of

The ultramodern Tijuana Cultural Center contains a museum, an omnitheater and a performing arts stage.

Lieutenant Guerrero, one of those who successfully quelled the 1911 revolution. The Héroes of 1911 Monument here is dedicated to the defenders of Tijuana.

Tijuana Cultural Center/Centro Cultural Tijuana *Paseo de los Héroes and Avenida Independencia. 01152 (66) 84-1111 or 84-1132.* Open daily 11 a.m. to 9 p.m. Museum: adults $1, children 50¢. This modern complex features a variety of cultural arts. The fine museum contains archaeological, historical and handicraft displays. An art gallery displays changing exhibits. Shops offer books and hand-crafted goods for sale. There is a restaurant on site. The 1000-seat concert hall offers varied musical and dramatic programs. The Tijuana Cultural Center was designed by the noted Mexican architect, Pedro Ramírez Vásquez. **Omnitheater**, a spherical theater located in the Cultural Center, presents large-format three-dimensional films on various subjects.

Torre de Tijuana *Boulevard Agua Caliente and Avenida Negrete.* This majestic Mediterranean arch tower set in a small park is a symbol of modern Tijuana. A stairway allows a good view of the city.

Wax Museum/Museo de Cera *Calle 1 near Avenida Revolución.* Open daily from 10 a.m. to 10 p.m. Adults $3; children ages 6 to 12, $2; under 6 free. Visitors are greeted by life-like figures from history, cinema and music, both Mexican and foreign. A few examples are Emiliano Zapata, Pedro Infante, Mahatma Gandhi, Laurel and Hardy and Mikhail Gorbachev.

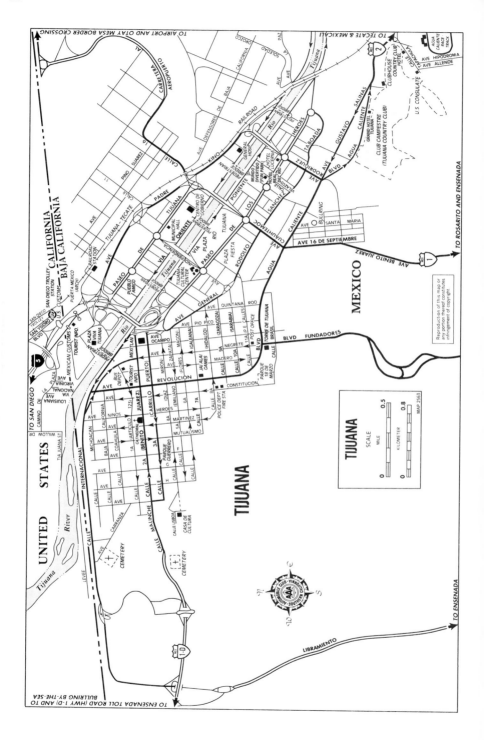

TIJUANA

TIJUANA

SCALE

MILE 0 0.5

KILOMETER 0 0.8

MAP 2565

Tom Dell

Plaza Monumental (Bullring-by-the-Sea) is located in the Playas de Tijuana development, six miles west of Downtown Tijuana via Highway 1D.

Spectator Sports

Bullfights

Some of the world's top matadors perform in Tijuana, with bullfights alternating between El Toreo and Plaza Monumental. The season is May through September; July and August are the busiest months. The spectacles are held on selected Sundays at 4 p.m. Ticket prices range from $15 to $42; the shaded side of the arena is more expensive. Tickets can be obtained from Five Star Tours, (619) 232-5049 and at the bullrings.

El Toreo *2 miles east of downtown Tijuana on Boulevard Agua Caliente. 01152 (66) 86-1510.*

Plaza Monumental (Bullring-by-the-Sea) *6 miles west of downtown Tijuana via Highway 1-D. 01152 (66) 80-1808.*

Charreadas (Mexican Rodeos)

These colorful equestrian events take place almost every Sunday afternoon from May through September, alternating among the several charro grounds in the Tijuana area. Most charreadas are free. For more information call the Asociación de Charros at 01152 (66) 81-3401.

Dog Racing

Agua Caliente Racetrack *3 miles east of downtown Tijuana off Boulevard Agua Caliente. (619) 231-1910.* Greyhounds run nightly at 7:45 p.m. and on Saturday and Sunday at 2 p.m. General admission is free; Turf Club seating is $5 (includes a $5 betting voucher). Wagering on U.S. horse racing and professional sports teams. (Horse racing has been discontinued at this facility.)

Jai Alai

Jai Alai is a fast-moving court game using a ball and a long curved wicker basket strapped to the wrist. Matches are held at the **Frontón Palacio** Avenida Revolución at Calle 7, phone 01152 (66) 85-2524 or (619) 231-1910. Monday and Tuesday from 12:30 to 6 p.m., Thursday through Sunday 8 p.m to midnight. Tickets range from $2 to $5, general admission; $20 *cancha club* (refundable with a wagering voucher).

Tijuana to Rosarito via Old Highway 1

(15 mi., 24 km.; 0:45 hrs.)

Highway 1—the old road—is a toll-free highway leading from the international border at Tijuana to Ensenada. The route passes through a modern maze of interchanges, southeast along Paseo de los Héroes, then south at the Cuautémoc monument (follow signs marked "Ensenada" or "Rosarito"). The 11 miles between Libramiento and Rosarito are four-lane divided highway. After curving through commercial areas, then low hills and farmland, Highway 1 crosses the toll road just north of Rosarito.

00.0	**Tijuana** (U.S. border crossing).
01.9	Boulevard Agua Caliente (Highway 2; see *Connecting Routes*). Ahead to the left are the downtown bullring and the Agua Caliente Racetrack.
05.7	Interchange with Libramiento, a bypass that skirts the southern part of Tijuana.
07.2	La Gloria (San Antonio de los Buenos), a village with a Pemex station and a few stores.
15.4	**Rosarito,** town center.

Rosarito

(See also *Lodging & Restaurants* and *Campgrounds & Trailer Parks*)

On a favored Pacific Ocean site fronting several miles of white sandy beach, Rosarito's mild semi-arid climate is similar to that of coastal San Diego County. Also known as Rosarito Beach/Playas de Rosarito, the town is situated at the junction of divided Mex-ico Highways 1 and 1D, both of which are four lanes from Tijuana. With its pleasant environment and proximity to Southern California, the town is one of the fastest growing in Baja California.

Rosarito's reputation as a vacation spot began in 1927 with the opening of the Rosarito Beach Hotel, the focus of recreational activities for many decades. The village became a destination for fly-in celebrities from the United States who sought seclusion. With the paving of the highway in 1930, a small stream of tourists started to travel the 15 miles south from the border to Rosarito's shores. Still a village in 1960, it has become a bigger boom town with each succeeding decade, with a current population of about 27,000. In the face of perpetual new construction, local leaders are striving to preserve the community's relaxed uncongested atmosphere, so attractive to locals and visitors alike.

Visitors along the wide Avenida Benito Juárez pass some three miles of restaurants, souvenir shops, food markets, an open-air bazaar, real estate offices, hospitals and a gasoline station. Quinta Plaza, in the northern part of town, has a *Comercial Mexicana* discount store, restaurants, shops and a convention center.

A growing number of hotels and motels serve tourists, and luxurious condominiums keep rising along the waterfront. A large oil-fueled power plant north of town supplies electricity to Tijuana and Rosarito. Favorite pastimes are swimming and surfing in the ocean, and horseback riding along the beach or inland; bicycle and motorcycle races start and finish here. (The Rosarito—Ensenada 50-Mile Fun Bike Ride takes place every April and September, attracting throngs of visitors.)

Take note . . . in Rosarito

Tourist Information and Assistance

The **Rosarito Convention and Visitors Bureau** is located in Quinta Plaza, in the northern part of town. Open daily from 10 a.m. to 4 p.m.; phone 01152 (661) 2-0396; (800) 962-2252 **(see ad inside front cover)**. The **State Tourism Office** is at Avenida Juárez and Calle Acacias next to the police station. Open Monday through Saturday from 9 a.m. to 7 p.m., Sunday 10 a.m. to 6 p.m.; phone 01152 (661) 2-0200. **Tourist Assistance,** which provides legal assistance to tourists, is in the same building and has the same hours and phone number.

R. Clark Hunter

View of the southern part of Rosarito, including Nuestra Señora del Rosario church.

Rosarito to Ensenada via Old Highway 1

(50 mi., 82 km.; 1:15 hrs.)

South of Rosarito, Mexico Highways 1 and 1D run parallel to one another for 24 miles along the rocky Pacific shoreline. At La Misión the old highway turns inland, climbs onto a level plateau, then curves gradually down to the coast at San Miguel, where it joins the divided highway leading into Ensenada. **Caution: Speed berms on**

Boulevard Teniente Azueta just west of downtown Ensenada can damage vehicles if taken too fast.

00.0   **Rosarito,** town center.

01.7   Popotla, a scattered seaside settlement with a large trailer park for permanent residents.

05.7   Calafia Resort, built on terraces overlooking the sea, has a popular restaurant and disco, a museum, and a mobile home park with overnight accommodations.

06.6   Las Gaviotas, a residential subdivision overlooking the ocean.

13.0   Cantamar, an oceanside resort complex with a Pemex station, and **Puerto Nuevo**, a community with over 30 restaurants specializing in lobster.

23.8   **La Misión** is a quiet village located in a steeply walled valley. On the south side of the valley are the ruins of Mission San Miguel, founded in 1787. The highway climbs out of the valley past abrupt volcanic bluffs via a series of narrow switchback curves.

43.0   San Miguel Village, a beach camp at the junction of Highways 1 and 1D. The rocky beach here is popular with surfers.

44.4   Junction with Highway 3, which leads northward to Guadalupe and Tecate (see *Connecting Routes*). Just past the interchange is El Sauzal, a sprawling community with a large fish cannery.

48.0   Junction. Although Highway 1 swings inland here, the preferred route into downtown Ensenada (signed *Centro*) follows the coastline to the right.

50.4   **Ensenada,** at the intersection of boulevards Teniente Azueta and Lázaro Cárdenas.

Tijuana to Ensenada via Toll Highway 1D

(68 mi., 109 km.; 1:30 hrs.)

The toll highway—a divided, fully access-controlled expressway—provides the fastest and safest route to Ensenada. Stopping along the highway is prohibited except in emergencies; call boxes are spaced along the expressway for travelers in distress. Many ramps offer access to seaside resorts and various points of interest. From the international border, follow the prominent "Ensenada Toll Road" (*Ensenada Cuota*) signs along Calle Inter-

TOLL RATES, TIJUANA TO ENSENADA (in dollars)

Car, Motorcycle, Van, Pickup Truck	$4.10
2 Axles: Motorhome, Cargo Truck	$8.30
3 Axles: Vehicle with Trailer (Tourist or Commercial), Cargo Truck	$12.40
4 Axles: Vehicle with Trailer, Cargo Truck	$16.40

The toll collected at each of the three toll gates is one-third of the above totals.

Tom Dell

At Punta Salsipuedes, just south of El Mirador, Highway 1D overlooks Baja California's scenic coastline.

nacional to Mexico Highway 1D. This route parallels the border fence and bypasses much of Tijuana's congestion. Detours are common, however, and traffic is sometimes routed through downtown streets. Highway 1D runs west to the first toll station at Playas de Tijuana, then turns south, following the scenic shoreline most of the way to Ensenada. **Caution: Speed berms on Boulevard Teniente Azueta just west of downtown Ensenada can damage vehicles if taken too fast.**

00.0 **Tijuana** (U.S. border crossing).
04.4 Exit for Playas de Tijuana and Bullring-by-the-Sea. No toll is charged to this point.
04.8 Toll station, Playas de Tijuana (*see* Toll Rates table).
12.0 Real del Mar, a resort complex with a hotel, tennis courts and a golf course.
13.0 Exit for San Antonio and Tijuana/Rosarito KOA.
17.4 Rosarito Norte interchange; junction with Highway 1 to Rosarito. (Although most

tourists take this highway to Rosarito, the town is described previously in the log for Old Highway 1, which passes directly through Rosarito.)
20.8 Rosarito Sur interchange; junction with Highway 1. To the east rises the impressive Mesa de Rosarito.
21.1 Toll station, Rosarito.
32.1 Exit for Cantamar and Puerto Nuevo; junction with Highway 1. Puerto Nuevo (Newport) is a fast-growing community with a hotel and over 30 restaurants specializing in lobster.
40.0 Exit for La Fonda, site of a popular restaurant, and the village of **La Misión,** which is 2.9 miles beyond.
44.4 Exit for **La Salina** (*see Campgrounds & Trailer Parks*).
47.4 Exit for Bajamar, a resort development with houses, condominiums, a hotel, tennis and a golf course, the Bajamar Country Club.

51.1 El Mirador, a rest stop with restaurant. An overlook provides a sweeping coastal panorama. At this point, Highway 1D makes a sharp turn, which requires a reduction in driving speed. The next several miles are subject to slides.

57.7 Exit for Playa Saldamando campground.

60.4 Toll station, San Miguel.

60.9 Exit for San Miguel Village; junction with Highway 1. The last eight miles to Ensenada are on a toll-free divided highway.

62.3 Junction with Highway 3, which leads northward to Guadalupe and Tecate (see *Connecting Routes*). Just past the interchange is El Sauzal, a sprawling community with a large fish cannery. Many hotels, motels and trailer parks are located along the beach between here and Ensenada.

68.3 **Ensenada,** at the junction of boulevards Teniente Azueta and Lázaro Cárdenas.

▬

Ensenada

(See also *Lodging & Restaurants* and *Campgrounds & Trailer Parks*)

The third largest city in Baja California, Ensenada, meaning cove or small bay, occupies a lowland that slopes gradually downward from scrub-covered hills to the shore of lovely Bahía de Todos Santos. Thanks to its scenic setting, beautiful beaches, numerous duty-free shops, excellent sportfishing, abundance of fine accommodations

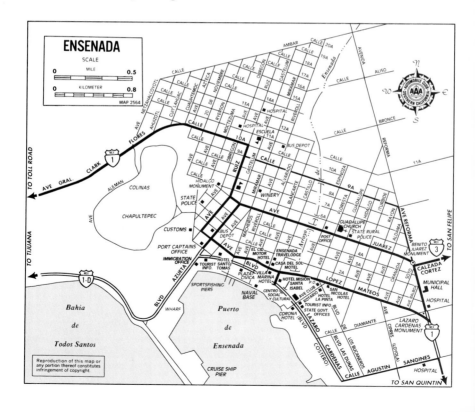

Take note . . . in Ensenada

Tourist Information and Assistance

The **State Tourism Office** is located on Boulevard Lázaro Cárdenas (Costero) and Calle Las Rocas, next to the other state government buildings. The office is open Monday through Friday 9 a.m. to 7 p.m., Saturday 10 a.m. to 3 p.m., Sunday 10 a.m. to 2 p.m.; phone 01152 (617) 2-3000 or 2-3022. **Asistencia al Turista/Tourist Assistance,** which provides legal assistance to tourists, is in the same building. The hours and phone number are the same as the tourism office. The **Tourist and Convention Bureau** has a booth on Boulevard Lázaro Cárdenas near the western entrance to the city. It is open Monday through Saturday 9 a.m. to 7 p.m. and Sunday 9 a.m. to 2 p.m; phone 01152 (617) 8-2411.

Newspapers

The English-language *Baja Sun* contains travel information, articles about Ensenada and other parts of Baja California, and numerous useful advertisements. California newspapers are available. The Spanish-language *El Mexicano* gives news of Ensenada and the state.

Radio and TV

Several American radio stations come in during the day, and more can be heard at night. Ensenada, of course, has its own radio stations. Radio Bahía Ensenada, 1590 AM, has an English/Spanish program on Saturday, 4 to 6 p.m. Most important hotels have satellite dish antennas to receive several American television stations, in addition to the Mexican channels.

Driving in Ensenada

Away from the heavily traveled arterial streets—those marked on the map with heavy black lines—Ensenada is not a difficult city for finding one's way; much of it is flat and laid out in a grid pattern. It is important, however, to watch for traffic lights and street signs; lights are often small and hard to see from a distance, and some streets are one-way. In most of the city there is little problem parking on the street or in the local shopping centers, although in the business districts street parking is scarce and parking meters require Mexican coins.

Local Transportation

Taxi service is readily available downtown and at hotels. In Mexico the ubiquitous taxi driver soliciting customers is sometimes an annoyance to the tourist, but once hired, he is usually friendly and courteous. Be sure to agree on the fare before getting in.

Local bus service is offered at low prices for those who wish to ride to the outlying districts and who enjoy mixing with residents. Inter-city buses follow both Highways 1 and 1D (the expressway) to Tijuana. Long-distance buses head south toward La Paz (see Bus Service in the Transportation section of the *Appendix*).

MEXICO HIGHWAY 1

and proximity to the United States, Ensenada is the peninsula's foremost summer resort. Hundreds of thousands of vacationers and weekend tourists flock to the city every year. The climate is very similar to that of San Diego, with mild, pleasant winters and sunny summers kept cool by refreshing sea breezes. Rainfall averages about 10 inches per year, most of which occurs from December through March.

With its protected harbor and modern dock facilities, Ensenada is also Baja California's leading seaport. It has become a major port of call for cruise ships. Some of the agricultural wealth of the Mexicali Valley is brought to Ensenada by truck, loaded onto ocean-going freighters and shipped to mainland Mexico and the Orient. Commercial fishing and seafood processing are other important contributors to the local economy; just west of the city is the largest fish cannery on Mexico's Pacific coast. Also in Ensenada is Bodegas de Santo Tomás—the nation's biggest winery.

In 1602, 60 years after Juan Rodríguez Cabrillo's voyage of discovery along the Pacific coast, Sebastián Vizcaíno sailed into the bay and was so enthralled by its beauty that he named it after all the saints—Ensenada de Todos los Santos. Lack of fresh water precluded the establishment of a permanent settlement for more than two centuries, but the bay was a frequent port of call for the treasure-laden Manila galleons and for the privateers who preyed on them, as well as for whaling ships and fur traders. In the early 19th century, ranchers moved into the area, and Ensenada became a supply point for the missionaries and pioneers trying to secure a foothold in Mexico's northern frontier. In 1870 gold was discovered at nearby Real de Castillo, and Ensenada boomed, soon

becoming an important supply depot for the miners. In 1882 it was made the capital of the territory, and two years later it became headquarters for a land company organized to colonize a huge land grant covering much of the peninsula. Shortly after the turn of the century, however, the mines gave out, the land company folded, the capital was moved to Mexicali, and Ensenada dwindled into a sleepy fishing village.

In the mid-1930s, two important factors combined to bring about a resurgence for Ensenada. First, agricultural reform and development in the Mexicali Valley created the need for a seaport to handle the export of farm products. And second, the completion of the paved highway from Tijuana permitted large numbers of American tourists to discover the area's rich recreational potential. Ensenada prospered and continues to grow; the city's population is about 230,000. Today it is the seat of government of the *municipio* of Ensenada, which extends south to the 28th Parallel and includes shoreline on both the east and west coasts of the state of Baja California.

Probably because of its dual position as both an important commercial center and a popular resort, Ensenada has two separate business districts. The downtown area, containing stores, banks, restaurants, cantinas and offices patronized primarily by local residents, is along avenidas Ruiz and Juárez. Tourist activity, on the other hand, centers on avenidas López Mateos and Lázaro Cárdenas (Costero), which are lined with motels, restaurants, nightclubs, sportfishing firms and dozens of shops catering to visitors.

Shopping

The city's easygoing, low-pressure atmosphere makes shopping in Ensenada an enjoyable experience for most tourists. In addition to the great savings on duty-free imported goods, Mexican-made items are also good buys. These include pottery, jewelry, baskets, ceramics, leather goods (jackets, sandals and purses), wrought-iron furniture and embroidered clothing. Most shops have fixed prices. **Centro Artesenal/Mexican Hand Crafts Center** is a large group of arts and crafts stores, located on Boulevard Lázaro Cárdenas (Costero) at Avenida Castillo.

In Ensenada along and near avenidas Ruiz, Juárez and Reforma, travelers can find many stores carrying a variety of consumer goods, including food, auto parts and camping supplies. The city also has many attractive supermarkets and discount stores.

Dining

Some of the restaurants listed here are AAA approved; more information about these can be found in the *Lodging & Restaurants* chapter of this book. Non-AAA-approved restaurants are also mentioned here as a service.

Among Ensenada's better-known eating establishments are **Casamar,** on Boulevard Lázaro Cárdenas (Costero) 987 (seafood); **El Rey Sol,** in town at avenidas López Mateos and Blancarte (French and Mexican cuisine); **El Campanario,** in Hotel Misión Santa Isabel (varied menu); **Enrique's,** on Highway 1D, 1½ miles north of town (Mexican and seafood specialties); **La Cueva de los Tigres,** on the beach 3 miles south of town via Highway 1 and gravel road (seafood, steaks and Mexican cuisine); the **Restaurant at Punta Morro** in the hotel of the same name (seafood and varied international cuisine); and **Viva Mexico Taquería** on Avenida López Mateos at Avenida Granada (tacos, steaks and carne asada). The widely known **Hussong's Bar,** on Avenida Ruíz near López Ma-

teos, has an old-fashioned rollicking cantina and a souvenir shop. In addition, Ensenada has many other large restaurants, plus numerous small cafes with reasonable prices.

Nightclubs

Ensenada is a lively place after dark. Many night spots and discos are found on or near Avenida López Mateos. The hotels Bahía, El Cid, La Pinta, Las Rosas and San Nicolás are well-known for live entertainment and dancing.

Points of Interest

Bodegas de Santo Tomás *Avenida Miramar at Calle 7. 01152 (617) 8-2509.* This winery offers tours and wine-tasting daily at 11 a.m., 1 and 3 p.m. Tour charge is $2.

Centro Cívico, Social y Cultural *Boulevard Lázaro Cárdenas at Avenida Club Rotario.* Formerly called Riviera del Pacífico, this building once served as a glamorous resort and casino renowned for its impressive Mediterranean architecture. Now it is a cultural center with an art gallery, a museum and attractive gardens containing historic monuments and plaques. It is also a site for many local civic and social events.

Chapultepec Hills *Via Avenida Alemán.* This attractive residential section overlooks the city and is an excellent vantage point for photographers. Another scenic viewpoint is the hill at Avenida Moctezuma and Calle 12.

Museo de Ciencias de Ensenada *Avenida Obregón between calles 14 and 15. 01152 (617) 8-7192.* Open Tuesday through Sunday from 9 a.m. to 5 p.m. Admission is $1.60. This science museum features astronomy, oceanography and marine life exhibits

MEXICO HIGHWAY 1

R. Clark Hunter

*Colossal heads of Benito Juárez, Miguel Hidalgo and
Venustiano Carranza oversee Ensenada's Plaza Cívica.*

for the region. A special exhibit stresses endangered animal species.

Nuestra Señora de Guadalupe
Calle 6 and Avenida Floresta. Built in the Spanish Colonial style, this church's impressive twin towers make it one of the most prominent structures in Ensenada.

Plaza Cívica *Boulevard Lázaro Cárdenas (Costero) at Avenida Riveroll.* This landscaped court contains 12-foot-high busts of Mexican heroes Juárez, Carranza and Hidalgo. Nearby at Avenida Alvarado is the Naval Base, which at sunrise and sunset has colorful flag ceremonies with a drum and bugle corps. Horse-drawn carriages for sightseeing depart from here.

Spectator Sports

Bullfights

Plaza de Toros *Calle Agustín Sanginés between Boulevard de los Bucaneros and Avenida Ciprés (Loyola),* hosts bullfights on an irregular schedule during the spring and summer. For de-

tails contact the State Tourism office, 01152 (617) 2-3000.

Ensenada to Colonet
(76 mi., 123 km.; 1:45 hrs.)

Leaving Ensenada, Highway 1 is an undivided four-lane road as far as Maneadero. It passes through commercial districts, then enters a coastal lowland where olives, vegetables and chili peppers are the principal crops. Beyond Maneadero, open countryside gives way to chaparral-clad slopes. The highway is quite narrow, and careful driving is essential. Thirty miles south of Ensenada, Highway 1 crosses the wide, beautiful Santo Tomás Valley, passing the vineyards of Mexico's largest winery. It then winds among steep hills and grassy valleys to San Vicente, where dairy and beef cattle graze. From here to Colonet, the landscape gradually becomes drier and less rugged.

00.0 Ensenada, at the intersection of boulevards Teniente

Azueta and Lázaro Cárdenas. Follow Lázaro Cárdenas south to its end, then turn left.

01.9 Junction with Highway 1, turn right.

04.9 El Ciprés, site of Ensenada Airport and a large military camp.

06.9 Turnoff to Estero Beach. The paved side road leads past several curio shops to a popular beach resort area. The sandy beaches and quiet waters of Bahía de Todos Santos are ideal for water sports.

09.4 Junction with road to Baja Country Club.

10.6 **Maneadero,** a community of about 30,000 people, at the junction with the paved road to Punta Banda (see *Side Routes*). This fast-growing agricultural market center has two Pemex stations, several small restaurants and many markets and other stores, including auto parts shops. Drivers should watch for unmarked speed bumps. South of Maneadero travelers are required to have validated tourist cards in their possession (see Mexican Tourist Cards in the *Tourist Regulations and Travel Tips* chapter).

21.6 Ejido Uruápan, which offers camping, hunting and hot springs.

26.5 Junction with the gravel road to La Bocana and Puerto Santo Tomás (see *Side Routes*).

28.9 **Santo Tomás** (see *Campgrounds & Trailer Parks*), a village that has become well-known because of the domestic wine of the same name. A Pemex station (*magna sin*) and general store are located here. Ruins of Mission Santo

R. Clark Hunter

Tourists walk along a sportfising pier in Ensenada after a day on Todos Santos Bay.

Tom Dell

The lush Santo Tomás Valley, site of the Santo Tomás Vineyards.

Tomás are located just west of the trailer park.

45.6 Junction with the paved road to Ejido Eréndira (see *Side Routes*).

51.9 A rough dirt road leads to the ruins of Mission San Vicente Ferrer, 0.6 mile to the west.

52.6 San Vicente, a busy farming center with a population of 6000. Facilities include two Pemex stations (*magna sin*), several stores, cafes, a motel, tire shops and an auto supply house.

75.6 Colonet, at the junction to San Antonio del Mar (see *Side Routes*). Colonet, a center for farmers and ranchers in the area, offers a selection of goods and services.

Colonet to San Quintín
(42 mi., 68 km.; 1 hr.)

South of Colonet the highway widens slightly as it crosses a level plateau dotted with occasional cultivated fields. After descending a steep hill into Camalú, Highway 1 reaches a flat, nearly featureless coastal plain. Approaching Colonia Guerrero, the motorist can glimpse the high Sierra San Pedro Mártir to the east; visible ahead are the ocean and the volcanic cones across Bahía de San Quintín. In this same area there is a narrow, reconstructed bridge over the Río Santo Domingo and some rough pavement due to flooding in winter 1993. Beyond Colonia Guerrero, the road runs in a straight line across level farmland to San Quintín.

00.0 Colonet, at the junction to San Antonio del Mar.

01.7 Junction with a good dirt road that leads to Cabo Colonet, site of a small fishing cooperative eight miles away.

07.8 San Telmo de Abajo, at the junction with an improved dirt road to San Telmo, Meling Ranch, the National Observatory and Mike's Sky Rancho (see *Side Routes*).

18.4 Camalú, which has a Pemex station, clinic and a variety of supplies and services.

27.1 **Colonia Vicente Guerrero** (see *Campgrounds & Trailer Parks*) is a busy, fast-growing agricultural center. Facilities include a motel, a hospital,

Pemex station (*magna sin*), telegraph and post office, stores and cafes.

27.5 Turnoff to Posada Don Diego and Mesón de Don Pepe trailer parks (tourist information is available at the latter).

41.5 San Quintín, Lázaro Cárdenas district, at the military camp.

San Quintín

(See also Lodging & Restaurants and Campgrounds & Trailer Parks)

The attraction of Bahía de San Quintín dates back to the late 19th century, when an English land company was authorized by the Mexican government to colonize the eastern shore of the bay. Crops were planted, and the colonists built a grist mill, a customs house and a pier. The enterprise was dependent on dry farming, however,

and a prolonged drought caused the colony to fail. Evidence of the past can be seen at the Old Mill Motel, which contains some of the original mill machinery, and farther south along the bay where pier pilings march into the water. A re-creation of a pioneer farm, with buildings and equipment reminiscent of the early 20th century, is located a short distance east of the Old Mill Motel. Another reminder is a collection of wooden English crosses in the lonely, windswept cemetery.

Today, San Quintín has two faces. One, the San Quintín Valley, has a population of about 22,000 in an urbanized area strung out haphazardly for several miles along the highway. The valley's two commercial zones, San Quintín and Lázaro Cárdenas, serve as market centers for a developing agricultural region. The many businesses here cater primarily to local residents, but services are available to travelers as well. Facilities include long-distance telephones, a movie theater, a large new church, numerous shops, motels, restaurants, banks, two clinics, two gasoline stations, mechanics and auto parts houses. Tourist information is available at the Motel Chávez Restaurant. The surrounding farmland produces large quantities of barley, tomatoes, strawberries, potatoes, peppers and other vegetables.

The other face of San Quintín is the nearby bay—probably the most popular tourist destination between Ensenada and Mulegé. The sheltered waters of the U-shaped inner bay separate the cultivated

Howard H. Goetzman

The old English cemetery at Bahía de San Quintín, as photographed in 1965. English settlers established a colony nearby during the 19th century, but were forced to abandon the project because of a lack of fresh water.

64

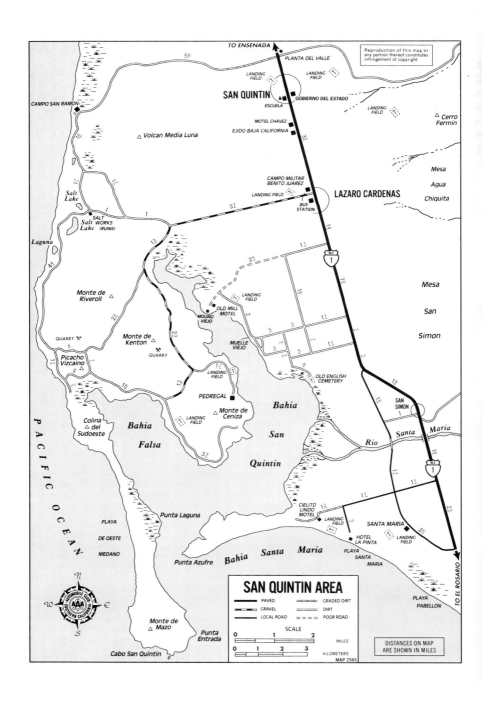

TO ENSENADA

PLANTA DEL VALLE

LANDING FIELD

LANDING FIELD

SAN QUINTIN

GOBIERNO DEL ESTADO

ESCUELA

CAMPO SAN RAMON

LANDING FIELD

△ Cerro Fermin

△ Volcan Media Luna

MOTEL CHAVEZ

EJIDO BAJA CALIFORNIA

Mesa

Agua

Chiquita

Salt Lake

SALT Salt WORKS Lake (RUINS)

Laguna

CAMPO MILITAR BENITO JUAREZ

LANDING FIELD

LAZARO CARDENAS

BUS STATION

1

Monte de Riveroll △

LANDING FIELD

Mesa

San

Simon

QUARRY

Monte de Kenton △

QUARRY

OLD MILL MOTEL

MOLINO VIEJO

MUELLE VIEJO

Picacho Vizcaino △

LANDING FIELD

PEDREGAL

OLD ENGLISH CEMETERY

SAN SIMON

Colina del Sudoeste △

LANDING FIELD

△ Monte de Ceniza

Bahia

San

Quintin

Bahia

Falsa

Rio Santa Maria

PACIFIC OCEAN

CIELITO LINDO MOTEL

LANDING FIELD

SANTA MARIA

LANDING FIELD

HOTEL LA PINTA

PLAYA SANTA MARIA

PLAYA

DE OESTE

MEDANO

Punta Laguna

Punta Azufre

Bahia Santa Maria

TO EL ROSARIO

N

W   E

S

AAA
AUTOMOBILE CLUB
SOUTHERN CALIFORNIA

Monte de Mazo △

Punta Entrada

Cabo San Quintin

PLAYA PABELLON

SAN QUINTIN AREA

	PAVED		GRADED DIRT
	GRAVEL		DIRT
	LOCAL ROAD		POOR ROAD

SCALE

0   1   2   MILES

0   1   2   3   KILOMETERS

MAP 2565

DISTANCES ON MAP ARE SHOWN IN MILES

fields of Valle de San Quintín from a row of volcanic cones to the west. Across a narrow sandspit to the south is the outer bay, which is more open to the winds and heavy surf of the Pacific Ocean. Bahía de San Quintín is a seasonal paradise for sportsmen. Black brant (a type of goose) migrate to the area each winter and are popular game. Good surf fishing and clam digging enhance the appeal of the beaches along the shore of the outer bay. Fishing from boats is excellent in both parts of the bay (see Fishing in *Recreation*). The quiet waters of the inner bay provide a fine, protected anchorage for small boats. Explorers with heavy-duty vehicles can make the adventurous trek to the western shore of the inner bay and the Pacific beaches beyond, where good primitive campsites can be found.

▬ San Quintín to El Rosario
(36 mi., 58 km.; 1 hr.)

Highway 1 narrows south of San Quintín. The road passes a group of roadside communities and a series of cultivated fields, then crosses a bridge spanning the bed of the intermittently flowing Río Santa María. Due to flooding in the winter of 1993, this and several other bridges in the region were reconstructed and may be narrow. Storm damage also caused some sections of rough pavement, which still remain. Thirty miles beyond San Quintín the road turns sharply inland, soon reaching a summit from which there are expansive views of the ocean and the countryside to the northeast. From the mesa, the highway drops into a wide valley and enters El Rosario.

00.0	San Quintín, at the military camp.
01.4	First turnoff to Bahía de San Quintín. This dirt road leads 3.6 miles to the shore. A better road follows.
03.2	Junction with the dirt road to Muelle Viejo, the ruins of a pier constructed by an unsuccessful English colony, and to the Old Mill Motel.
04.4	Highway 1 crosses a bridge over the Río Santa María.

Tom Dell

El Rosario is still an important reference point for travelers. Highway 1 turns inland here and enters the rugged central desert of Baja California.

Bill Cory

Cirios begin to appear about eight miles beyond El Rosario. These unique plants grow only in Baja California in a belt extending from here to below Punta Prieta on Highway 1 and to Bahía de los Angeles on the eastern coast.

07.9 Junction with the paved road to the Hotel La Pinta and the Cielito Lindo Motel.

09.0 Turnoff on a dirt road to El Pabellón RV Park.

16.1 Junction with the unmarked short dirt road to El Socorrito, a seaside village that offers sportfishing and scuba diving.

35.8 Rosario de Arriba, the primary settlement of El Rosario. The much smaller Rosario de Abajo, which contains the ruins of Mission Nuestra Señora del Rosario, lies about a mile west via a dirt road. The total population for both communities is about 4000. Before the completion of the Transpeninsular Highway and the peninsula's microwave telephone system, El Rosario was considered the last outpost of civilization in northern Baja California. It is now a quiet agricultural community and highway stop, with gasoline (*magna sin*), auto parts, restaurants, two motels, and groceries. A museum containing a nice variety of items from northern Baja California is located on Highway 1 in the center of town. For entrance to the museum, inquire at Mamá Espinoza's Restaurant on the bend of the highway.

El Rosario to Cataviña

(76 mi., 122 km.; 2 hrs.)

Leaving El Rosario, Highway 1 turns east and follows the wide, cultivated Arroyo del Rosario for a few miles, then crosses the valley and climbs into a region of low, deeply eroded hills.

Soon the terrain begins to conform to the armchair traveler's notion of Baja, with cirio trees and giant cardón cacti appearing alongside the highway. With its blue skies, expansive views and abundance of unique vegetation, the Central Desert of Baja California is one of North America's most fascinating desert regions. After continuing southeast through ranges of hills and wide valleys, the highway enters a spectacular landscape of large boulder formations interspersed with dense thickets of cirio, cardón and other varieties of desert vegetation. Here Highway 1 crosses several deep arroyos that are subject to flash flooding. At present these arroyo crossings or *vados* contain potholes from storm damage during winter 1993. Many other parts of the highway from El Rosario to south of Cataviña are rough and require very careful driving. In the heart of this "rock-garden" zone are Cataviña and Rancho Santa Inés.

00.0 El Rosario.

04.8 A bridge carries Highway 1 across Arroyo del Rosario.

08.1 Cirio trees begin to appear, their weird forms reaching skyward in a profusion of shapes. Aside from a small stand in Sonora on the Mexican mainland, these plants grow nowhere else in the world.

14.5 Junction with a good dirt road leading 39 miles to Punta San Carlos and a network of roads which provides access to several fishing camps.

31.3 Junction with a rough dirt road to Rancho El Cartabón.

38.3 Signed junction with an unpaved road to the adobe ruins of Mission San Fernando Velicatá, founded in 1769 by Father Junípero Serra, who went on to establish Alta California's chain of missions. Passenger cars can make this trip in dry weather.

39.8 El Progreso, which has a cafe. Once a busy construction camp, El Progreso is now all but abandoned.

46.8 Junction with the road to Santa Catarina and Punta Canoas (see *Side Routes*).

55.2 San Agustín, which consists of an abandoned government-built trailer park and a

MEXICO HIGHWAY 1

Bill Cory

Just north of Cataviña, Highway 1 enters a spectacular boulder-strewn landscape, part of the Desierto Central de Baja California Natural Park.

The Hotel La Pinta at Cataviña, built shortly after the completion of the highway, offers comfortable accommodations and meals to travelers.

highway maintenance camp. From behind the camp a sandy road leads to Rancho San Agustín.

57.1 Junction with a good dirt road leading to El Mármol (see *Side Routes*). Near the junction are two cafes.

59.4 Highway 1 now enters a region of impressive boulder-strewn countryside. The Mexican government has created a park here, and the natural environment is protected by federal law.

74.1 Arroyo de Cataviñacito, a deep arroyo with tall blue palms and occasional pools of water. The first elephant trees are seen near here, their short, fat trunks seemingly squatting among the boulders.

76.3 **Cataviña** (see *Lodging & Restaurants*), set in the midst of "rock-garden" scenery. A Pemex station, a market, two cafes and a mechanic's shop

are on the left; on the right is a government-built trailer park and the Hotel La Pinta, which sometimes sells gasoline (*magna sin*). Hikes over beautiful desert landscape may be taken in any direction from the village.

Cataviña to Bahía de los Angeles Junction

(65 mi., 105 km.; 1:30 hrs.)

From Cataviña, the highway continues to lead southeast through interesting rock-strewn country. After crossing a narrow arroyo, the road climbs to a 2700-foot summit, then descends quickly to the edge of a dry lake. Beyond here the landscape becomes more barren as Highway 1 meanders through low hills, ascends a 2200-foot saddle and drops onto the basin of Laguna Chapala. This vast, desolate dry lake becomes a sea of mud following heavy rains. After crossing another range of low barren hills, the highway traverses a sandy plain to the junction with the road to Bahía de los Angeles. This region is a showcase for the typical vegetation of Baja California's central desert: cirio, cardón, cholla cactus, ocotillo, elephant trees and yucca válida.

00.0 Cataviña.

00.7 Junction with the 0.8-mile paved road to Rancho Santa Inés, which offers a clinic, motel, campground, cafe, a paved airstrip and information for off-road explorers.

07.4 Rancho San Ignacito. In late 1973, road crews working north and south met here as they completed the paving of Highway 1. A small monument on the west side of the highway marks the spot.

18.6 El Pedregoso, a mountain composed entirely of jumbled boulders. Before the completion of the paved highway, this was an important land

mark for peninsula travelers.

33.7 Laguna Chapala Junction. Here a graded dirt road, signed Calamajué, provides access to Bahía San Luis Gonzaga and other points along the northeastern shore of the peninsula. At the junction is a cafe.

34.5 Rancho Chapala. Stretching away to the east is the broad expanse of Laguna Chapala, with its bed of cracked clay.

50.8 Junction with a rough road to Campo Calamajué, a fish camp.

65.3 Junction with the paved road to **Bahía de los Angeles** (see *Side Routes* and *Campgrounds & Trailer Parks*). Here there are a gasoline station (*magna sin*) and a highway patrol station. The junction is sometimes called Punta Prieta, although the original settlement bearing this name is eight miles to the south.

Bill Cory

Laguna Chapala, a vast, desolate dry lake bed. Solid and driveable in dry weather, it becomes a huge expanse of mud after storms.

Bill Cory

Near Punta Prieta, the barren Sierra de la Asamblea overlooks a sandy plain covered with abundant desert vegetation.

Bahía de los Angeles Junction to Guerrero Negro

(80 mi., 129 km.; 1:45 hrs.)

For the first 15 miles after leaving the Bahía de los Angeles junction, Highway 1 continues to cross a level, sandy plain. It then climbs into hilly country sparsely vegetated with cirio and elephant trees. Extra caution is required in this section, which is characterized by steep dropoffs, sharp curves and a narrow roadway. Near Rosarito, several flat-topped buttes dot the horizon to the east. Turning almost due south, the highway descends gradually onto the windy Vizcaíno Desert, one of the most desolate portions of the entire peninsula. Only hearty yucca válida and scattered clumps of saltbrush interrupt the uniformity of the sandy landscape.

00.0 Junction to Bahía de los Angeles.

08.4 Junction with the short paved road to the village of Punta Prieta. Once a bustling construction camp during the paving of Highway 1, Punta Prieta is now a sleepy little hamlet. Facilities include a store, a cafe, a small military camp and a highway maintenance station. On the east side of the highway is a paved airstrip.

18.3 Brief view of the Pacific Ocean from a low summit.

24.0 Junction with a gravel road to Santa Rosalillita (see *Side Routes*).

32.3 Rosarito, a village with a store, a cafe and a shrine. Rosarito also marks the junction with the dirt road to Mission San Borja (see *Side Routes*).

39.2 Junction with a dirt road leading north along isolated beaches for 18 miles to Santa Rosalillita. This area is popular with surfers.

42.7 Junction with a rough dirt road to El Tomatal.

49.4	Turnoff to Rancho San Angel.	**80.3**	Junction with the paved road

49.4 Turnoff to Rancho San Angel.

59.0 Villa Jesús María, a farming village with a Pemex station (*magna sin*), two cafes and a small store. A paved road leads west to Ejido Morelos, a government-sponsored cattle-raising project, and Laguna Manuela, a lagoon with a fish camp and a sandy beach.

78.4 The 28th parallel separates the states of Baja California and Baja California Sur. Erected on the latitude line is a 140-foot-high steel monument in the form of a stylized eagle, commemorating completion of Highway 1 and the uniting of northern and southern Baja California—a major milestone in the peninsula's history. On the west side of the monument are Hotel La Pinta and a trailer park. The 28th parallel also marks the boundary of the Pacific and Mountain time zones.

80.3 Junction with the paved road to the town of **Guerrero Negro,** 2 miles to the west.

Guerrero Negro

(See also *Lodging & Restaurants* and *Campgrounds & Trailer Parks*)

Located in the midst of the vast Vizcaíno Desert, this hospitable community of about 11,000 residents plays a significant role in the economy of Baja California. Essentially a company town, Guerrero Negro is the world's leading producer of salt, according to the firm Exportadora de Sal. South of town are thousands of evaporating ponds, each about 100 yards square and from three to four feet deep when flooded with sea water. The desert sun evaporates the water quickly, leaving a residue of pure white, hard salt, which is scooped up by dredges and taken by trucks to a nearby wharf. The salt is then loaded by conveyor belt onto barges and carried to Cedros Island, where it is transferred into oceangoing freighters. Salt from Guerrero Negro is

MEXICO HIGHWAY 1

Tom Dell

This huge steel monument straddles the 28th parallel, the imaginary line dividing the states of Baja California and Baja California Sur.

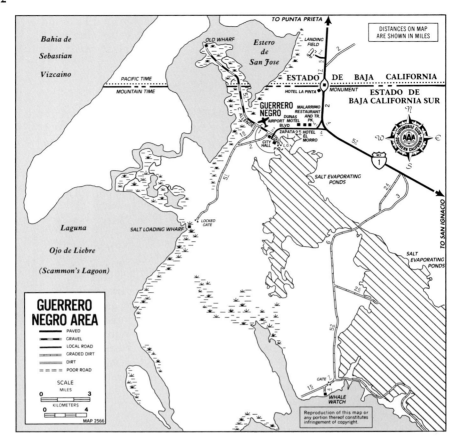

GUERRERO NEGRO AREA

PAVED
GRAVEL
LOCAL ROAD
GRADED DIRT
DIRT
POOR ROAD

SCALE
MILES
0 — 3
KILOMETERS
0 — 4
MAP 2566

used in Mexico, the United States, Canada and Japan.

A wide variety of services and facilities is available in Guerrero Negro, including several motels and trailer parks, restaurants, stores, two Pemex stations, several auto parts houses, mechanics, markets, a hospital, banks and an airport.

During most of the year, Guerrero Negro offers little in the way of recreation, although good surf fishing can be found along the remote beaches to the north. In January, February and early March, however, nearby Scammon's Lagoon (*Laguana Ojo de Liebre*) is the destination of the spec-

tacular run of gray whales, who migrate annually from the Bering Sea (see Fauna in *Introduction*).

Good spots from which to see the whales are the old salt wharf, located seven miles west of Guerrero Negro via a dirt road, and the shore of Scammon's Lagoon, which has been designated a natural park by the Mexican government (see *Side Routes* chapter, Highway 1 to Scammon's Lagoon).

Once an endangered specie, gray whales are now protected by the Mexican and American governments. The name Guerrero Negro is the Spanish translation of *Black Warrior,* an American whaling ship that was wrecked at the entrance to the lagoon in the late 19th Century.

Isla Cedros

Isla Cedros is a barren, rugged island situated about 55 miles west of the Guerrero Negro coastal area. Its inhabitants are supported mostly by a fish-packing plant. It also plays the role of transshipment point for the salt mined at Guerrero Negro, which has no deep water harbor. Ocean-going ships load the salt for export at the port of Cedros (also called El Pueblo), where most of the population of about 6000 live.

Virtually untouched by tourism, Cedros has the character of a typical older Mexican coastal town. Facilities include restaurants, a bank, a church, taxis and a couple of low-priced inns. Visitors are able to find beaches, hire fishing boats and hike over trails to observe the unspoiled natural environment of most of the island. Cedros is

accessible by a local airline, with flights leaving from both Ensenada and Guerrero Negro a couple times a week.

Guerrero Negro to San Ignacio
(89 mi., 142 km.; 1:45 hrs.)

From the junction to Guerrero Negro, Highway 1 turns inland, heading southeast across the barren Vizcaíno Desert. Near the town of Vizcaíno, however, yucca válida, cardón cacti and dense thickets of low shrubs begin to appear alongside the highway. About 20 miles from San Ignacio, the road passes a group of flat-topped volcanic cones; the dark reddish-brown rocks in this region give further evidence of past volcanic activity. Finally, after winding through low, cactus-covered hills, the highway brings the traveler to the junction with the paved road to San Ignacio. Much of this section of Highway 1 is rough or narrow; drive with care.

MEXICO HIGHWAY 1

Tom Dell

Between Guerrero Negro and San Ignacio, Highway 1 cuts a streamlined swath across the vast Vizcaíno Desert.

00.0   Junction to Guerrero Negro.

05.6   Junction with the graded road to the shore of Scammon's Lagoon, signed *Laguna Ojo de Liebre* (see *Side Routes*).

17.1   Junction with the gravel highway to El Arco (see *Side Routes*).

45.4   Vizcaíno (sometimes called Fundolegal), with about 2000 inhabitants, has a Pemex station (*magna sin*), two motels, an RV park, cafes, a market, a pharmacy and auto parts. A paved side road leads five miles to Ejido Díaz Ordaz (sometimes called Vizcaíno). This *ejido* is a major government-assisted farming cooperative. Water from deep wells has turned a section of forbidding desert into productive fields and orchards; principal crops include spices, cotton, figs, grapes and oranges. The *ejido* has a clinic, a market and a variety of small stores. Pavement on the side road ends after 16 more miles. From this point, the road is graded earth and leads onto the remote Vizcaíno Peninsula (see *Side Routes*); this side trip is only for adventurous well-prepared travelers with the proper vehicles and equipment.

52.4   A paved road leads to Emiliano Zapata, a large dairy-farming *ejido* or collective agricultural settlement.

57.4   Estación Microóndas Los Angeles, the first of 23 microwave relay stations along Highway 1 in Baja California Sur. The stations are closed to the public.

61.3   Junction with graded dirt road to San Francisco de la Sierra (see *Side Routes*).

73.6   Junction with a graded dirt road to Punta Abreojos (see *Side Routes*). A cafe is located at the junction.

Tom Dell

San Ignacio, with its magnificent 18th-century mission, occupies a palm-lined arroyo surrounded on all sides by harsh desert terrain.

85.8	Junction with a 0.6-mile paved road to a good paved airstrip.
88.6	Junction with the 0.9-mile paved road to San Lino and Paredones, two villages on the outskirts of San Ignacio.
88.9	Junction with the 1.1-mile-long paved road to **San Ignacio.** Opposite the junction is a Pemex station offering *magna sin.*

▬
San Ignacio

(See also *Lodging & Restaurants* and *Campgrounds & Trailer Parks*)

For the traveler who has motored through mile after mile of inhospitable terrain, the first view of San Ignacio is one of Baja California's great delights. A forest of date palms and one of the most charming towns on the peninsula are set in the bottom of a wide arroyo surrounded by arid desert. Northernmost of Baja California's major oasis communities, San Ignacio is an attractive, tranquil settlement of about 2000 inhabitants. Its thatched-roof dwellings and pastel-colored business structures are clustered around an imposing stone mission and a tree-shaded plaza. The paved road leading from Highway 1 into San Ignacio passes over a small dam, impounding an underground river that emerges to the earth's surface here. It provides sustenance for an economy based on agriculture. Dates are the chief crop, but figs, oranges and grapes are also grown commercially. San Ignacio also serves as the market center for the isolated cattle ranches to the north and south. To the visitor, it offers hotels and trailer parks, cafes, gasoline, mechanical assistance, telephone service, supplies and an airstrip.

Before the arrival of European explorers, this was the site of a large Indian settlement. Seeing a fertile field for their work, the Jesuits founded a mission here in 1728 and planted the date palms that now cover the floor of the arroyo. After the expulsion of the Jesuits from Mexico, the Dominicans came to San Ignacio and built the present church, which was completed in 1786. Thanks to lava-block walls four-feet thick, it remains in an excellent state of preservation and still serves as a parish church.

In the rugged, remote mountains both north and south of San Ignacio are hundreds of mysterious cave paintings by prehistoric Indians. Large figures of humans and animals in a variety of colors appear on high ledges and on the ceilings and walls of shallow caves. The origin, age and meaning of this rock art are unknown. One good road leads to the area, and arrangements for mule trips to many of these sites can be made at the hotels in San Ignacio.

South of San Ignacio a dirt road leads 30 miles to Laguna San Ignacio, a site for whale watching. From there a long graded dirt road travels 100 miles south along the Pacific coast to the agricultural oases of San José de Gracia and Ejido Cadeje and the large fishing village of San Juanico. Bahía San Juanico has beach campsites and good surfing. From here the road continues to Ciudad Insurgentes in the Santo Domingo Valley.

▬
San Ignacio to
Santa Rosalia

(45 mi., 73 km.; 1:15 hrs.)

Leaving the palm groves of San Ignacio behind, Highway 1 re-enters arid countryside, winding through low hills toward Las Tres Vírgenes, a large mountain mass with three volcanic

Tom Dell

Just east of San Ignacio, Highway 1 skirts the base of Las Tres Vírgenes.

cones rising majestically above the surrounding desert. After skirting the base of the volcanoes, the road drops onto a cactus-covered plateau. At the end of the plateau is the steepest grade on the entire length of Highway 1; here the road drops via sharp switchbacks for seven miles to the shore of the Gulf of California. (Drivers should exercise caution, watching particularly for trucks rounding the curves.) Then the highway turns south and follows the coastline for 4.7 miles to the junction with the main street of Santa Rosalía.

00.0	Junction with the paved road into San Ignacio.
08.8	Junction with a rough dirt road to Rancho Santa Marta, a departure point for mule trips to ancient Indian cave paintings in the rugged mountains north of San Ignacio.
24.0	Excellent viewpoint for Las Tres Vírgenes.
34.1	First view of the Gulf of California.
34.4	Beginning of a series of steep grades and tight curves, as the highway plunges 1000 feet to the shore of the gulf.
40.6	The shore of the Gulf of California.
45.2	Junction with the main street of Santa Rosalía.

Santa Rosalía

(See also *Lodging & Restaurants* and *Campgrounds & Trailer Parks*)

Santa Rosalía, with a population of 11,000, is a bustling city with narrow, congested streets and a businesslike atmosphere. It used to be a mining town, having been established in the 1880s by the French-owned El Boleo Copper Company. After discovering rich copper deposits here, the mining company imported Indian labor from Sonora, built a pipeline to bring water to the city and constructed a port to handle shipments of processed ore. Mining operations were very prosperous for several decades, but ore deterioration and low demand forced the closure of the mines in 1954. A few efforts have been made since then to revive the industry.

With its row upon row of uniform frame buildings and its large smelters, Santa Rosalía looks like a company-owned mining town, quite different from any other town in Baja California. Even the church of Santa Bárbara seems incongruous, constructed of flat galvanized iron shipped in sections from France. The town consists of three sections, with two plateaus separated by a flat-bottomed arroyo. The northern plateau, with its many French-colonial buildings and its panoramic view of the smelter, is especially interesting. Commercial fishing boats are based in the small harbor, which also serves as the terminus for ferry service to Guaymas across the gulf (see *Appendix,* Transportation).

Bill Cory

This prefabricated iron church, designed by A. G. Eiffel for the 1898 Paris World's Fair, was shipped in sections around Cape Horn to Santa Rosalía.

Santa Rosalía is the seat of government for the *municipio* of Mulegé, which also contains Guerrero Negro, San Ignacio and Mulegé. Although Santa Rosalía is not a tourist town, it does offer a variety of facilities, including overnight accommodations, many stores and restaurants, an excellent

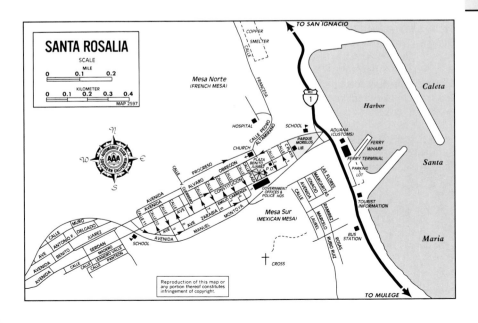

Tom Dell

A ferry lands at Santa Rosalía after an eight-hour voyage from Guaymas. The ferries are vital supply lines between Baja California and the mainland of Mexico.

bakery, a Pemex station, auto parts, mechanical service, banks, telephone and telegraph. Biblioteca Mahatma Gandhi, the public library at Calle Playa and Avenida Constitución, displays historical account ledgers from the mining company and photographs of past mining and shipping.

Santa Rosalía to Mulegé

(38 mi., 61 km.; 1 hr.)

From Santa Rosalía, Highway 1 heads south along the gulf shore for about four miles, offering excellent views of Isla San Marcos, where gypsum is mined and shipped to the United States. After swinging inland, the highway soon returns to the gulf, then turns inland again, passing through barren countryside before rapidly descending to Mulegé.

00.0   Junction with the main street of Santa Rosalía.

05.2   Junction with the 7.5-mile dirt road to Santa Agueda, a quaint farming village that produces papayas, mangos and dates, and has a spring that is the source of Santa Rosalía's water. Although graded its entire length, the road has a rough, washboard surface and a couple of bad spots that could damage a passenger car.

09.0   San Lucas, a fishing village situated on an attractive, palm-lined cove. Good camping beaches can be found both north and south of the village. A signed turnoff leads to San Lucas RV Park.

14.3   San Bruno, a village with an airstrip that has grown up around a fishing cooperative on the gulf shore, 0.8 mile from Highway 1.

17.5   Junction with the dirt road to San José de Magdalena (see *Side Routes*).

22.0   Entrance to the Santa Rosalía Airport.

25.6   A gravel road leading to **Punta Chivato,** site of a seafront hotel (see *Lodging &*

Restaurants). Nearby are a good dirt airstrip, a cluster of vacation homes and a camping area on a sandy beach.

38.5 **Mulegé.** Turn left to enter the main part of town.

Mulegé

(See also *Lodging & Restaurants* and *Campgrounds & Trailer Parks*)

The oasis community of Mulegé is located near the bottom of a lushly vegetated river valley surrounded by barren hills. Its name is a contraction of Yuman Indian words meaning "large creek of the white mouth." The town, which has a population of about 5000, sits on the north bank of the Río Mulegé (Santa Rosalía) about two miles upstream from the Gulf of California. One of the oldest towns in southern Baja California, it began as a mission settlement in 1705. With its air of tranquility, abundance of date palms and many old-style houses, Mulegé exudes the atmosphere of a quiet, traditional town. Dates are the principal crop, but figs, oranges, bananas and olives are also grown here.

Since the completion of the paved Transpeninsular Highway, Mulegé has become a popular tourist destination. Its extensive facilities include hotels, trailer parks, restaurants, banks, markets, gift shops, a laundromat, two Pemex stations, an auto supply store, mechanical assistance and a clinic. Tourist information and assistance are available at the Hotel Serenidad). The downtown streets, although in good condition, are narrow and restricted to one-way traffic.

Points of Interest

Misión Santa Rosalía de Mulegé
Just upstream from the bridge that carries Highway 1 across the river. Founded in 1705 and completed in 1766, the mission has been restored with the help of the government and now functions as a Catholic church. Nearby, rocky steps lead up a hill that

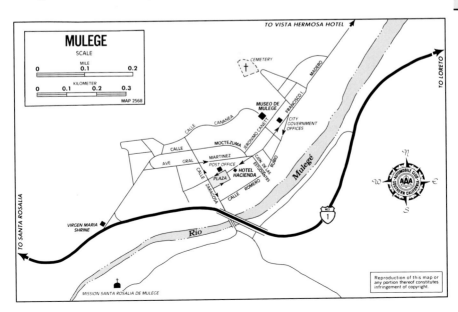

Tom Dell

Mulegé is the gateway to beautiful Bahía de la Concepción, famous for its fine camping beaches, excellent fishing and spectacular scenery.

affords a bird's-eye view over the oasis. To reach the mission from town, follow Calle Zaragoza (the longest north-south street in Mulegé) south, cross the river on a small bridge under the elevated highway bridge, turn sharply back to the right and follow a dirt road, first through palm groves then up a barren grade to the mission.

Museo de Mulegé *On a hilltop overlooking the town.* A classic building that was formerly a federal prison now houses displays of the history of Mulegé and other places in Baja California Sur. It contains fine artifacts of Cochimí Indians and Mexican settlers, religious objects and paintings by local artists.

Shrine of La Virgen María *At the west end of town.* The shrine includes a panoramic painting of Mulegé.

Mulegé to Loreto

(84 mi., 136 km.; 2 hrs.)

Beyond the junction with Mulegé's main street, Highway 1 crosses the river and veers eastward toward the Gulf of California, then heads south through barren coastal hills. A dozen miles past Mulegé, the highway reaches the shore of beautiful Bahía de la Concepción, one of the scenic highlights of Baja California. For the next 25 miles, the road parallels the shore of the bay, providing a series of breathtaking panoramas of sparkling blue-green waters, volcanic islands and inviting campsites. From the head of the bay, Highway 1 climbs a low saddle, then emerges onto a long, sandy plain. The rugged backbone of the Sierra de la Giganta is visible to the west. Finally, after winding through scrub-covered hills, the highway drops to a coastal plain near the junction to Loreto. There is no gasoline available on this long stretch of highway.

00.0   Junction to Mulegé.

00.7   Junction with a road leading to Mission Santa Rosalía de Mulegé.

01.7   Junction with the entrance road to the Villa María Isabel RV/Trailer Park.

02.4   Junction with the road to the Hotel Serenidad.

13.3   Playa Santispac, a developed public beach on an attractive cove.

14.6   Posada Concepción, a campground on the shore of Bahía Tordillo.

17.1   Rancho El Coyote, opposite a pair of lovely coves with enticing public beaches.

Photos by Tom Dell

Mission Santa Rosalía de Mulegé, founded by the Jesuits in 1705, has been extensively restored. It is located just west of Highway 1 via a narrow, unpaved road.

The Río Mulegé (Santa Rosalía) flows lazily just upstream from its mouth. The palm-lined banks of the river give this scene an idyllic tropical appearance.

27.0   El Requesón, a small island connected to the shore by a sandspit. The narrow spit is a *playa pública.*

36.3   Junction with a lonesome dirt road that loops around the southern end of Bahía Concepción, then goes north along the eastern side of the bay for 36 miles to Punta Concepción. The road passes a few fish camps and much pristine desert. The last few miles are very rough.

45.7   Rancho Rosarito, a ranch in a small oasis.

46.8   Junction with a road across the Sierra de la Giganta to San Isidro, La Purísima, San Jose de Comondú and San Miguel de Comondú (see *Side Routes*).

R. Clark Hunter

Cardón cacti on the lonesome eastern shore of Bahía Concepción.

54.1   Junction with a scenic dirt road to San Juanico and Bahía San Basilio.

65.2   Junction with a dirt road to Rancho San Juan Londo, 0.2 miles from the highway in a palm grove. This is the site of a Jesuit *visita,* or visiting station, dating from 1705.

84.1   Junction with the paved road to **Loreto.**

▬
Loreto

(See also *Lodging & Restaurants* and *Campgrounds & Trailer Parks*)

Loreto enjoys a scenic setting in a grove of palms and other subtropical trees on the shore of the Gulf of California. The jagged peaks of the Sierra de la Giganta rise abruptly from the coastal plain, forming a dramatic backdrop to the west. Directly offshore is Isla del Carmen, site of a salt works that has operated since the Spaniards first settled. A branch road leads from Highway 1 to the center of Loreto, which is built around a picturesque central plaza and a graceful stone mission. On the shore of the gulf, Calle de la Playa and the *malecón* (sea wall) walkway have recently been refurbished and paved. A stroll along the malecón reveals impressive sights: crashing surf, pelicans and other birds diving for fish and a vista of azure waters and the rugged island beyond.

Despite its impressive mission church, Loreto gives little indication of the key role it has played in the history of Baja California. Loreto is the oldest permanent settlement in the Californias. It dates back to October 25, 1697, when the Jesuit padre Juan María Salvatierra arrived and founded Mission Nuestra Señora de Loreto. For the next 132 years, Loreto served as the capital of Baja California, as well as the commercial and military hub of the peninsula. It was the base from which Junípero Serra began the exploration

Take note . . . in Loreto

Tourist Information and Assistance

The **Municipal Tourism Office** on the Plaza Cívica in the municipal hall, offers information and brochures about the region.

and colonization of what is now California in 1769; on his journey northward he founded the chain of missions in Alta California. In 1829, after Loreto was devastated by a hurricane, the capital was moved to La Paz. After more than a century of peaceful slumber, Loreto has rebounded—thanks to its location on Highway 1 and the discovery by sportsmen that fishing off Loreto was good even by Gulf of California standards. Since the completion of the paved highway in 1973, the warm waters of the area have attracted increasing numbers of anglers and tourists each year. Loreto Airport receives regular commercial flights from Los Angeles. FONATUR, a government-managed development group,

has also targeted the Loreto area for a major tourist development, patterned after similar projects in Mexico at Cancún and Ixtapa. To date, FONATUR has assisted in developments in the town of Loreto and in resort facilities at Nopaló, 5 miles to the south. In addition a marina is being developed at Puerto Escondido (Puerto Loreto), 15 miles south of Loreto.

In this town of about 9000, fishing and tourism are the bulwarks of the local economy, with tourism playing an ever-increasing role. Facilities include a variety of hotels, trailer parks, numerous shops, two supermarkets, restaurants, a hospital, a bank, a laundromat, gasoline, diesel fuel, mechani-

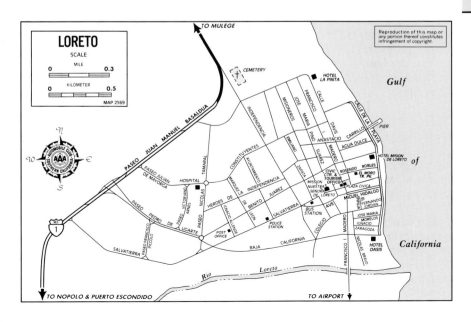

Clark Hunter

Loreto's historic municipal hall faces the Plaza Cívica.

cal service and auto parts. Typical Mexican articles for sale include shawls, women's clothing, pottery and leather crafts. In 1992 the city became the seat of government for the new *municipio* of Loreto.

Points of Interest

Misión Nuestra Señora de Loreto
Center of town. The current building was completed in 1752. It has withstood numerous hurricanes, floods and earthquakes, and is still an active church after extensive restoration and remodeling.

Museum *Next door to the mission.*
Open Monday through Friday, 9 a.m. to 12:30 p.m. and 1 to 4 p.m. Admission $1.60. Fascinating displays about missions and horse and wagon equipment are presented in this museum.

Plaza Cívica *Avenidas Salvatierra and Francisco Madero, just east of the mission.* Laid out in traditional Mexican style, it faces the municipal hall, the tourism office and several stores.

Loreto to Ciudad Constitución
(89 mi., 143 km.; 2 hrs.)

South of Loreto, the Sierra de la Giganta rises abruptly from the deep-blue waters of the gulf. For several miles, Highway 1 runs along the base of the reddish-brown mountains, following the dramatic coastline past fine beaches and offshore islands. Then the highway turns inland and climbs rapidly via sharp switchbacks. On approaching the summit, unusual hat-shaped mountain peaks are visible nearby. After the summit, the road begins a gradual descent along the edge of a deep canyon. Continuing southwest, the highway levels out onto the broad, gently sloped Santo Domingo (Magdalena) Valley. Though extremely arid, this sandy, cactus-covered lowland has developed into a major agricultural center—thanks to water from deep wells. Highway 1 passes several large farms and a pair of federal water projects before arriving in Ciudad Insurgentes, where it turns south and runs in a straight line along irrigated fields to Ciudad Constitución. Slow-moving vehicles are a common hazard in this final stretch; pass with care.

00.0 Junction with the paved road into Loreto.

01.1 Junction with a rough dirt road to Mission San Javier (see *Side Routes*). This road should only be attempted by sturdy high-clearance vehicles.

01.7 Junction with the paved road to Loreto's airport. Aero California flies here from Los Angeles. (See *Appendix,* Transportation Schedules section.)

05.2 Nopoló, site of a government-sponsored FONATUR resort complex, which is now being developed. Currently in operation are the Hotel Mercure El Cortés and a clinic.

10.0 A dirt road to Playa Notrí, a sandy beach.

14.0 Junction with the short dirt road to Juncalito, a fishing village, where boats for sport-fishing are available. The road continues beyond the village to a *playa pública.*

15.2 Junction with the 1.5-mile paved road to Puerto Escondido (Puerto Loreto), a deep-water port once used for shipping products. This beautiful, nearly landlocked bay is slowly being developed by FONATUR. Tourist facilities include the Tripui Resort RV Park (see *Campgrounds and Trailer Parks*) and a marina with a boat ramp.

34.0 A steep, scenic dirt road leads southeast to Agua Verde, a fishing village on the Gulf of California. Campsites are available on nearby beaches.

44.6 Turnout overlooking a rugged canyon.

63.0 Entrance to Ley Federal de Aguas #1, a government-

R. Clark Hunter

The bold front of Sierra de la Giganta is a distinctive landmark when viewed from Playa Juncalito, south of Loreto on the Gulf of California.

sponsored water project that provides fresh water for nearby farms. It has a large Pemex station.

67.5 Buenos Aires and Ley Federal de Aguas #2, a collection of prosperous-looking farms.

73.3 A red, white and green monument marks the junction with Ciudad Insurgentes, an agricultural settlement of about 12,000 with stores, cafes, two gasoline stations, banks, an auto parts store and mechanical assistance. The center of town is to the right. The main street continues north as a paved road for 66 miles, then as a graded dirt road following the coast for 139 more miles to San Ignacio; branches lead to San Javier, Comondú and La Purísima (see *Side Routes*).

88.3 Entrance to the Ciudad Constitución airport. *Ciudad Constitución,* at the junction with the paved road (Mexico Highway 22) to San Carlos (see *Side Routes*).

Ciudad Constitución

(See *Campgrounds & Trailer Parks*)

In the 1960s the Santo Domingo Valley (sometimes called Magdalena Plain) was opened to rapid agricultural development, and within two decades Ciudad Constitución grew from a village into a booming modern city. With a current population of about 48,000 it is the second largest population center in the state of Baja California Sur and the seat of government for the *municipio* of Comondú, which also includes Ciudad Insurgentes. The region is extremely arid, but water trapped for centuries far beneath the earth's surface has been tapped by deep wells, transforming the desert into a checkerboard of attractive farms. The leading crops are wheat and garbanzo; also important are cotton, sorghum, alfalfa, corn and citrus fruits. Some farms also raise livestock. The agricultural products are shipped to the mainland from San Carlos, 36 miles to the west.

Ciudad Constitución is not oriented toward tourism, but offers extensive facilities including hotels, a trailer park,

Bill Cory

The main street of Ciudad Constitución, an agricultural market town in the Santo Domingo Valley.

supermarkets, a large public market, large and varied stores, hospitals, banks, an ice house, laundromats, automobile dealerships, gasoline stations, auto supply stores and auto repair shops. Among a large number of restaurants and cafes, Restaurant Sancho Panza in the Hotel Maribel offers a variety of fine Mexican dishes. Prices in Ciudad Constitución are lower than in the tourist towns.

Ciudad Constitución to La Paz

(134 mi., 216 km.; 2:45 hrs.)

After leaving Ciudad Constitución, Highway 1 runs absolutely straight for more than 30 miles across virtually flat terrain. It then turns southeast and traverses a region of seemingly endless chalk-colored hills and mesas and deeply eroded gullies; numerous sharp curves present driving hazards in this section. Finally, at a high bluff marked by a tepee-shaped shrine, the Gulf of California and Bahía de La Paz come into view, with the city a cluster of white buildings on the far side of the bay. Descending rapidly, the highway

soon reaches a wide, heavily vegetated coastal plain. After passing through the small bayside settlement of El Centenario, Highway 1 follows the curve of the bay into La Paz, capital of Baja California Sur.

00.0	Ciudad Constitución, at the junction with the highway to San Carlos.
01.5	Junction with the dirt road to Campestre La Pila, a large farm that contains a trailer park and a swimming pool (see *Campgrounds and Trailer Parks*).
07.9	Villa Morelos, a tiny farming community with a cafe.
10.1	Junction with the dirt road to El Ihuagil Dam and Mission *San Luís Gonzaga* (see *Side Routes*).
14.0	Colonia Nuñes, another agricultural settlement. Highway 1 now leaves the region of irrigated farms and enters open desert.
35.6	Santa Rita, a village with a store, cafe and a church. At the north end of the village a dirt road branches west to

Tom Dell

Between Ciudad Constitución and La Paz, Highway 1 crosses open desert punctuated with chalk-colored mesas and buttes.

Tom Dell

La Paz occupies a shelf between barren foothills and the curving shore of the bay. The city is both the state capital and a busy seaport.

Puerto Chale (see *Side Routes*).

53.9 Junction with a mostly graded dirt road to a cattle and goat-raising region that includes the villages of San Pedro de la Presa, Las Animas and El Bosque. Winding along streams through the scenic Sierra de la Giganta, the road descends to San Evaristo on the gulf coast, 68 miles to the northeast.

61.8 Las Pocitas, a village with a picturesque church, a clinic and a cafe. A graded road leads northeast to La Soledad and San Evaristo.

71.3 El Cien, a settlement with a Pemex station, highway department camp and a cafe.

83.9 Junction with the 12-mile dirt road to El Conejo, a wind-blown Pacific beach that is popular with surfers. Any high-clearance vehicle can make the trip.

99.8 A good graded dirt road to Conquista Agraria and the Pacific coast.

113.3 A summit with a sweeping panorama of Bahía de La Paz and the mountains beyond; a turnout leads to a tepee-shaped shrine. Highway 1 now begins a sharp descent.

123.9 Junction with a scenic paved road leading 24.7 miles north along the shore of Bahía de La Paz to the mining settlement of San Juan de la Costa. Phosphorus mined here is shipped by freighter to processing plants elsewhere in Mexico for use in the production of fertilizer. The town has gasoline and groceries. A graded dirt road follows the coast 45 miles farther north to the village of San Evaristo; its economy is based on fishing and salt evaporation and it has a protected cove. From there a road winds southwest through the Sierra de la Giganta and connects with Highway 1.

124.4 El Centenario, a small town of about 2000 inhabitants on the shore of the bay, has a Pemex station (*magna sin*). The skyline of La Paz is visible across the water.

129.2 Chametla, a settlement at the junction with the 2.1-mile paved road to La Paz International Airport. Aero California and Aeromexico fly here from Los Angeles and Tijuana (see Air Service in *Appendix,* Transportation).

130.2 At a "Dove of Peace" monument, Camino a las Garzas veers to the right, providing a convenient bypass of central La Paz for motorists bound for the Los Cabos region.

133.5 La Paz, at the intersection of calzadas Abasolo and 5 de Febrero. Turn right here for Highway 1 south to Cabo San Lucas; straight ahead,

the road along the bay's shore leads to downtown La Paz and to Pichilingue, the terminal for the Mazatlán and Topolobampo ferries (see *Appendix,* Transportation Schedules).

La Paz

(See also *Lodging & Restaurants* and *Campgrounds & Trailer Parks*)

La Paz is picturesquely sandwiched between cactus-covered foothills and the curving shore of beautiful Bahía de La Paz—largest bay on the west side of the Gulf of California. Directly opposite the city is El Mogote, a narrow

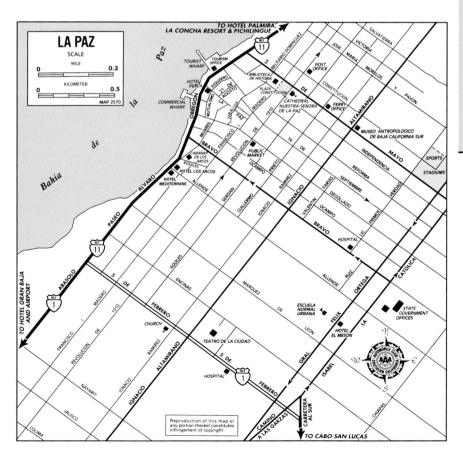

Take note . . . in La Paz

Tourist Information and Assistance

The **State Tourism Office,** which is staffed by helpful bilingual personnel, is located on the Tourist Wharf at Paseo Alvaro Obregón and 16 de Septiembre (see map). The office is open Monday through Friday, 8 a.m. to 8 p.m. Phone 01152 (112) 4-0100 or 4-0103. **Protección al Turista/Tourist Protection,** which provides legal assistance to tourists, is located in the same office and has the same hours and the same phone number. Another office for tourist information may be reached at 01152 (112) 4-0199.

Newspapers

The *Baja Sun* is an English-language newspaper with recreational articles and advertisements covering the municipalities of La Paz and Los Cabos, plus additional material about the rest of Baja California. Several publications in English are for sale at the bookstore Librería Contempo on Agustín Arreolo near Paseo Alvaro Obregón. Two Spanish dailies in La Paz—*el Sudcaliforniano* and *Diario Peninsular*—serve the city and the remainder of Baja California Sur.

Radio and Television Stations

La Paz has several radio stations. XERT, 800 AM, has a varied selection of international music; 90.1 FM, *Radio Alegría,* presents traditional Mexican music. A few American radio stations come in at night. As in other parts of the Baja California peninsula, large hotels have satellite dish antennas which bring in several American TV stations in addition to the local channel and the national TV networks from Mexico City.

Driving in La Paz

Traffic flows smoothly on most of the long, straight streets of La Paz. Other than an abrupt terrace which rises from the bay, the city has level topography. To avoid being disoriented, drivers should closely follow the La Paz map, which reveals that the grid pattern of streets is oriented northeast-southwest. The old business section near the *malecón* (bay-front drive) has congested irregular streets and is better covered on foot. The city has several rental car agencies.

Local Transportation

La Paz has numerous taxis, especially along the *malecón* and near the hotels. Before getting in a cab, be sure to understand the fare to be charged. The rate for two miles is about $4, and from central La Paz to the airport (about 8 miles) approximately $11. Local city buses run frequently to all parts of La Paz. The fare is only about 30¢. Bus riders should know some Spanish and understand the layout of the city. The central depot for local buses is by the public market at Revolución de 1910 and Degollado. Service to Pichilingue and Los Cabos is provided by Transportes Aguila at 125 Paseo Alvaro Obregón.

Long-distance travel is provided by Tres Estrellas de Oro bus lines to all other cities on the Baja peninsula; the terminal is at Jalisco and Héroes de Independencia (see *Appendix,* Transportation section).

Ferry Transportation

Ferryboats, carrying passengers and vehicles to the mainland, sail out of Pichilingue, deep water port for La Paz. Grupo Sematur, the principal ferry company, has its ticket office on Guillermo Prieto at Cinco de Mayo (see *Appendix,* Transportation section).

sandspit separating the main body of the bay from Ensenada de los Aripes, a shallow inlet to the west. Because of its location at the southeastern end of the bay, La Paz's shoreline faces northwest—a fact that becomes readily apparent during one of the city's magnificent sunsets. With its fine beaches, superlative sportfishing, numerous duty-free shops and abundance of tourist facilities, La Paz is fast becoming one of the top resorts on Mexico's west coast. The ideal time to visit La Paz is November through May, when days are warm and sunny and nights

are cool. Summers can be uncomfortably hot, but often a welcome afternoon breeze known as the *coromuel* refreshes the city. Late summer to early fall is the rainy season. Rainfall is scant, varying from year to year, and most of it comes during short, violent tropical storms called *chubascos*.

La Paz has the longest history of any settlement in the Californias—and one of the most turbulent. The bay was discovered by a Spanish expedition in 1533, but the leader and several of his soldiers were killed by Indians shortly

Tom Dell

La Paz's palm-lined malecón, *or sea wall, is a pleasant place for a relaxing stroll. Thousands of local residents join in the customary promenade every Sunday evening.*

after landing. Two years later Hernán Cortés, the conqueror of Mexico, attempted to colonize the site of La Paz; supply problems, however, caused him to fail. The rich oyster beds in nearby gulf waters brought numerous seekers of wealth during the 17th century, and pearls from La Paz found their way into the Spanish royal treasury, but none of the colonies survived more than a short time. The task of colonization fell to the Jesuits, who founded a mission here in 1720. The padres withstood a series of Indian uprisings, but after disease virtually wiped out the Indian population the mission was abandoned in 1749. Today the Cathedral of La Paz stands on its site. Not until 1811 did La Paz become a permanent settlement. In 1829, after Loreto was destroyed by a hurricane, the fledgling village of La Paz became the territorial capital. American troops occupied La Paz during the Mexican War and battles were fought in the streets of the city, but the soldiers returned to the United States after the treaty was signed. The notorious William Walker also attempted a takeover, but he was quickly expelled.

After years of existence as a remote territory, Baja California Sur—one of Mexico's two newest states—has made rapid economic strides, with tremendous gains in population, productivity and tourism. As a result, La Paz has evolved from a sleepy little port into a vigorous, modern state capital. It is also the seat of government for the *municipio* of La Paz, which also encompasses Todos Santos. This jolt into the Mexican mainstream has not come without a few growing pains, such as the traffic snarls that occur daily in the narrow downtown streets. The current population numbers about 176,000. Still, there is something of a small-

town atmosphere in La Paz, and the city retains touches of colonial grace and charm. Interspersed with contemporary structures and paved streets are colorful gardens, arched doorways and cobblestone sidewalks. Some businesses continue to observe the traditional siesta hour, closing their doors in the early afternoon. And on Sunday evenings, local residents join in the customary promenade along the palm-lined *malecón* (sea wall).

Shopping

La Paz is a free port and offers the careful shopper good buys on imported merchandise, as well as on Mexican handicrafts. Shops catering to tourists are clustered along **Paseo Alvaro Obregón** opposite the *malecón.* Bargains can also be found in small stores scattered throughout the downtown area just behind the waterfront. Hand-woven cotton and woolen articles are made and sold at **Artesanía Cuautémoc/The Weaver;** it is located on Abasolo (Highway 1) between calles Jalisco and Nayarít. **Centro de Arte Regional,** on Chiapas at Calle Encinas, is a pottery workshop offering a variety of goods at reasonable prices.

Travelers who wish to replenish their supplies will find several large supermarkets, as well as many small grocery stores, bakeries and fruit markets. At the **Public Market** merchants sell a wide assortment of goods from individual stalls; it is located on Avenida Revolución de 1910 at Degollado. **La Perla de La Paz** is a downtown department store on Mutualismo offering a variety of high-quality merchandise. Other department stores include **Dorian's** downtown and **CCC,** with two stores near the state capitol and on Colima near Highway 1.

Dining

(These restaurants are not all AAA approved but are shown as a convenience to travelers.) Well-known establishments include **Bermejo,** in Hotel Los Arcos (seafood, steak and Mexican dishes); **Kiwi,** on the beach near Paseo Alvaro Obregón and 5 de Mayo (seafood); **El Taste,** two blocks southwest of Hotel Los Arcos on Paseo Obregón (seafood and steaks); **Jardín Yee,** on Highway 1 about a mile southwest of the junction of Abasolo and 5 de Febrero (Cantonese cuisine); **Lapa de Carlos 'n Charlies,** on the waterfront at Paseo Obregón and de León (varied menu); **El Molino Steak House,** on the waterfront at Legaspy and Topete; **Hotel Plaza Real,** at Esquerro and Callejon La Paz in downtown (varied menu); **Samalú,** in southwest La Paz on Rangel, between Colima and Jalisco (seafood); **Caballo Blanco de La Paz,** 1½ miles southwest of downtown at Abasolo and Jalisco (steak and seafood); **La Terraza,** a sidewalk cafe in the Hotel Perla on Paseo Obregón (varied menu); and **Nuevo Pekín,** on Paseo Obregón, ¼ mile northeast of downtown La Paz (Chinese food).

Nightclubs

La Paz' nightlife is rather tame by resort standards, but the city does have a few establishments offering dancing and/or live entertainment. These include discotheques at the **Hotel Palmira** and the **Hotel Gran Baja;** the night club **La Cabaña,** on the lobby floor of the Hotel Perla; and **Quinto Patio,** on Alvaro Obregon near Bravo.

Points of Interest

Biblioteca de Historia de las Californias *North side of Plaza Constitución. 01152 (112) 2-0162.* Open Monday through Friday from 8 a.m.

to 8 p.m. Free admission. This library, occupying the old government center, has a display of vivid paintings about early Baja California Sur and a collection of books in Spanish and English about the history of Baja California and California.

Boat Tours *Tourist Wharf at Paseo Alvaro Obregón and 16 de Septiembre.* Several companies offer boat trips around Bahía de la Paz. Trips to Isla Espíritu Santo are available for those who wish to kayak around the island and enjoy its unspoiled natural environment. Call or visit the State Tourism office on the wharf for details; 01152 (112) 4-0100. Some hotels and travel agencies also have information on boat tours.

Dove of Peace Monument *Junction of Highway 1 and Camino a las Garzas, the bypass to Los Cabos.* As a gateway to La Paz, the large contemporary sculpture bears an inscription which translates, "And if you want peace (*paz*), I offer it to you in the sunny peace of my bay."

Museo de Antropología e Historia de Baja California Sur *Ignacio Altamirano and 5 de Mayo. 01152 (112) 2-0162.* Open Tuesday through Friday from 8 a.m. to 6 p.m., Saturday 9 a.m. to 2 p.m. Donation. This outstanding museum features exhibits on geology, geography, flora and fauna. Displays on anthropology explain Indian cultures with dioramas and replicas of cave paintings. History is covered through Spanish mission settlement, Mexican ranch life, and the struggle during the wars of independence. There is also a good book store.

Nuestra Señora de La Paz *South side of Plaza Constitución.* This cathedral began as one of the original missions. Large bilingual plaques describe the history of the church and some of the early settlement of La Paz. Across Calle Revolución is an attractive plaza park.

Teatro de la Ciudad *Miguel Legaspy and Héroes de Independencia. 01152 (112) 5-0207.* The theater offers a variety of performing arts and also contains an art gallery.

La Paz to Los Barriles
(65 mi., 105 km.; 1:45 hrs.)

After leaving the outskirts of La Paz, Highway 1 crosses level countryside with dense growths of cardón and pitahaya (organ pipe) cacti and various trees and shrubs. Just south of the village of San Pedro is the junction with Highway 19 to Todos Santos and Cabo San Lucas. At this point, the main highway bears left and climbs into the foothills of the Sierra de la Laguna. After passing through El Triunfo, the road descends to San Antonio in the bottom of a narrow valley. It then crosses another arm of the mountains and follows the course of a steep-walled canyon to San Bartolo.

Emerging from the mountains, Highway 1 soon reaches Los Barriles on the shore of Bahía de Palmas, famous for its superlative sportfishing.

00.0 La Paz, at the intersection of Calzadas Abasolo and 5 de Febrero. To proceed south on Highway 1, take 5 de Febrero southeast for one mile to Carretera al Sur, then bear right.

01.4 Junction with the paved road (BC 286) to San Juan de los Planes (see *Side Routes*).

16.0 San Pedro, a small community serving the surrounding farms and ranches.

19.0 Junction with Mexico Highway 19 to Todos Santos and Cabo San Lucas (see *Connecting Routes*).

32.3 El Triunfo, a picturesque mountain village with a cafe and a church. El Triunfo was once a rich gold- and silver-mining camp and at one time was the largest settlement in the south of Baja California.

R. Clark Hunter

An Auto Club field mapping reporter stops at a roadside fruit stand in San Bartolo.

The mines closed in 1926, but with the increase in precious metal values, mining has resumed at some locations. Numerous old buildings line the highway, and on a hill just south of the village are the remains of the old smelter. Hand-woven baskets are for sale on the north side of the highway.

36.8   San Antonio, an attractive farming center located in the bottom of a deep arroyo. San Antonio's history also includes a mining boom. Facilities include groceries, eating establishments and gasoline. Past the junction with the village's main street, Highway 1 climbs sharply out of the canyon.

53.8   San Bartolo, a sleepy town strung out along a palm-lined canyon, produces guavas, oranges, avocados and other fruits. Groceries, local fruits and meals are available.

65.2   Junction with a dirt road signed "Ramal El Cardonal." This road leads 0.8 mile to another junction; the road to the left is nine miles of a rough and narrow but scenic coastal route to the resort community of **Punta Pescadero.** The road goes on to the village and resort of El Cardonal, to Boca del Alamo and farther northwest to San Juan de los Planes.

Just south of the junction is **Los Barriles** (see *Campgrounds & Trailer Parks*), a rapidly growing tourist community on Bahía de Palmas with two hotels, two trailer parks, a Pemex station (*magna sin*), an airstrip, cafes, markets, auto parts, a clinic and sportfishing boats.

Los Barriles to San José del Cabo
(50 mi., 81 km.; 1:30 hrs.)

The highway skirts the coastline for a few miles, then crosses a long cactus-covered plain. The high Sierra de la Laguna looms dramatically to the west; cattle are frequently encountered on this section of highway. At San José del Cabo the road again reaches the shore of the Gulf of California (Sea of Cortez). Starting at Los Cabos Airport, the highway is four-lane divided all the way to Cabo San Lucas.

1.9   Junction with the entrance road of the Hotel Rancho Buena Vista.

4.4   Junction with a dirt road to the Hotel Buena Vista Beach Resort.

12.3   Junction with a paved road to **La Ribera,** then graded roads to Punta Colorada, Cabo Pulmo and Los Frailes (see *Side Routes*). To the right is Las Cuevas, a quiet farming village with no tourist facilities.

17.4   Junction with the paved road to **Santiago.** This attractive agricultural community of about 4000 people sits on a pair of hills separated by a shallow palm-forested canyon. On the northern hill, 1.7 miles from Highway 1, is the town plaza, along with a gasoline station, an inn with a restaurant and several cafes and stores. Just beyond the southern hill is the Santiago Zoo, the only one in Baja California Sur, with a variety of wildlife native to Mexico.

19.4   The Tropic of Cancer, marked by a spherical concrete monument representing the 23.5° North Latitude parallel.

26.1 A Pemex station at the junction with the 1.7-mile paved road to Miraflores, a farming town known for its vegetables and cheeses. By the end of the paved road at the town entrance is a leather shop that does retail sales. Facilities in Miraflores include stores and cafes.

29.4 Junction with the graded dirt road to Caduaño, another small farming community. The town center is about a mile from the main highway.

36.3 Junction with a winding scenic road signed "Los Naranjos," which goes across the tree-covered landscape of the Sierra de la Laguna to El Pescadero and Todos Santos on Mexico Highway 19. Sturdy, high-clearance vehicles are necessary.

41.6 Santa Anita, a sleepy little town with a cafe and a small store.

43.3 Junction with the 0.9-mile paved road to Los Cabos International Airport (see *Appendix,* Transportation).

47.9 Santa Rosa, a rapidly growing community of about 3000, has a Pemex station, cafes and stores.

50.1 Junction with Calle Zaragoza, which leads to the center of San José del Cabo.

SAN JOSE DEL CABO

Take note . . . in San José del Cabo

Tourist Information

The **Municipal Tourism Office** in San José's plaza park offers information and printed materials about the Los Cabos region.

San José del Cabo

(See also *Lodging & Restaurants* and *Campgrounds & Trailer Parks*)

At the spot where Highway 1 meets the Gulf of California, San José del Cabo occupies low hills and an attrac-tive, narrow coastal lowland. Founded in 1730, its contrasting buildings suggest that it is an old settlement with much recent growth. Tropical agriculture—coconuts, mangos, spices and citrus fruits—plus fast-growing tourism have brought the population to about 11,000. San José del Cabo is the seat

R. Clark Hunter

Los Cabos Municipal Hall in San José del Cabo was built in 1927.

of government of the *municipio* of Los Cabos, which encompasses the East Cape and Cabo San Lucas.

The town center includes an attractive plaza park. Numerous stores and restaurants are open to the visitor, particularly along Calles Zaragoza and Mijares. The town also has auto parts, mechanical service and two hospitals. Immediately south of town, a new FONATUR resort development fronts directly on the beautiful beaches of the Gulf of California. To date, six large hotels are in operation; a golf course and a shopping center are open; and several condominium developments are finished.

Points of Interest

Estero de San Jose *End of Paseo San Jose, just east of Hotel Presidente Los Cabos.* The estuary of the Río San José is bordered by palm groves and is replete with aquatic plants. It is a protected sanctuary, home to a variety of birds. Facilities are being developed for visitors to hike along the shores and take boat rides.

Plaza Park *Calle Zaragoza and Boulevard Mijares.* This small town square has the atmosphere of old Mexico. Facing the shaded plaza are the church, the tourism office and a monument to General José Antonio Mijares.

Palacio Municipal/Municipal Hall *One block south of the plaza.* Dating from 1927, the traditional structure has offices that face on an interior patio.

San José Church *West side of the plaza.* Founded in 1730, this active church has been rebuilt according to the original style. It has classic twin steeples.

San José del Cabo to Cabo San Lucas

(21 mi., 34 km.; 0:30 hr.)

A recently completed four-lane expressway leads southwest to Cabo San Lucas, passing many hotels and restaurants, winding along the gulf through low, scrub-dotted hills, and occasionally offering tantalizing glimpses of beautiful beaches and azure waters. Several public beaches are accessible from the highway via side roads. Finally, just before arriving in Cabo San Lucas, travelers get the first view of Land's End (*Finisterra*), the tip of the Baja California peninsula. At the Cabo San Lucas wharf, 1059 miles from the U.S. border, Highway 1 ends.

00.0	Junction with Calle Zaragoza into San José del Cabo.
01.3	Junction with a palm-lined boulevard leading to the beach resort development marked *"zona de hoteles."*
01.8	Playa Tropical, site of Brisa del Mar Trailer Park. The highway swings to the southwest at this point.
03.8	Entrance road of the Hotel Palmilla resort.
06.7	On the north side of the highway is Cabo Real Golf Course. On the south side is Hotel Meliá Cabo Real.
11.0	Entrance road of the Hotel Cabo San Lucas.
12.8	Entrance road of the Hotel Twin Dolphin.
15.4	Cabo del Sol Golf Club.
16.9	Junction with the paved road leading to the Cabo Bello development, which includes the Hotel Calinda Beach Cabo San Lucas. At this point, Land's End comes into view.
20.4	Cabo San Lucas, at the junction with Calle Morelos, which is the beginning of Mexico Highway 19 leading

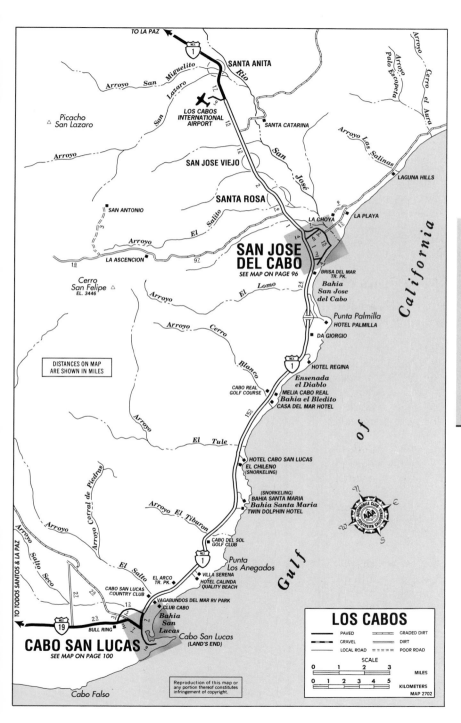

TO LA PAZ

SANTA ANITA

Arroyo San Miguelito

San Lazaro

Rio

LOS CABOS INTERNATIONAL AIRPORT

Picacho San Lazaro △

SANTA CATARINA

Arroyo Palo Escopeta

Arroyo

Cerro el Aura

Arroyo

SAN JOSE VIEJO

San

Arroyo Las Salinas

José

LAGUNA HILLS

SANTA ROSA

SAN ANTONIO

El Salito

Arroyo

LA CHOYA

LA PLAYA

SAN JOSE
DEL CABO
SEE MAP ON PAGE 96

Arroyo

LA ASCENCION

BRISA DEL MAR TR. PK.

Cerro San Felipe △
EL. 3446

El Lomo

Bahia San Jose del Cabo

California

DISTANCES ON MAP ARE SHOWN IN MILES

Arroyo

Cerro

Punta Palmilla
HOTEL PALMILLA

Arroyo

DA GIORGIO

Blanco

HOTEL REGINA

Arroyo

CABO REAL GOLF COURSE

Ensenada el Diablo
MELIA CABO REAL
Bahia el Bledito
CASA DEL MAR HOTEL

El Tule

of

HOTEL CABO SAN LUCAS
EL CHILENO
(SNORKELING)

(SNORKELING)
BAHIA SANTA MARIA
Bahia Santa Maria
TWIN DOLPHIN HOTEL

Arroyo Corral de Piedras

Arroyo El Tiburon

CABO DEL SOL GOLF CLUB

Arroyo

Gulf

El Salto

Punta Los Anegados

EL ARCO TR. PK.

VILLA SERENA
HOTEL CALINDA
QUALITY BEACH

Arroyo

Arroyo Salto Seco

CABO SAN LUCAS COUNTRY CLUB

VAGABUNDOS DEL MAR RV PARK
CLUB CABO

TO TODOS SANTOS & LA PAZ

BULL RING

Bahia San Lucas

Cabo San Lucas
(LAND'S END)

CABO SAN LUCAS
SEE MAP ON PAGE 100

Cabo Falso

LOS CABOS

PAVED		GRADED DIRT
GRAVEL		DIRT
LOCAL ROAD	= = = = =	POOR ROAD

SCALE

0   1   2   3
MILES

0 1 2 3 4 5
KILOMETERS

MAP 2702

north to Todos Santos, San Pedro and La Paz (see *Connecting Routes*). Boulevard Marina, on the left, leads to the waterfront.

Cabo San Lucas

(See also Lodging & Restaurants and Campgrounds & Trailer Parks)

The town of Cabo San Lucas fronts a small harbor on the gulf side of the rocky peninsula that forms the southernmost tip of Baja California. The bay, which in the 16th and 17th centuries was a favorite hiding place for pirates who lay in wait for Spanish treasure ships, now serves as an anchorage for fishing boats and private yachts. Because of its renowned sport-

fishing and the increasing popularity of its many luxury hotels, Cabo San Lucas has changed from a quiet, unassuming cannery village into an internationally known resort. From only 1500 inhabitants in 1970, the town has grown to about 12,000 at present.

Signs of this rapid growth are everywhere. Impressive condominiums spread over the hillside and the waterfront. A marvelous view of the waterfront and Land's End can be seen from the Hotel Finisterra or the Pedregal condominium zone on Camino del Mar. Facilities include trailer parks, many restaurants and cafes, markets, gift shops, shopping centers, Pemex stations, auto repairs and parts, and a marina. The once-busy ferry terminal at Cabo San Lucas is now idle; ferry

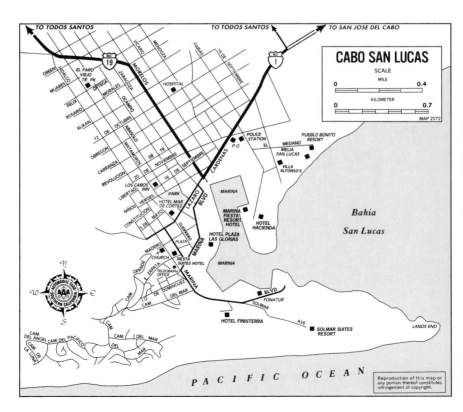

Take note . . . in Cabo San Lucas

Tourist Assistance
The U.S. Consular Agent, on Boulevard Marina y Pedregal No. 3, offers assistance to U.S. citizens in the Los Cabos region. The phone is 01152 (114) 3-3566.

Newspapers
Two informative newspapers which provide information and advertisements covering the Los Cabos region are the bilingual *El Tiempo Los Cabos Times* and the English-language *Baja Sun,* which also has material about the rest of the peninsula. Radio 96 FM, Cabo Mil, plays a variety of fine international music.

R. Clark Hunter

The attractive harbor of Cabo San Lucas, looking northeast.

service to Puerto Vallarta is suspended indefinitely.

Nightclubs

Cabo San Lucas vibrates at night. Many night spots and discos are located in the tourist area along boulevards Lázaro Cárdenas and Marina. Three popular ones with bizarre names are **Cabo Wabo, Squid Roe** and **The Giggling Marlin.**

Points of Interest

Galería El Dorado *Boulevard Marina near Guerrero.* This arts and crafts store displays a nice collection of paintings and ceramics by local artists. Visitors are welcome to browse.

Land's End/Finisterra *The rocky, extreme southern end of the penin-*

sula is situated at 22 degrees, 50 minutes north latitude. Its rugged, wave-eroded rock formations, including The Arches/Los Arcos, may be viewed from Highway 1 on the approach to Cabo San Lucas or from any slightly-elevated spot in town.

Land's End and its beaches may be reached by boat, or on foot by starting on the beach by Solmar Suites Resort and climbing over a rough rocky saddle. (This climb should be made only by those in good physical shape, traveling with a partner.) ■

Tom Dell

Land's End, where the Gulf of California meets the Pacific Ocean.

Mexico Highway 5

From Mexicali—the bustling capital city of the state of Baja California—Highway 5 leads southward past the verdant patchwork of one of Mexico's most productive agricultural regions, then crosses open desert backed by rugged, barren mountains. The route has a good paved surface to San Felipe, a resort town on the shore of the Gulf of California (Sea of Cortez), and for a short distance beyond. Between Punta Estrella and Puertecitos the road is paved but rough. From Puertecitos a graded but bumpy road extends farther south to Bahía San Luis Gonzaga. An ambitious highway construction project calls for the paving of the entire San Felipe to Bahía Gonzaga road sometime in the near future. This would bring rapid development to a region which, until very recently, was inaccessible to most tourists. The highway would also provide an alternate route for those who wish to travel from the California border south to the central desert region. Ample accommodations and facilities can be found in Mexicali and San Felipe, while rustic lodging, eating and camping facilities are scattered along the gulf coast. Fishing in the Gulf of California is excellent.

CROSSING THE BORDER

California State Route 111 leads through the Imperial Valley town of Calexico to the international border at Mexicali. Tourist cards can be obtained and processed in the designated building on the east side of the border gate (see *Tourist Regulations and Travel Tips* chapter).

Mexicali

(See also *Lodging and Restaurants*)

Mexicali is unique among Mexico's large border cities in that its size and economic well-being do not result from either its proximity to the United States or its ability to attract tourist dollars. Instead, this mushrooming metropolis of about 775,000 owes its prosperity and phenomenal growth to its position as capital of the state of Baja California, and as the seat of government of the *municipio* of Mexicali, which extends south to San Felipe. It is also the hub of one of Mexico's most important agricultural regions. Many tourists pass through Mexicali en route to San Felipe or to the Mexican mainland, but relatively few pause to examine this bustling, interesting city.

In the early 20th century Mexicali developed as a farm market center, and in 1915 it became the capital of the territory of Baja California Norte. For a couple of decades legalized alcohol and gambling and land speculation attracted visitors from across the border. In the late 1930s, under the leadership of Mexican president Lázaro Cárdenas, the fertile land of the Mexicali Valley was distributed among Mexican farmers and collective agricultural colonies, called *ejidos*. Also, the flow of irrigation water from the Colorado River was guaranteed by international treaty. These factors contributed to the economic bases of farming and industry.

Water has been the key to Mexicali's growth. The Mexicali Valley is extremely arid: the pleasant winters and torrid summers bring only about three inches of rain per year—not enough to exploit the rich, silt-laden soil deposited throughout the centuries by the Colorado River. So Mexico developed an elaborate irrigation complex tied to Morelos Dam, on the Colorado River just south of the border. The result is an agricultural empire in the midst of the desert, served by a proud

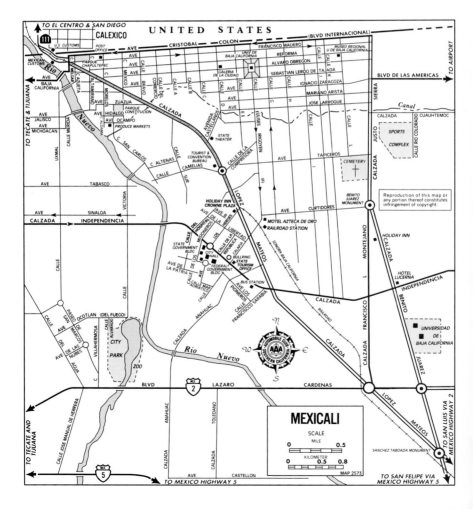

MEXICALI

Take note . . . in Mexicali

Tourist Information and Assistance

The **Mexicali Tourist and Convention Bureau** is on Calzada López Mateos at Calle Camelias. Hours are Monday through Friday, 9 a.m. to 7 p.m.; Saturday 9 a.m. to 3 p.m.; phone 01152 (65) 57-2376 or 57-2561. The **State Tourism Office** is located near the corner of Calle Calafia and Calzada Independencia, next to the Restaurant California in the Centro Cívico-Comercial. It is open Monday through Friday, 8 a.m. to 7 p.m., Saturday 9 a.m. to 3 p.m., and Sunday 9 a.m. to 1 p.m.; phone 01152 (65) 56-1072 or 56-1172. **Asistencia al Turista/Tourist Assistance**, providing legal aid and general information to tourists, is in the same office and has the same phone number.

Newspapers

Mexicali has no English-language newspaper, but tourist brochures in English are available at the tourism offices. The AAA-approved hotels in town often have California newspapers. Two Spanish-language newspapers are *La Voz de la Frontera* and *Novedades de Baja California*.

Radio and Television Stations

Many California radio stations are received all through northern Baja California. Among the several Mexicali stations, XED at 1050 AM broadcasts a rich variety of traditional folk music. A few American television stations are received, along with the Mexicali stations.

Driving in Mexicali

Before crossing the border into Mexicali, be sure to obtain Mexican auto insurance (see Automobile Requirements in the *Tourist Regulations and Travel Tips* chapter). Tourists driving in Mexicali find wide, flat streets, many of which are one way. Unfortunately, many streets lack signs. Mexicali has no expressway bypass like Tijuana, but three wide boulevards—calzadas López Mateos, Justo Sierra and Benito Juárez—usually allow traffic to move through the city at moderate speeds. Traffic circles, or *glorietas*, found along these boulevards pose a challenge for new visitors. When entering a traffic circle, drivers should bear right, then follow the flow of traffic counterclockwise. It is important to watch for traffic lights and street signs; lights are often small and hard to see from a distance. Stop signs are sometimes not very noticeable.

Parking is scarce in the business district near the border and around the government center, but it does not pose a problem in other parts of the city. Visitors planning to shop in the border business district should park on the Calexico, California, side and walk across. Most of the tourist-oriented stores are within a few blocks.

MEXICO HIGHWAY 5

Local Transportation

Traveling a few miles in town by taxi costs about $6, although sometimes bargaining can lower the fare. It is wise to agree on the price before getting into the cab.

As in other large Baja California cities, Mexicali bus fare is extremely cheap. Riders should know a little Spanish, have an idea of the city's layout and not mind traveling in old coaches. For long-distance travel, Mexicali is an important departure point for bus and train lines to Mexico City.

city with modern commercial and industrial complexes, palm-lined boulevards, lush parks and quiet residential neighborhoods with neatly manicured shrubs and gardens. Permeating present-day Mexicali is a distinct aura of growth and vitality.

A good example of this vitality is the new **Centro Cívico-Comercial de Mexicali**—an innovative center for government and commerce along Calzada Independencia in the central part of the city. Included in this ambitious urban development are municipal, state and federal government offices, three hospitals, the bus terminal, a bullring, movie theaters, hotels, restaurants, private offices and shopping centers.

R. Clark Hunter

Shopping

The largest commercial area of Mexicali is the **border business district,** located in a rough rectangle bounded by avenidas Cristóbal Colón, Alvaro Obregón, the Río Nuevo and Calle C. This typical Mexican commercial district contains shops and restaurants catering to the tourist trade, along with businesses oriented to local consumers. Articles for sale that appeal to tourists include pottery, wrought iron, leather goods, blankets, silver, jewelry and works of art.

Other important, newer commercial strips spread southward along **calzadas López Mateos, Justo Sierra** and **Benito Juárez.** Plaza

Calzada Independencia in the Centro Cívico-Comercial de Mexicali. Visible are the bullfight arena, a large Chinese restaurant, and a sign pointing to the U.S. border.

Cachanilla is an impressive shopping mall 1.7 miles from the border on the northeast side of López Mateos. Neon signs on these streets present an impressive spectacle after dark. A growing business district is the **Centro Cívico-Commercial,** near the government center.

Dining

Mexicali has a long list of fine Mexican and International eating places. A few of them are **9 Dragones,** on Calzada Benito Juárez just south of Lázaro Cárdenas, in the Plaza Mandarín (Chinese cuisine); **Sakura** on Calzada Francisco Montejano and Boulevard Lázaro Cárdenas (Japanese food); **Rívoli** in Hotel Lucerna (varied menu, including steak and seafood); **Los Arcos** on Calle Calafia near the bull ring (seafood); **El Vaquero** in Centro Cívico-Commercial on Avenida de los Héroes near Independencia (steak, carne asada); **Los Búffalos,** in the Plaza Cachanilla shopping center (ranch-style cooking); and **El Sarape** in the border business district on Calle México between Colón and Madero (Mexican food).

Nightclubs

Numerous piano bars and discotheques lie within walking distance of the international border. Live entertainment and dancing are offered at hotels **Lucerna** and **Holiday Inn** on Calzada Benito Juárez, and at **Forum Discotheque** at Calzada Justo Sierra and Avenida Reforma.

Points of Interest

City Park/Bosque de la Ciudad
Avenida Ocotlán (del Fuego) and Calle Alvarado, in southwest Mexicali. 01152 (65) 55-2833. Open Tuesday through Friday 9 a.m. to 5 p.m., Saturday and Sunday 9 a.m. to 5 p.m. Admission $1. The easiest approach is from the north along calles

R. Clark Hunter

El Bosque de la Ciudad provides a shady retreat for Mexicali residents.

MEXICO HIGHWAY 5

Victoria and Alvarado. The park contains a zoo, a museum of natural history, a picnic area and a children's playground.

Galería de la Ciudad *1209 Avenida Alvaro Obregón between calles D and E. 01152 (65) 53-5044.* Open Monday through Friday, 9 a.m. to 8 p.m. Free admission. Housed in what was formerly the state governor's residence, the art gallery features works of Baja California painters, sculptors and photographers.

Glorieta Monuments The traffic circles on Mexicali's main boulevards contain impressive monuments. Crosswalks lead to the landscaped islands where the monuments stand.

Museo Regional Universidad de Baja California *Avenida Reforma and Calle L. 01152 (65) 54-1977.* Open Tuesday through Friday 9 a.m. to 6 p.m., Saturday and Sunday 9 a.m. to 2 p.m. Free admission. This fine museum contains comprehensive exhibits on geology, rocks and minerals, anthropology of American Indians, and the missions and ranches of early Baja California.

Parque Industrial *Avenida Brasil and Boulevard de las Americas between Calzada Justo Sierra and the airport.* Like Tijuana, Mexicali has *maquiladoras.* This area contains industrial plants that are owned by Americans and other foreigners attracted to Mexican border areas because of low production costs.

State Theater/Teatro del Estado *Calzada López Mateos, 1½ miles south of the U.S. border. 01152 (65) 54-6418.* Plays, musicals and dance presentations are featured here. The Mexicali Convention and Tourist Bureau also has programs and schedules.

Spectator Sports
Bullfights

Plaza de Toros Calafia Calle Calafia in the Centro Cívico-Comercial. 01152 (65) 57-0681. Bullfights are held every autumn and sometimes in spring.

Charreadas (Mexican Rodeos)

Charro grounds, 3.7 miles east of Calzada Justo Sierra on Carretera a Compuertas (the road to the airport). There is no set schedule for these colorful equestrian events, but charreadas average once a month during the winter and spring, usually on Sunday and major Mexican holidays.

Mexicali to San Felipe
(124 mi., 198 km.; 2:30 hrs.)

The most direct route to San Felipe follows Calzada López Mateos from the international border to Mexico Highway 5. Upon leaving the Mexican port of entry, turn 45 degrees to the right and follow Calzada López Mateos in a southeasterly direction to the traffic circle at the intersection with Highway 5. An alternate route, popular in previous years, follows Avenida Francisco I. Madero eastward to Calzada Justo Sierra, which leads south to Highway 5. Motorists returning to the United States from Mexicali must approach the U.S. Customs facility along Avenida Cristóbal Colón, a one-way westbound street immediately south of the international border. After leaving Mexicali, the highway skirts the western edge of one of Mexico's most productive farming regions for about 30 miles. To the southwest is the imposing mountain wall of the Sierra de los Cucapá.

Plumes of steam, visible to the east, rise from the Cerro Prieto geothermal

Bill Cory

About 40 miles south of Mexicali, Highway 5 crosses open desert. This route is similar to Highway 1, with good striping and signing but a general lack of shoulders.

electric plant. (Mexico is one of the world's leading producers of geothermal electricity, and some of this electricity is exported to the United States.) Mexico Highway 5 then continues southward through extremely arid desert. After about 45 miles, the road runs atop an 11-mile-long earthen levee while crossing an arm of the intermittent lake, Laguna Salada. Then it passes through the Sierra Pinta, whose dark volcanic basalt hills have an otherworldly appearance. As the highway nears San Felipe, the high Sierra San Pedro Mártir, capped by 10,154-foot Picacho del Diablo, is visible to the west. On the outskirts of San Felipe the flat, straight highway bends toward the gulf, passing under big white gateway arches.

00.0	Mexicali (U.S. border crossing).
03.0	Junction with Calzada Independencia.
04.1	Junction with Calzada Lázaro Cárdenas.
05.1	Traffic circle at Sánchez Taboada Monument. Bear right, then take the right fork, which heads south.
05.7	Junction with Highway 2 west to Tecate and Tijuana (see *Connecting Routes*).
07.7	A paved road branches west to Club Deportivo Campestre de Mexicali, which has a golf course and other sports facilities.
25.2	Junction with the paved road to the farming communities of Zakamoto and Ejido Nayarít.
26.1	La Puerta, a roadside farming center with a Pemex station (*magna sin*), cafe and store.
29.3	Junction with highway BC 4, a paved route that crosses the Mexicali Valley to Coahuila (Colonia Nuevas) and continues to El Golfo de Santa Clara on the Sonora side of the gulf (see *Side Routes*).
37.0	Campo Sonora, the first of several rustic trailer camps along Río Hardy.
38.3	Río del Mayor, a village with an Indian museum under development. Located by the police station, it is called Museo Comunitario, Centro Cultural Cucapá.
44.2	At this point, the highway, elevated by a levee, sets out across the southern end of Laguna Salada.

71.2 La Ventana, which has a Pemex station and café.

92.7 El Chinero (Crucero la Trinidad), junction with Highway 3, which leads westward to Valle de Trinidad and Ensenada (see *Connecting Routes*). At the junction is a government-built restaurant and picnic area. About 0.7 mile south of the junction is a Pemex station (*magna sin*) and a café.

111.0 A dirt road branches left to Campo Don Abel, the first of a string of rustic trailer camps on the gulf shore north of San Felipe. Facilities in these camps are usually modest.

114.8 A graded 1-mile road to El Paraíso/Pete's Camp, a long-established popular camp with tent and RV spaces, showers, a disposal station and a restaurant-bar.

123.6 San Felipe, at the junction of Highway 5 and Avenida Mar de Cortez.

San Felipe

(See also *Lodging & Restaurants* and *Campgrounds & Trailer Parks*)

This major winter resort and fishing center occupies a site where the shimmering waters of the Gulf of California

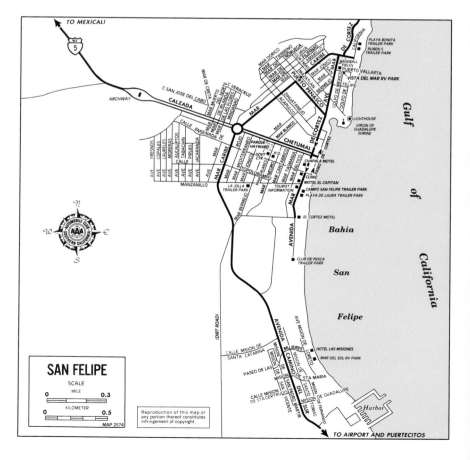

Take note . . . in San Felipe

Tourist Information

The **State Tourism Office** is located on Avenida Mar de Cortez at Manzanillo (see map). Hours are Monday through Friday 8 a.m. to 7 p.m., Saturday and Sunday 9 a.m. to 2 p.m.; phone 01152 (657) 7-1155. **Tourist Assistance** can be reached through the same office.

lap against the shores of a forbidding desert. Clearly visible across the sandy coastal plain to the west is the steep eastern wall of the Sierra San Pedro Mártir—highest range on the peninsula. The town itself is nestled beneath 940-foot-high Punta San Felipe, a rugged headland that provides a partial shelter for boats and forms the northern end of shallow Bahía San Felipe. From this point, the shore of the bay makes a crescent-shaped dent in the coastline, then swings southeastward in a line of wide, attractive beaches to Punta Estrella, 12 miles distant. An interesting natural phenomenon here is the extreme tidal range, which can reach more than 20 feet; this makes boating a tricky proposition for those without experience in these waters.

San Felipe is a friendly community of about 15,000, with modest dwellings, sandy side streets and little vegetation. The wide variety of facilities include numerous hotels and trailer parks, markets, bakeries, restaurants, bars, launch ramps, banks, clinics, auto mechanics and two Pemex stations. Curio shops sell a great variety of goods, including blankets, shawls, shoes, beach wear, shirts and pottery. Highway 5 ends at Avenida Mar de Cortez, which parallels the shore and

R. Clark Hunter

San Felipe's broad beach faces the Gulf of California. The Sierra San Pedro Mártir rises in the background.

forms the main street of town; its many businesses cater to local residents and tourists alike.

Although nomadic fishermen were attracted to this area as early as the mid-19th century, San Felipe did not become a permanent settlement until the 1920s. Large-scale fishing began in earnest during World War II, and the completion of the paved highway from Mexicali in 1951 brought a surge of American sports enthusiasts. In the years that followed, San Felipe gradually evolved from a sleepy fishing village into a popular resort. Rapid expansion during the 1980s, with the addition of many new hotels, condominiums and trailer parks, is continuing in the 1990s. The recently modernized airport has gained international status.

November through April is the ideal time to visit San Felipe. Days are usually warm and sunny, and nights are refreshingly cool. Summers, however, can be unbearably hot, with daytime temperatures sometimes exceeding 115 Fahrenheit. Rainfall is less than two inches per year. U.S. vacation periods (Washington's Birthday, Easter week, Memorial Day, Labor Day, Thanksgiving, etc.) are extremely crowded, and accommodations, trailer parks and even beach campsites are likely to be jammed. San Felipe tends to attract a somewhat unruly brand of tourist, and annoyances caused by motorcycles, dune buggies and loud parties are common during holiday periods. Litter is also a problem. The town is relatively peaceful the rest of the year.

Points of Interest

Valle de los Gigantes *13½ miles south of town center, then about three miles southwest on a sandy road.* There is no sign pointing to this attraction, but look for one that points in the opposite direction to Colonia Gutierrez Polanco. The title of this place translates "Valley of the Giants," and this cluster of very large cardón cacti has specimens more than 100 years old. Sturdy high-clearance vehicles should be used on this road.

R. Clark Hunter

Looking north from the San Felipe lighthouse along the shore of the bay toward rugged Punta San Felipe.

R. Clark Hunter

Stately cardón cacti stand in El Valle de los Gigantes south of San Felipe.

Virgin of Guadalupe Shrine *Situated on a hilltop just north of San Felipe.* A panoramic view of the town and the coastline is offered. Adjacent is a lighthouse (not open to visitors).

San Felipe to Puertecitos

(52 mi., 83 km.; 2 hrs.)

This route through rapidly developing and changing territory has been paved as far as Puertecitos. Plans call for additional paving south to Bahía San Luis Gonzaga sometime in the near future. Some of the pavement on the southern end of this route is rough, ranging from broken surfaces to large potholes.

The first eight miles run close to the bay through part of San Felipe's resort area, with a number of hotels, campgrounds and condominiums; more are under construction. The pavement is good on this first section, but drifting sand is a problem in a few spots; drive with caution to avoid skidding. The remaining 44 miles follow a route a little inland from the Gulf of California, with turnoffs leading to numerous campos that contain small communities of American and Canadian vacation homes and trailer camps. As yet, virtually no facilities exist for motorists on this long section, but there is much indication of land development for recreation. Along the route, the terrain changes very little; level to rolling countryside is interspersed with low, barren hills. Ocotillo, mesquite, cholla cactus and smoke trees are the most common forms of vegetation, although a few elephant trees and cardón cacti may be seen.

00.0 Junction of Highway 5 and Avenida Mar Caribe (street name for the beginning of the route.)

00.5 Junction with a graded road which also leads to Puertecitos; in the past this inland route was the preferred road for some travelers.

00.9 Entrance to Hotel Las Misiones and Mar del Sol RV Park.

01.4 Entrance to the commercial harbor.

05.5 Junction with the paved road to San Felipe International Airport.

07.3 La Hacienda, a condominium development.

09.7 Turnoff to Faro Beach and Punta Estrella, at the southern end of Bahía San Felipe.

13.5 An unsigned sandy road leads southwest to Valle de los Gigantes, a group of very large cardón cacti. In the opposite

Tom Dell

*Mobile homes overlook a shallow bay at Puertecitos,
a community with a predominantly American population.*

direction a sign points to Colonia Gutierrez Polanco.

19.0 A sandy spur road leads 2½ miles to Laguna (Rancho) Percibú, a growing community of American beach houses, a campground and a restaurant.

25.4 Turnoff to Campo Santa María, a large collection of trailers and vacation homes.

28.2 The village of Ejido Delicias, with a clinic and a small store. On the beach opposite are a lighthouse and Campo El Vergel, a large settlement.

40.7 Junction with the inland road leading north toward San Felipe.

51.6 **Puertecitos**, overlooking a small bay. At the northern entrance is a municipal delegation and a small Mexican community called Ejido Matomí. Most of Puertecitos, however, is inhabited by Americans who lease their homes and trailer sites from the owners of the land. Facilities include a motel, a cafe and bar, a small general store, a Pemex station (not

always open) and an airstrip. Arrangements can be made for camping, cabaña rentals, fishing boats, trailer rentals and boat launching. Fishing is good outside the shallow bay, which becomes dry during extreme low tides. The short road branching to the southeast point of the bay passes a rocky footpath leading to natural hot springs; depending on the tide, three separate pools are filled with water of varying temperatures.

Puertecitos to Bahía San Luis Gonzaga

(45 mi., 72 km.; 4 hrs.)

Long notorious as one of Baja California's roughest routes, this graded dirt road along the Gulf of California was greatly improved in 1987. The surface is rough washboard, however, and sturdy high-clearance vehicles are recommended. Carry adequate emergency equipment, as this is a lonely stretch of road. Vegetation is sparse along this arid route, but interesting rocks can be seen in shades of orange, red and brown. Much of the road has been realigned, but motorists can see the former tortuous, rocky route alongside. Between 11 and 19 miles the road crosses several hills, with spectacular views of canyons and the gulf. The treacherous Huerfanito Grade is now bypassed. Between Nacho's Camp and Punta Bufeo are numerous signs advertising undeveloped campsites and lots for sale. The road here is level, running close to shore. For the last six miles it crosses sandy arroyos and passes among hills before reaching the shore of the bay.

Bahía San Luis Gonzaga, not to be confused with the mission of the same name in Baja California Sur, is a beautiful, pristine body of water. Although the landscape is barren, Bahía Gonzaga typifies an isolated, peaceful seaside spot in Baja California, with brilliant sun by day and a million stars by night.

00.0	Puertecitos.
04.8	Campo La Costilla, a small private camp at the edge of an attractive cove, where the natural slope of the beach makes an excellent launch ramp. Refreshments can be purchased here.
11.6	The first of many good camping spots along the rocky gulf shore.
17.7	Nacho's Camp, a group of homes owned by Americans.
20.0	San Juan del Mar, a growing beach settlement with an airstrip.
35.1	Campo Salvatierra, an abandoned private campground with several good primitive camping spots.
37.8	Junction with the road to Las Encantadas.
39.4	Junction with a 1.3-mile dirt road to Campo Punta Bufeo, a collection of homes owned by Americans and an airstrip. Refreshments and simple meals are available.
42.5	Junction with the 0.9-mile road to Papa Fernandez' camp, located on Bahía San Luis Gonzaga. The resort offers meals, refreshments, boats and motors for rent,

John P. Skinner

This rocky, rough road between Puertecitos and Bahía San Luis Gonzaga used to torment the hardiest of drivers prior to 1987; it is now replaced by a greatly improved parallel route.

MEXICO HIGHWAY 5

Tom Dell

The road along the Gulf of California is a scenic, lonely route suited to sturdy vehicles. From the top of the grade is a dramatic panorama of the coastline and offshore islands.

and occasionally gasoline and oil. The level grassy field to the west makes a good natural airstrip. Fishing is excellent.

00.0   Bahía San Luis Gonzaga, at the junction to Papa Fernandez.

Bill Cory

Bahía San Luis Gonzaga to Highway 1

(39 mi., 63 km.; 2 hrs.)

With careful driving, this graded dirt road can be traveled by passenger cars and small RVs. After passing the shore of Bahía San Luis Gonzaga near Punta Willard, the route comes to the junction to Punta Final, on the southern end of the bay. For the first few miles after the bay, the road ascends through gently sloping desert terrain where wildflowers form carpets of color during early spring. Then the road enters a range of hills containing numerous elephant trees. Just beyond a rocky canyon with a windy road is Rancho las Arrastras. A short distance past the ranch, the route forks to the left and then meets a road leading southwest to Highway 1.

The road from Bahía San Luis Gonzaga to Highway 1 is full of scenic variety. Through river canyons, over hills and through dense stands of cirio and elephant trees, it winds through the heart of the central Baja California wilderness. Here an ocotillo stands sentinel over the vast, quiet desert.

02.6 Rancho Grande, a water purification/ice plant and a campground. A 1.6-mile side road leads to Alfonsina's Camp, located on a narrow sandspit facing the bay. Facilities include a small hotel, a campground, a restaurant, an airstrip and gasoline. Vacation homes line the sandspit next to the camp.

11.7 Junction with the road to Punta Final, a private beach community.

22.0 Rancho las Arrastras de Arriola, which has radiator water and cold drinks.

26.0 Junction with the road leading 13 miles southwest to Highway 1. It joins the highway just north of Laguna Chapala, 33.7 miles south of Cataviña. From the junction, turn right for Highway 1. A left turn leads east, then north to Hermenegildo Galiana and to Campo Calamajué on the gulf.■

Connecting Routes

Two of the three Mexican federal highways described in this section link Highways 1 and 5. The first, Highway 2, leads eastward from Tijuana to Tecate and Mexicali, then continues into Sonora, eventually connecting with Highway 15 to Mexico City. The second is Highway 3, with two major sections: the northern section connecting Tecate with El Sauzal, which is the shortest link between Mexicali and Ensenada; and the southern section running from Ensenada to a junction with Highway 5 at a point about 31 miles north of San Felipe. The third connecting route is Highway 19, which forms part of a loop with Highway 1 in the extreme southern portion of the peninsula. Travel time between La Paz and Cabo San Lucas is about one hour shorter on this route than via Highway 1. All three of these routes are paved over their entire lengths.

CROSSING THE BORDER

The Tecate border crossing, which connects the village of Tecate, California with Tecate, Baja California, gets relatively little use by tourists entering Mexico. For those return-ing to the United States from Ensenada and points farther south, however, it is a popular alternative to the crowded crossing at Tijuana. Delays are seldom encountered here by motorists in either direction. The border gates are open daily from 6 a.m. to midnight.

MEXICO HIGHWAY 2

Tijuana to Tecate via Highway 2

(34 mi., 54 km.; 1 hr.)

Mexico Highway 2 starts in Tijuana as Boulevard Díaz Ordaz, passes through the bustling industrial and commercial zone of La Mesa, then crosses a dam and enters rural countryside that is evolving into an industrial district. Then the road climbs gradually into low rocky hills, past olive orchards, dairy farms and cattle ranches on the way to Tecate. Highway 2 is four-lanes undivided to La Presa, then becomes a good two-lane road the rest of the way. Traffic is heavy in La Mesa, so Boulevard Insurgentes may be preferable. It is a divided road that starts in La Mesa, parallels Highway 2 for seven miles, then merges with it.

00.0   Tijuana (San Ysidro border crossing). Proceed

	straight ahead and follow signs for Mexicali.
03.9	Agua Caliente Racetrack. On the hills to the south is one of the city's most attractive residential neighborhoods.
06.1	Boulevard Lázaro Cárdenas, which goes northeast to Boulevard Insurgentes, the central bus station and Tijuana Airport.
11.5	La Presa, the easternmost district in the Tijuana urbanized area.
11.8	Rodríguez Dam and lake, once the sole source of Tijuana's water supply. The road follows the top of the dam and is quite narrow.
15.4	El Florido, a large housing development; three miles farther is a dairy-farming village with the same name.
30.1	Rancho La Puerta, a nicely landscaped resort and spa specializing in physical fitness. It offers pleasant accommodations and strictly vegetarian meals.
33.6	Tecate, a friendly town clustered around a tree-shaded plaza. Highway 3 leads south from Tecate to El Sauzal and Ensenada (see description, Mexico Highway 3).

Tijuana to Tecate via Toll Highway 2D

(22 mi., 35 km.; 0:30 hr.)

Opened in 1992, this toll highway—a divided fully controlled-access expressway—provides a fast alternative to Highway 2. It begins in the Otay Mesa district of Tijuana. After crossing the border, drive 1.2 miles straight south to the first main boulevard, then turn east (left). Follow Boulevard Industrial (Eje Oriente-Poniente) through Ciudad Industrial, the *maquiladora* (industrial)

district. After about 2 miles the boulevard becomes the toll highway.

After passing sprawling poor housing developments, the expressway heads into rural landscape. It first follows a canyon where falling rocks are a possibility. Then it goes over rolling landscape, passing occasional farms and ranches. After about 18 miles it enters the Tecate Basin, where Highway 2D presently ends at the entrance to Tecate. This route is also called Autopista Tijuana-Mexicali, because it is the western section of a planned expressway that will, in the near future, link Tijuana with Mexicali. At press time, the expressway was under construction between Tecate and La Rumorosa, 41 miles to the east.

The toll road is lightly traveled, because rates are quite high–$3.90 for cars, pick-up trucks and vans; $7.80 for motorhomes; and $9.70 for vehicles with trailers.

00.0	Tijuana (Otay Mesa).
03.6	Toll station.
16.1	Exit for Highway 2 and west entrance to Tecate.
21.8	Exit for Highway 3 and south entrance to Tecate.

Tecate

Lacking proximity to any large population center in the United States, Tecate has never had much of a border-town atmosphere. Instead, this pleasant city of about 50,000 is a typical Mexican community, where life centers around a tranquil tree-shaded plaza. At an elevation of 1690 feet, Tecate sits in a bowl-shaped valley surrounded by rocky hills; because of its inland location, the city has hot, dry summers and cool winters with occasional frost.

Tecate came into being in the late 19th century, when farmers and

Take note . . . in Tecate

Tourist Information and Assistance

The **State Tourism Office** is located at 1305 Callejón Libertad, on the south side of the plaza. Hours are Monday through Friday 8 a.m. to 7 p.m., Saturday and Sunday 9 a.m. to 3 p.m. 01152 (665) 4-1095. **Tourist Assistance** is also located in this office.

ranchers, attracted by its abundant water and fertile soil, settled the area. Tecate has long been a farm market center for a productive region that yields grapes, olives and grain. Industries—beer, instant coffee and *maquiladoras* (assembly plants)—have been growing in importance. Its diversified facilities and location at the junction of two major Mexican routes (Highways 2 and 3) have made Tecate a favorite stopover for travelers. Several accommodations can be found here, along with a variety of stores and restaurants, a hospital, gasoline stations, and auto parts and repairs. The

city is the seat of government of the *municipio* of Tecate.

Points of Interest

Parque Hidalgo *On Avenida Juárez and Calle Ortiz Rubio.* The town plaza is an attractive retreat. An impressive monument to Benito Juárez is located at the northeast corner of the park.

Cuauhtémoc Brewery *Avenida Hidalgo and Calle Carranza.* Beer garden open Tuesday through Saturday 10 a.m. to 5 p.m. Brewery tours are given on Saturday mornings; call

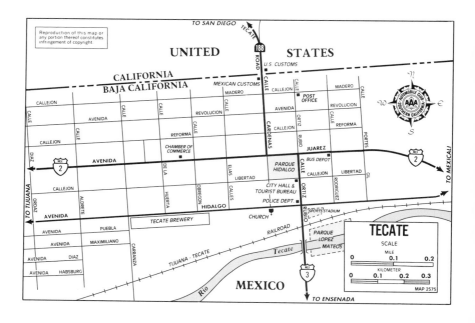

R. Clark Hunter

Locals and visitors are welcome in Tecate's pleasant, shady plaza.

01152 (665) 4-2011 for reservations. Home of Tecate beer.

Tecate to Mexicali

(89 mi., 144 km.; 2:45 hrs.)

Continuing east from Tecate, Highway 2 begins a long, gradual climb onto a high plateau. It passes small farms and ranches and several rustic resorts and campgrounds, visited mainly by Mexicans. Near La Rumorosa, at an elevation of more than 4000 feet, the highway can become impassable after heavy snows, but these rarely occur. Just east of La Rumorosa is the Rumorosa (Cantú) Grade, one of the most spectacular mountain highways on the continent, where the road makes an abrupt switchback descent past strangely jumbled rock formations to the floor of the barren desert. Strong winds, slow-moving trucks and many sharp curves call for reduced speeds and careful driving in this 15-mile section; passing can be difficult. After reaching the base of the grade, Highway 2 skirts the vast bed of Laguna Salada, which since 1977 has held water. The road now sweeps through low hills, then enters the Mexicali Valley—one of Mexico's richest farming areas. Although Highway 2 bypasses the center of Mexicali, well-marked paved roads lead into the city.

00.0   Tecate, at the junction of Highways 2 and 3.

13.6   Loma Tova, a village with a cafe.

21.2   Colonia El Hongo, a fast-growing farming community with cafes and stores. A partially paved road winds seven miles southwest to Hacienda Santa Verónica, a cattle ranch with a hotel and trailer park.

31.6   El Condor, a settlement with a Pemex station and restaurant, at the junction with a graded road to Laguna Hanson in the Sierra de Juárez (see *Side Routes*).

41.0   La Rumorosa, elevation 4300 feet, located on a high boulder-strewn plateau. Facilities in the town include stores, cafes, a gasoline station (*magna sin*) and mechanical assistance. Just east of La Rumorosa, Highway 2 begins its steep winding drop to the desert floor.

65.8   Junction with a graded dirt road along the edge of Laguna Salada to Cañon de Guadalupe. This lovely palm canyon is 27 miles south, then 8 miles west. The road is suitable for passenger cars and small RVs. The canyon features hot springs, hot tubs,

R. Clark Hunter

Highway 2 makes a very steep climb over the rugged Rumorosa Grade.

a small store and a developed campground; rates are $10 per vehicle. For information call (714) 673-2670.

79.4 Colonia Progreso, a village with a large municipal building, a motel, restaurant and a Pemex station.

83.4 Junction with Calle Guadalajara, the shortest route to downtown Mexicali and the U.S. border. The sign says "Centro, Calexico."

88.9 Mexicali, at the traffic-circle intersection of Highways 2 and 5 (see *Mexico Highway 5*).

Mexicali to La Rumorosa via Toll Highway 2D
(31 mi., 50 km.; 0:45 hr.)

This expressway, the eastern part of the Autopista Tijuana-Mexicali, is at present open only to westbound (upgrade) traffic. Beginning at a Solidari-

dad monument 15 miles west of Mexicali, it crosses level desert floor, then winds up the steep Rumorosa Grade, paralleling old Highway 2. This two-lane one-way road has a very good surface, but be cautious on sharp curves and abrupt drop-offs. This part of Highway 2D ends with a toll station at the top of the grade, next to the entrance to La Rumorosa. Just beyond the toll gate there are rest rooms. Tolls are high—$5.00 for cars, pickup trucks and vans; $10.10 for motorhomes; and $15.10 for vehicles pulling trailers. Few vehicles choose to travel it. This route is a subject of controversy—the government is considering charging tolls on both highways, with old Highway 2 becoming one-way eastbound.

Mexicali to San Luis R.C., Sonora
(41 mi., 66 km.; 1 hr.)

From the traffic circle on the southern outskirts of Mexicali, Highway 2 tra-

*Cañón de Guadalupe is a lovely palm oasis, where thermal waters
flow from natural hot springs on the rocky canyon walls.*

verses an industrial area, then strikes out across the flat Mexicali Valley, one of Mexico's most important farming areas. Irrigated farms and small communities line the highway in this section. Cotton production, from field to gin, is in evidence. Also important are sorghum and hay crops. Although the highway has two lanes in each direction, motorists should be alert for slow-moving farm vehicles entering and leaving the roadway.

After crossing a toll bridge over the Colorado River, Highway 2 enters the state of Sonora and the booming border town of San Luis R.C.

00.0 Mexicali, at the junction of Highways 2 and 5.

06.0 Junction with a paved road to Ejido Puebla (stores, cafes, Pemex station) and the Cerro Prieto Geothermal Zone, site of a large geothermal electrical generating facility.

14.0 Double junction with BCN 1, a paved highway. To the left it goes to Mexicali International Airport. To the right it leads south past the farming towns of Nuevo León and Ledón, then intersects BCN 4, which turns eastward to Coahuila. From here, another paved road crosses into Sonora (see Side Routes).

24.6 Bataques, which has a Pemex station.

27.4 Junction with a paved highway (BCN 2) to the agricultural center of Ciudad Morelos. Ten miles northeast on BCN 8 is the pleasant border town of Algodones. With a population of about 5000, **Algodones** has gasoline, a hotel, cafes, pharmacies, dentists, optometrists, souvenir crafts, a park and a state tourism office. Near Al-

godones is Morelos Dam, where irrigation water for the Mexicali Valley is taken from the Colorado River. From Andrade, at the international border, California State Route 186 takes the traveler to Interstate 8 at a point 7 miles west of Yuma, Arizona.

38.3 Toll bridge ($0.90 for cars and pickups) across the Colorado River, which forms the boundary between the states of Baja California and Sonora.

40.6 **San Luis Río Colorado.** "Río Colorado" is used to differentiate the city from other Mexican towns named San Luis. With a population of 135,000, the city thrives from agriculture (cotton and wheat), highway transportation and the international border trade. Tourist facilities are concentrated near the international border, which is 23 miles south of Yuma, Arizona. It has an attractive plaza park which is surrounded by businesses, a classic church and government buildings, including a state tourism office. From San Luis, Highway 2 heads eastward across barren desert to Highway 15, providing the fastest, most direct link between Southern California and the interior of Mexico. For travel on the mainland car permits are required. Car permits can be obtained in San Luis at the international border (see Tourist Regulations and Travel Tips, Automobile Requirements section). Those traveling beyond San Luis should refer to the AAA Travel Guide to Mexico.

MEXICO HIGHWAY 3

Tecate to El Sauzal
(66 mi., 107 km.; 1:30 hrs.)

After leaving Tecate this two-lane highway climbs into a region of boulder-strewn, scrub-covered mountains and small upland valleys, some of which are under cultivation. Several sharp curves and steep grades in this section call for extra caution. On the southern third of the route the highway runs past olive orchards and miles of vineyards through a level valley bordered by low hills to the junction with Highway 1 at El Sauzal. Because this is the shortest route from the farms of the Mexicali Valley to Ensenada's port, large trucks are sometimes encountered along this section of Highway 3.

00.0	Tecate, at the junction of Highways 2 and 3.
01.8	Junction with Mexico Highway 2D, the Tijuana-Mexicali Expressway.
05.7	Rancho Tecate, a new resort with a golf course.
17.8	Valle de las Palmas, an agricultural community with gasoline (*magna sin*), stores and restaurants.
31.0	El Testerazo, a village with a cafe. To the west are prominent rocky peaks, 3000 to 4200 feet in elevation.
46.2	Domecq Winery; tours are given from Tuesday through Saturday, 9 a.m. to 1 p.m. At this point the highway enters a region containing extensive, well-maintained vineyards. A short distance north is L.A. Cetto Winery, which also conducts tours.
48.3	Guadalupe. Next to the elementary school are the ruins of Mission Nuestra Señora de Guadalupe (1834), last of the Baja California missions. Russian immigrants founded an agricultural community here early in the 20th century. Museo Comunitario del Valle de Guadalupe has a collection of pictures and artifacts about these Russian-Mexican settlers. This museum is located 1½ miles west of the junction of Highway 3 and the main road into town. Hours are Wednesday through Sunday 9 a.m. to 4 p.m.; donation. Guadalupe and Francisco Zarco, an adjacent village, have two cafes, groceries, an inn and a clinic.
59.4	Villa Juárez, a town with a restaurant and a market. In the vicinity are new real estate developments.
66.1	El Sauzal, at the junction with Highway 1. Ensenada is six miles to the southeast.

Ensenada to El Chinero (Crucero La Trinidad), Junction with Highway 5
(123 mi., 198 km.; 3 hrs.)

Sometimes known as the Ensenada-San Felipe Road, this section of Highway 3 usually has a good paved surface. Together with Highways 1 (or 1D), 2 and 5, this scenic route with very light traffic offers visitors an opportunity for an interesting loop trip through the northern portion of Baja California. The first 24 miles east of Ensenada are narrow and winding, as the highway climbs and crosses a range of chaparral-covered hills before dropping into wide green Valle de Ojos Negros—a productive farming and ranching center. Beyond the turnoff to the village of Ojos Negros, the pavement becomes wider. Heading south, then southeast, Highway 3

126

R. Clark Hunter

Ocotillo, brush and wildflowers decorate the desert floor near San Felipe.

climbs through semiarid foothills to a plateau known as Llano Colorado. The landscape gradually becomes drier as the highway winds through more hills and descends along the edge of Valle de Trinidad, an important agricultural development. After leaving the fields and cattle grazing lands of the valley, Highway 3 follows a canyon called San Matías Pass, after which it drops to the floor of arid Valle de San Felipe. To the south the rugged face of the Sierra San Pedro Mártir is clearly visible, capped by Picacho del Diablo (elevation 10,154 feet), the highest point in Baja California. After crossing open desert bordered by low barren hills, Highway 3 meets Highway 5 at El Chinero, 32 miles north of San Felipe.

00.0 Ensenada, at the intersection of Avenida Benito Juárez (Highway 1), Avenida Reforma and Calzada Cortez. Follow Calzada Cortez eastward from the traffic circle.

08.1 El Gran 13, a new amusement park with rides and playground equipment, a picnic ground, a swimming pool and spa.

16.4 Junction with a 5.2-mile dirt road to Agua Caliente, a rustic tourist resort. This road should not be attempted in wet weather.

24.7 Junction with the paved road leading 1.2 miles to Ojos Negros, a farming and cattle-raising community with two markets and a nice park. Restaurant Oasis has tourist information. A graded road leads eastward from Ojos Negros to the Sierra de Juárez and Laguna Hanson (see *Side Routes*).

34.7   Junction with a signed road to Parque Nacional Constitución de 1857; the road from Ojos Negros is preferable.

57.5   Héroes de la Independencia, a scattered settlement on Llano Colorado. The town has groceries, pottery stores, cafes, auto parts and a Pemex station (*magna sin*). A dirt road branches north to the ruins of Mission Santa Catarina, founded in 1797.

75.5   Junction with the short, paved road to Valle de Trinidad. A small village in 1980, it is now a farm market center of 3000 with stores, cafes, a bank, an ice house, schools, an unusual conical church, a mechanic, tire repair and gasoline station.

86.2   Junction with a good dirt road to Mike's Sky Rancho, which is 22.5 miles to the south (see *Side Routes*).

92.5   San Matías Pass, elevation 2950 feet.

95.9   Junction with a dirt road leading first to *ejidos* Villa del Sol and Colonia San Pedro Mártir, then southeast to San Felipe. This rugged route passes close to the base of the Sierra San Pedro Mártir; Cañón El Diablo, 20 miles south of the junction, is where many climbers begin the difficult ascent of Picacho del Diablo.

123.4   El Chinero (Crucero la Trinidad), junction with Highway 5 (see *Mexico Highway 5*). At the junction is a government-built restaurant and picnic area. About 0.7 mile south of the junction is a Pemex station (*magna sin*) and a cafe.

MEXICO HIGHWAY 19

Highway 1 to Todos Santos

(32 mi., 51 km.; 0:45 hr.)

This route leaves Highway 1 at a point 19 miles south of La Paz and offers the possibility of a scenic loop trip from La Paz to Cabo San Lucas and back. Since 1986, when it became completely paved, Highway 19 has been the most direct route between La Paz and Cabo San Lucas. It is about an hour (and about 30 miles) shorter than Highway 1, the old traditional route. From its junction with Highway 1 the road leads southward across flat, cactus-covered countryside toward Todos Santos.

00.0   Junction with Highway 1, just south of the village of San Pedro.

06.0   Club Campestre El Carrizal, a local country club with a pool and a restaurant.

26.5   Signed road to Presa de Santa Inéz, a dam.

31.8   Todos Santos, town center.

Todos Santos

(See also *Campgrounds & Trailer Parks*)

With its red brick buildings and wide streets, Todos Santos is still a tranquil town, despite the increasing impact of tourism. Almost directly on the Tropic of Cancer, this town of about 6000 inhabitants is laid out on a small, rolling coastal plain called the Valle del Pilar, a couple of miles from the Pacific Ocean shore.

Founded in 1733 as a mission settlement, Todos Santos remained a village until the latter nineteenth century. At this time ample supplies of underground water were tapped to develop

Tom Dell

Along Mexico Highway 19 lies a succession of beautiful, unpopulated beaches, such as this wave-lashed cove near Todos Santos.

agriculture, especially sugar cane. When the sugar market collapsed in recent times, farmers diversified into growing vegetables, mangos, coconuts, papayas and other tropical fruits. Fishing also contributes to the economy. Ruins of sugar mills may be seen on Avenida Juárez about a block south of the ISSTE general store, and at El Molino Trailer Park.

Facing the pleasant plaza are the church, Nuestra Señor del Pilar (successor to the early mission); a theater; the town hall; and Restaurant Santa Fé (Italian dishes and seafood). An excellent museum, Casa de la Cultura, is located near the center of town at Calles Topete and Pilar. It contains materials on the history of Baja California Sur and Mexico, as well as items that reveal Todos Santos' civic pride. Several

buildings in town bear plaques honoring noted residents who fought in various struggles for Mexican independence. Hotel California, built in 1926, exhibits a Mexican colonial style. It is on Calle Juárez, a block west of the plaza. Todos Santos has markets, restaurants, a bank, medical clinics, a gasoline station and a park. For visitors there are three hotels and two trailer parks. A lighthouse stands at Playa Punta Lobos, an attractive beach two miles west of town.

Todos Santos to Cabo San Lucas

(45 mi., 72 km.; 1:30 hrs.)

Beyond Todos Santos, Highway 19 parallels the coastline over rolling terrain and provides access to some of

Baja California's most beautiful, unspoiled Pacific beaches. Many of these are *playas públicas* (public beaches) and are notable for good surfing.

00.0 Todos Santos, town center.
01.7 Junction with a dirt road to Playa Punta Lobos, used by fishermen and also a popular picnic spot with local residents.
03.6 El Pescadero (see *Campgrounds & Trailer Parks*), a farming and fishing town of 1500 located just east of the highway. Several dirt roads lead from the pavement to the center of town, where stores and cafes ring a small plaza. El Pescadero is a junction with a road leading across the Sierra de la Laguna to Highway 1, 5 miles north of Santa Anita.
07.5 Junction with a good dirt road to Playa Los Cerritos, a wide, beautiful beach with a private trailer park and public beach camping.
14.9 Colonia Elías Calles, a small farming community surrounded by fields and orchards. Several nice beaches lie just to the west.
26.8 Rancho Migriño, a cattle ranch.
42.2 Junction with a dirt road to Cabo San Lucas airstrip.
44.5 Cabo San Lucas, at the junction with Highway 1.■

John Austerman

The back roads of Baja California offer properly equipped
explorers a wealth of solitude and rugged beauty.

Side Routes

Wandering off the main highway is part of the excitement of traveling in Baja California. Many of the most rewarding side trips are described in this section; they are listed from north to south. For their exact locations, refer to the maps at the beginning of this book.

Although some of these side trips can be made in a standard passenger car, most require a high-clearance, heavy-duty utility vehicle with special equipment and emergency supplies. Before planning any extended off-highway travel in Baja California, read the section entitled Backcountry Travel in the *Introduction*.

Highway 5 to El Golfo de Santa Clara, Sonora

(69 mi., 112 km.; 2:30 hrs.)

This route encompasses rich agricultural land in the Mexicali Valley, the Sonoran Desert and a picturesque fishing town on the Gulf of California. Just beyond El Faro, 26 miles south of Mexicali on Mexico Highway 5, turn east on state highway BC 4 where the sign points to Colonia Nuevas. (State highways are not usually indicated on signs, but the abbreviation is printed on occasional roadside posts.) This paved highway leads across pasture land and grain fields to Ejido Durango, a farm village with gasoline.

At mileage 10 is Ledón (Colonia Carranza), which has gasoline (*magna sin*) and a few stores. Crossing flat land planted in cotton, the road reaches Murguía, turns south, then eastward. Four miles past Murguía the highway crosses the Colorado River by means of a culvert. Due to irrigation demands the river is usually a shallow narrow stream. After an occasional rain, however, the crossing may be flooded. (The highway formerly shared the railroad bridge to the north, but this route is closed for an indefinite time.) The last town in Baja California on this route, 21 miles east of Highway 5, is Coahuila, also called Colonia Nuevas. Drive slowly on the graded dirt streets. Turn left, cross the railroad and follow the signs to Sonora.

One hundred yards beyond the railroad, travelers enter the state of Sonora; there is no checkpoint. Sonora is on Mountain Time, and the urban area of Coahuila continues under the name of Luis B. Sánchez. The two towns constitute a sizeable farm market center, containing two Pemex stations (*magna sin*), auto parts, a clinic and several markets and restaurants. After one more mile the road runs into state highway SON 40. A left turn leads north to San Luis, Sonora; a right turn leads southeast to El Golfo. After passing a secondary school and some farmland, the road to El Golfo comes to Riíto, a small agricultural center at the end of the cultivated area. Here are gasoline and diesel and a few stores. Between Riíto and El Golfo de Santa Clara are 43 miles of the barren Sonoran Desert, with no services. The only real settlement is El Doctor, a railroad work station with a few buildings and a rustic cafe. The highway is very flat and in good condition most of the way. The road becomes quite rough, however, 12 miles southeast of El Doctor. Heavy rains in 1993 caused potholes and broken pavement for 9 miles. Shortly before coming to the town the road smoothes out, curves and drops quickly to a small coastal basin. Pavement ends at the entrance to El Golfo.

Another route to El Golfo starts in the city of San Luis R.C., Sonora. From Mexico Highway 2, turn south on Calle 2, which becomes highway SON 40 to Riíto. From Riíto follow the route previously described to El Golfo.

El Golfo de Santa Clara is a fishing town of about 3000 residents, with a fish-processing plant, Pemex station (gasoline and diesel), a grocery store, a general store, a church and several cafes. The streets are sandy and cars can easily get stuck. The motorist should greatly lower tire pressure before driving these streets. Several shops advertise "*aire*/air" for refilling the tires later. The harbor has many fishing boats, large and small, that catch shrimp, clams and sierra. Arrangements can sometimes be made for sportfishing. The tidal range is great here at the head of the Gulf of California, with sandy beaches at high tide and mud flats exposed at low tide. Across the gulf the mountains of Baja California are visible.

A graded sandy road extends southeast of town, passing side roads to two RV parks and an area where signs announce a planned beach community. At 1.7 miles there is a large public beach camping area (no facilities), backed by sand dunes, hills and a lighthouse. This spot is sometimes used by Americans with ATVs.

Ojos Negros to Laguna Hanson
(27 mi., 43 km.; 1:45 hrs.)

This unpaved side route offers visitors a chance to explore the high plateau country of the Sierra de Juárez—a land of cool mountain air and thick forests of ponderosa pine. In the heart of this rugged region is a Mexican national park highlighted by Laguna Hanson, a small, intermittent lake surrounded by tall pines, unusual rock formations and excellent primitive campsites. Another attraction of this trip is solitude; despite its fine scenery and its proximity to the international border, the park gets very few tourists.

Laguna Hanson can be reached from El Cóndor, west of La Rumorosa on Highway 2, but the preferred route—usually accessible in dry weather by passenger cars—begins at Ojos Negros, 25 miles east of Ensenada via Highway 3 and a paved spur road. From the end of pavement in Ojos Negros, turn right onto a wide graded road running eastward toward the mountains. For the first few miles the road passes Puerta Trampa and other prosperous farms and ranches, then enters brush-covered foothills. At mile 7.8 is a major junction; bear right here. Beyond the junction the road begins to climb steadily, but there are no steep grades. After another eight miles the road leaves the chaparral belt and

John Austerman

La Bufadora

traverses forests of ponderosa pine. At mileage 20.4 is another important junction; bear left. From this point the route swings north and enters Aserradero, a village of wooden buildings; the road leaves Aserradero ahead to the left. Just beyond the village the road crosses the southern boundary of Parque Nacional Constitución de 1857. Four miles beyond Aserradero is Laguna Hanson. Park regulations prohibit hunting, but camping is permitted. From Laguna Hanson, the road continues northward for another 37 miles, eventually meeting Highway 2 at a junction just west of La Rumorosa.

Maneadero to Punta Banda and La Bufadora

(14 mi., 23 km.; 0:30 hr.)

(See also *Campgrounds & Trailer Parks*)

This short side trip is an ideal excursion for visitors to the Ensenada area and is a popular family outing for local residents. Since the paved road to Punta Banda leaves Highway 1 north of Maneadero, travelers who are in Mexico for less than 72 hours do not need tourist cards to make this trip.

From its junction with Highway 1, BCN 23 winds through olive orchards and cultivated fields for a few miles, then leads onto Punta Banda, the rocky peninsula that forms the southern end of Bahía de Todos Santos. Seven miles west of Maneadero is the turnoff to Baja Beach and Tennis Club, a private resort. Another mile west is a group of trailer parks and campgrounds on the shore of the bay; La Jolla Beach Camp and Villarino Camp offer extensive camping facilities.

Beyond the trailer parks and campgrounds, the road has numerous curves and grades as it climbs to the summit of the peninsula and drops to the edge of a small rocky cove that is popular with skin and scuba divers. The road is badly potholed towards the end. Located here are three small restaurants and a shop offering diving supplies. Near the western tip of Punta Banda, the road ends at a parking lot (fee). From this point, steps lead to the main attraction of the trip—*La Bufadora*—a natural sea spout that shoots spray high into the air. Its most dramatic activity occurs during incoming tides. At the base of the steps are a bazaar and food stands.

Santo Tomás to La Bocana and Puerto Santo Tomás
(15 mi., 24 km.; 1 hr.)

Visitors are attracted to this route by the scenic, rocky Pacific coastline. The graded road, suitable for sturdy passenger cars, follows the Santo Tomás Valley west to La Bocana, then winds along the coast northwest to Puerto Santo Tomás.

The road branches off Highway 1 at Ejido Ajusco, just north of Santo Tomás. After passing vineyards, fenced pastures and grain fields it follows the contours of the northern wall of the valley; an old route can be seen meandering along the sandy stream bed below.

The road reaches a junction at 15.6 miles. The fork to the left goes to a campground and a cement plant. The right fork leads to the tourist village of La Bocana de Santo Tomás, which offers rustic cabins with gas stoves and electricity, a small store, boats for rent and a small freshwater lagoon; a minimal charge is made for camping. The drive north from La Bocana offers good views of sharply eroded cliffs, offshore rocks and the rugged coastline. A number of attractive American vacation houses face the sea. The road has some rough spots as it approaches Puerto Santo Tomás, a small fishing village with rustic houses and campsites for rent. Trails suitable for motorcycles and four-wheel-drive vehicles crisscross the area.

Highway 1 to Ejido Eréndira, Puerto San Isidro and Points North
(13 mi., 21 km.; 0:45 hr.)

The signed junction with the paved road to Ejido Eréndira is 6.9 miles

American vacation houses overlook the rocky Pacific Coast at La Bocana. Across the bay is Puerto Santo Tomás.

north of San Vicente. From its junction with Highway 1 the road follows the east wall of a narrow, attractive tree-lined canyon past chaparral-clad slopes similar to those of many parts of Southern California. About 6.4 miles from the main highway the road crosses a bridge as the canyon empties into a larger wider arroyo, which the road follows for 4.3 miles to a junction.

To the right is Ejido Eréndira, a farming community located just inland from the ocean. Facilities include two cafes, some stores and a Pemex station. Cabins, RV spaces and fishing boats are available for rent. Two miles beyond Ejido Eréndira the road reaches the beach, changes to a rough dirt surface, then turns northward and soon arrives in Puerto San Isidro, site of a government-operated oyster and abalone hatchery and a small cluster of dwellings overlooking the coast. The road continues northward along the rocky coastline for five miles to Punta Cabras, a collection of rustic beach homes and an electric plant under construction. There is little sandy beach along this stretch, but explorers will enjoy the cliffs, the rock shelves jutting into the water and the many seawater spouts. North of Punta Cabras is a long sandy beach on crescent-shaped Bahía Almejas.

Colonet to San Antonio del Mar

(8 mi., 12 km.; 0:30 hr.)

This partly graded dirt road, which leaves Highway 1 at a signed junction on the northern outskirts of Colonet, is in fairly good condition all the way to the coast and can be traveled in dry weather by all types of vehicles. It follows sparsely vegetated, gently rolling terrain for 4.3 miles. At this point there is a sweeping view of the coast

before the road makes a brief, steep descent to the coastal lowland. At 4.7 miles is a junction with a dirt road to Johnson Ranch, 0.6 mile to the right. Proceed straight ahead for San Antonio del Mar. A number of beach houses and permanent trailers are located here and primitive campsites are available for a small fee. The beach area, backed by high dunes, is beautiful and affords good clamming and surf fishing.

Highway 1 to Meling Ranch

(31 mi., 50 km.; 1:45 hrs.)

Wide and graded most of the way to Meling Ranch, this road can be driven in a passenger car during dry weather. From the village of San Telmo de Abajo on Highway 1, about 8 miles south of Colonet, the road winds between low, scrub-covered hills for 5.8 miles to the small village of San Telmo, which is picturesquely nestled in a small bowl-shaped valley. Beyond San Telmo the road passes Ejido Sinaloa and enters hilly country. At mileage 16.9 is the junction with a road on the left leading to Rancho Buenavista. The route to Meling Ranch now ascends a rocky arroyo, emerges onto a high ridge and winds through low hills to a junction at mileage 31.1. The turnoff for Meling Ranch is 0.4 mile ahead; the main road continues to the National Observatory.

Meling Ranch, also known as San José, is the product of a marriage uniting two pioneering families—the Melings and the Johnsons. Both families settled in northern Baja California in the early 1900s. The ranch house, rebuilt after the ranch was destroyed during the 1911 revolution, is a model example of the structures of that era. The 10,000-acre cattle ranch offers its

R. Clark Hunter

El Picacho del Diablo, the highest peak on the peninsula of Baja California, crowns the Sierra San Pedro Mártir at 10,154 feet.

guests comfortable accommodations, family-style meals, a swimming pool and horseback riding; pack trips into Sierra San Pedro Mártir National Park can be arranged by reservation. A 3500-foot graded airstrip is just east of the ranch. The daily rate for two persons—room and meals—is $110. For information and reservations call (619) 758-2719 or write Apartado Postal 1326, Ensenada, Baja California, Mexico.

Meling Ranch to the National Observatory

(30 mi., 48 km.; 1:15 hrs.)

The remarkably clear air atop the high Sierra San Pedro Mártir has prompted the Mexican government to build a modern astronomical observatory on a rounded summit 9000 feet in elevation, across from Picacho del Diablo, highest point on the peninsula. Thanks to the graded road built to aid con-

struction of the observatory, visitors now have a chance to explore Sierra San Pedro Mártir National Park—a magnificent region of rocky peaks, forests of pine and fir, freshwater streams and mountain meadows. The graded road to the observatory is somewhat rough and steep, requiring high-clearance vehicles. Snow is a regular occurrence in winter, and the road can be impassable after heavy storms.

From the turnoff to Meling Ranch the road curves through rolling fields, then climbs steadily into the mountains. At beautiful forest-rimmed Corona de Abajo Meadow the road enters Sierra San Pedro Mártir National Park. No hunting is permitted in the park, but fishing, camping, hiking and backpacking are allowed. An entrance fee is sometimes charged at the gate for day use and overnight stays. Beyond the entrance station the road continues for 12.7 miles to a highway work station; from here visitors must walk the last mile to the observatory. The observatory is not open to the public, but near it is a viewpoint with a breathtaking panorama of Picacho del Diablo, the barren desert far below and the Gulf of California on the distant horizon. The return descent toward the west allows a view of broad ranges of hills extending to the Pacific Coast.

Highway 3 to Mike's Sky Rancho

(23 mi., 37 km.; 1:30 hrs.)

This route to a secluded backcountry lodge begins at a signed junction at a point 10.7 miles southeast of Valle de Trinidad. Sturdy high-clearance vehicles are necessary. The first half of the trip is over a dirt road rising gradually over semi-arid landscape. Cerro San Matías (elevation 7100 feet) is visible to the east. The road becomes rougher and more winding as it approaches a junction at mileage 13.8. Here is found a 6000-foot graded airstrip that belongs to Mike's. A rough road to the right goes to Ejido Los Pocitos. Bear left to continue 8.2

miles farther over rough surface to the ranch. (Another road to Mike's, coming from the vicinity of Meling Ranch, is almost impassable due to storms in 1992.)

Mike's Sky Rancho rests on a knoll overlooking Arroyo San Rafael, a wooded valley flanked by steep, brush-covered mountains. The ranch offers motel-type accommodations for about $25, family-style meals, a swimming pool, horseback riding, sycamore-shaded campsites and information about trips into the rugged country to the east. The small stream that flows through the valley yields occasional catches of small rainbow trout. Hunters can go after deer, rabbit, quail and mountain lion.

Highway 1 to Punta Canoas and Puerto Catarina

(46 mi., 74 km.; 2:30 hrs.)

This trek, which descends through scenic desert to unspoiled Pacific shores, actually has two destinations.

SIDE ROUTES

Tom Dell

Mike's Sky Rancho, nestled in the foothills of the rugged Sierra San Pedro Mártir. The surrounding area is popular with hikers and motorcycle enthusiasts.

The branch to Punta Canoas is used to measure the mileage and time given above. This is a trip for seasoned, well-prepared adventurers in high-clearance, heavy-duty vehicles; four-wheel drive is desirable. There are no facilities so travelers should carry plenty of food, water and gasoline, and be prepared to camp out. Sites and experiences include rich displays of ocotillos, cardóns and elephant trees; remote Pacific beaches offer opportunities for clam digging, shell collecting and tidepool exploring; and solitude. Surfers occasionally visit, lured more by lack of surfers than by quality waves.

From its junction with the highway 5.6 miles southeast of Rancho Santa Cecilia (or 29 miles northwest of Cataviña), the road is graded and in good condition for the first 7 miles. Although its quality gradually deteriorates, a few sandy stretches present the only obstacles to passenger vehicles as far as Rancho Santa Catarina. This friendly settlement houses families who raise cattle and a few crops. Fresh water is available for washing and for radiators. After leaving the ranch the road climbs to a plateau. At mileage 20.9 is a junction. To the right, via 16.6 miles of rough road, is Puerto Catarina, once the shipping port for onyx from El Mármol. Bear left for Punta Canoas. The road becomes narrow and rough as it crosses the coastal hills. At mileage 40.2 is another junction; bear left. At mileage 41.9 is a fork. To the right the road leads 3.3 miles to Punta Canoas, site of a seasonally occupied fish camp. Campsites on a shelf high above the rugged coastline are plentiful.

Highway 1 to El Mármol
(10 mi., 16 km.; 0:30 hr.)

The signed junction with the road to El Mármol is 2.2 miles southeast of San Agustín on Highway 1. The road is smooth, graded and easily passable during dry weather in any type of vehicle. After leaving the main highway, the road runs 0.4 mile to a junction with a remnant of the old peninsular road; on the right is a wooden corral and small gravel quarry. At mileage 0.9 the road passes a windmill and another corral, then veers to the right. After crossing open countryside that is sparsely covered with cacti and brush, the road flanks an abandoned airstrip, then enters El Mármol, 9.6 miles from Highway 1.

El Mármol was once an active onyx-mining concern, but a drop in the demand for onyx caused the camp to be abandoned in 1958. In 1993 limited mining began again. Blocks and chips of onyx lie strewn across the barren landscape alongside the quarry. A walk through the remains of the camp reveals the ruins of adobe buildings, a schoolhouse made of unpolished onyx, the carcasses of long-abandoned trucks and an interesting cemetery. Caution: several deep, uncovered wells present hazards; use care when walking here.

Highway 1 to Bahía de los Angeles
(42 mi., 68 km.; 1 hr.)

(See also *Campgrounds & Trailer Parks*)

This scenic seaside town is reached via a very rough paved highway that suffered damage in the winter storms of early 1993. The road starts 8.4 miles north of Punta Prieta at a junction that has a Pemex station and a cafe. From this point it heads east across a sandy plain where the typical vegetation of Baja California's central desert is particularly abundant; it includes cardón, cholla and garambullo cacti, as well as cirio, ocotillo and yucca válida. Brightly colored wildflowers carpet the

Tom Dell

*The deep blue waters of Bahía de los Angeles present a striking
contrast to the barren slopes of huge Isla Angel de la Guarda.*

floor of the desert in early spring. Barren mountains are on the horizon. After about 10 miles, the road veers slightly to the right, passes through a gap in the mountains, then descends to the edge of a large dry lake. At mileage 28 is the signed junction with a rough dirt road to Mission San Borja; the road to the mission from Rosarito on Highway 1 is better and easier to drive. After a gentle downhill run through a canyon, the highway drops quickly to the shore of the Gulf of California.

With high, barren mountains as a dramatic backdrop to the west and several offshore islands jutting up from the deep blue waters of the gulf, Bahía de los Angeles is one of the beauty spots of Baja California. The bay, which is protected by 45-mile-long Isla Angel de la Guarda, offers a fine sheltered anchorage for boats. Sportfishing is excellent. Fishing trips can be arranged, and there are several launch ramps for private boats. Facilities include a paved airstrip, gasoline station

(fuel supply unreliable), stores, restaurants, a bakery, three trailer parks, three motels and an inn. In the center of town are a plaza park, town hall, and a museum that displays sea life and artifacts relating to the mining and history of the region. Isla Raza, a reserve for migratory waterfowl, is a bird-watcher's paradise. Dirt roads run both north and south of the town past vacation homes to remote beaches where good campsites can be found. In addition, a graded road winds southeastward from Bahía de los Angeles to remote San Francisquito.

Bahía de los Angeles to San Francisquito
(81 mi., 130 km.; 3:45 hrs.)

A journey through scenic desert hills and valleys to a secluded bay on the Gulf of California (Sea of Cortez) is graded all the way. Because it is isolated, a motorist can travel great distances without seeing another automobile, so a fully equipped, sturdy high-clearance vehicle is a must. The road travels inland most of the way due to the rugged coastline. Numerous subtropical desert plants grow along this route, especially cardón, elephant tree, ocotillo, cholla and sagebrush.

In the southern part of the village of Bahía de los Angeles the road turns right, then soon bears left. For several miles the bayshore, lined with houses and a trailer camp, is visible. Heading south between two mountain ranges, the road later climbs through hills. At 27 miles a side road goes north to Las Animas Camp, used by fishermen. Follow the large sign that points southeast toward Punta San Francisquito. The road now climbs through hills, then drops almost to Bahía San Rafael. Visible in the gulf are several small islands, and in the distance is the large Isla Tiburón. The road once more heads inland, climbs a steep grade, then gradually descends toward the coast in an easterly direction. At 68 miles is a junction; to the right is a road to El Arco. Turn left and drive 13 miles to San Francisquito. On the way

two roads branch southeast to El Barril, a large cattle ranch that includes many Mexican ranchers and several American vacation homes. Keep left at each junction; the direction to the coast is mostly northeast.

On Bahía Santa Teresa, a small attractive bay with a long sandy beach, is the rustic fishing resort named Punta San Francisquito. It has cabañas, a restaurant and bar, electricity during the evening hours, fishing boats and an airstrip. Most guests arrive by airplane. About a mile north of the resort, on Bahía San Francisquito, is a beautiful cove sheltered by rugged head-lands. Here is found a fish camp with a mechanic's shop. Camping is permitted for a small fee, and fishing is good.

Highway 1 to Santa Rosalillita
(10 mi., 16 km.; 1 hr.)

A wide gravel road, negotiable in a passenger vehicle, now leads to the Pacific coast and the settlement of

Tom Dell

The single-track road to Mission San Borja winds among cirio and cacti; only sturdy high-clearance vehicles should attempt this route.

Santa Rosalillita. Leaving the highway 15.6 miles south of Punta Prieta the new road follows the shoulder of a wide arroyo, above the old road in the sandy wash below. At mileage 8.2 is a junction with a gravel road leading north that connects with the rugged road following the Pacific coast. The road crosses a dirt airstrip at mileage 8.4 and then loops down onto the beach and into Santa Rosalillita, 9.9 miles from Highway 1. Here a government-assisted fishing cooperative harvests abalone and other varieties of shellfish. There are no tourist facilities, but the nearby beaches offer excellent opportunities for shell collecting.

An alternate return route, which is not suitable for standard automobiles, leads south from Santa Rosalillita to several beautiful, isolated beaches. For 15 miles the road meanders along the coastline past beaches covered with small, smooth stones, volcanic rocks and pearly white turban shells. Surfing is good near the rocky points. At Playa Altamira, a good open camping spot, the road turns inland and runs about three miles to meet Highway 1 at a point 6.5 miles south of Rosarito.

Rosarito to Mission San Borja
(22 mi., 35 km.; 2 hrs.)

This, the best route to Mission San Borja, is totally unsuited to travel in a passenger car. There are no steep grades, but the single-track road has a high crown and numerous rough and rocky spots, calling for a sturdy high-clearance vehicle. For those with the proper equipment the trip to this magnificent mission is well worth the time and effort. The road to San Borja begins in Rosarito, a village in the southern part of the state of Baja California.

A visit to remote Mission San Borja is a worthwhile expedition for the properly equipped explorer.

Rosarito has a store and a cafe, and it should not be confused with the booming tourist town of Rosarito in the northern part of the state. The route bears right just past a small weather station and leads northeast through open desert past several flat-topped buttes. At mileage 13.6 is a junction; bear left. About 2 miles beyond the junction is Rancho San Ignacito, a large cattle ranch with a stone-walled corral and a deep well. Beyond the ranch the road makes a rough climb out of a small arroyo, then descends gradually to Mission San Borja, located in a broad valley at the base of high barren mountains.

Mission San Francisco de Borja was founded by the Jesuits in 1759, shortly before the order's expulsion from the New World. The stone church at San Borja was completed by the Dominicans in 1801. At one time the mission served more than 3000

Indians, but the diseases of the white man decimated the native population and the mission was abandoned in 1818. The mission is largely intact and has been restored by the Mexican government. Behind the church are several adobe ruins, including the remains of an irrigation system built by the mission friars. A few families live and farm nearby.

Another road leads north from the mission for 23 miles to a junction with the paved road connecting Highway 1 with Bahía de los Angeles. This road is even rougher than the one described previously; it is steep and narrow, with numerous rocky arroyo crossings.

Highway 1 to Scammon's Lagoon (Laguna Ojo de Liebre)
(15 mi., 24 km.; 0:45 hr.)

During January through early March this side trip offers travelers an opportunity to see California gray whales, which make a 6000-mile annual migration from the Bering Sea to bear their young in the shallow waters of Scammon's Lagoon. This route also reveals a wealth of bird life, such as cormorants, herons and pelicans. *The second part of the route, about 9 miles through salt company property, is open to the public only from January 4 through March 30.* The dirt road to the southeastern arm of the lagoon branches off Highway 1 at a point 5.6 miles south of the turnoff to Guerrero Negro; the junction bears the signs "Laguna Ojo de Liebre" and "Parque Natural de la Ballena Gris/ Gray Whale Natural Park." While it is wide and graded its entire length, the road is quite sandy for the first couple of miles and corrugated part of the way. During dry weather, however, a passenger car can make the trip if it is driven at a slow, even pace.

After leaving Highway 1 the road passes several junctions, at some of which are signs with a picture of a whale and an arrow pointing the way. The side roads in this area belong to Guerrero Negro's salt company and are closed to public use. A salt company checkpoint is 3.7 miles west; after this the road to Scammon's Lagoon crosses a levee between two evaporating ponds, where large salt dredges can occasionally be seen at work harvesting the salt. After another 10 miles the road comes to a small shack, which bears the sign "Parque Natural de la Ballena Gris/Gray Whale Natural Park." Sometimes admission of about $3 is collected. Just beyond the shack is a fork; the road to the left leads to the best beach from which to observe the massive marine mammals. Binoculars help, since the whales are usually some distance offshore. Tours in small boats are available during whale season for about $10 an hour. Overnight camping is permitted here, although no facilities have been installed.

Highway 1 to El Arco
(26 mi., 43 km.; 1 hr.)

The road to El Arco, designated Mexico Highway 18, leaves Highway 1 at a well-signed junction located 17.1 miles southeast of Guerrero Negro. The highway is elevated, with a surface of gravel and broken pavement. There are no meals or lodging on this route nor those that follow it out of El Arco. Leading northeast from the junction the road runs through flat, barren terrain until mileage 6.6, when dense desert vegetation suddenly appears; cardón, yucca válida, elephant trees, cholla cacti and several brushy shrubs all grow in this "living desert." After continuing gently uphill for several miles, the road rounds a small range of steep, barren hills, then drops into El Arco.

El Arco is a small, scattered settlement situated about a mile north of the 28th parallel—the imaginary line dividing the states of Baja California and Baja California Sur. El Arco began as a gold-mining camp, and for many years was a way-stop on old Highway 1. Now it is a peaceful if worn-looking community that serves as a center for the surrounding ranches. Within the village are a military camp, gasoline pumped from drums and a church. A little copper mining is done in the vicinity. A landing field is located just south of town. From El Arco, dirt roads lead to numerous points of interest.

El Arco to Mission Santa Gertrudis
(23 mi., 37 km.; 1:30 hrs.)

Although this road is wide and graded for the first 17 miles and is in reasonably good condition for its entire length, an ordinary passenger car could have trouble clearing the high center crown and several rough spots. For the properly equipped explorer, however, this is a worthwhile side trip. The road to the mission begins where the paved road through El Arco makes a hard right turn and the pavement ends. Just beyond is a metal sign that at one time indicated the direction to the mission; veer right at this point. From El Arco the road traverses barren desert, passes two large cattle ranches, then meanders through an arroyo to Mission Santa Gertrudis.

Located in a narrow canyon, Mission Santa Gertrudis was founded by the Jesuits in 1752 and was an important supply center during the mission era. After the Jesuits were expelled from Baja California in 1768, the Domini-

cans arrived here and built the small stone church in 1796. Almost from the beginning, Santa Gertrudis was plagued by insufficient fresh water, and the local Indian population suffered greatly from diseases; the mission was finally abandoned in 1822. In addition to the chapel, which is still in use, the site contains several other stone ruins, including the remains of an irrigation system dating from the 18th century and a restored adobe belfry. A few ranchers now occupy the area.

El Arco to San Francisquito
(48 mi., 77 km.; 2:30 hrs.)

The road to Bahía San Francisquito is generally good by off-road standards and is suitable for high-clearance vehicles. Until recently, however, four-wheel drive was necessary to make the trip because of the infamous grade known as La Cuesta de la Ley. This harrowing plunge, which dropped 400 feet in only 0.4 mile, has been re-graded to accommodate most high-clearance vehicles. To locate the route, proceed northeast at the junction by the town hall in El Arco. After 2.3 miles, during which the road negotiates a steep narrow arroyo, the route passes through Pozo Alemán, which many years ago was an important gold-mining center but now looks like a ghost town. Beyond Pozo Alemán, the road traverses a flat plain, then enters a region of rocky arroyos dotted with huge cardón cacti. At mileage 7.9 a road leads left to Rancho La Unión; bear right. The road to the gulf now runs through a series of steep-sided valleys, then ascends a plateau. At mileage 29 La Cuesta de la Ley begins its descent. A major fork is located at mileage 34.9; to the right is Rancho El Barril, a privately owned cattle ranch, while the left branch leads to San Francisquito.

Punta San Francisquito is a rustic fishing resort located on Bahía Santa Teresa (San Francisquito). For details about this community, see the "Bahía de los Angeles to San Francisquito" description in *Side Routes*.

Loop Trip From Highway 1 Around the Vizcaíno Peninsula

Because of the great distances involved and the remote nature of the territory, this trip is unique among Baja California's side routes. The trek onto the Vizcaíno Peninsula should be attempted only by serious off-road adventurers who are equipped to handle the worst that Baja California has to offer—isolation, poor roads, scarcity of fresh water, lack of facilities, frequent dust storms, desert heat and heavy coastal fog.

For the most part, the main routes are well signed, periodically maintained and fairly good by Baja California off-pavement standards. The main highway from Vizcaíno to Bahía Tortugas via Rancho San José de Castro may be traveled by well-supplied, light front-wheel-drive vehicles, but a high-clearance sturdy vehicle is recommended. The other roads on the peninsula contain bad spots that can trap or damage a passenger car or low-clearance vehicle. It is advisable to use the "buddy" system, with a caravan of two or more vehicles traveling together. Plenty of extra water, food and gasoline should be carried, and equipment should be checked against the Suggested Supply Lists in the *Appendix*.

For those prepared for the rigors of this journey, the remoteness of this huge hook protruding westward from the central spine of Baja California is the principal lure. Most of the Vizcaíno Peninsula has seen relatively little human intrusion. The desert scenery, though barren, is unusual and striking. Along the coast are attractive bays and coves, rugged headlands and miles of wide, beautiful beaches. Fishing and beachcombing are excellent.

The peninsula is not devoid of habitation. There are four fair-sized cannery towns, along with numerous small ranches and fish camps. But none of these settlements is prepared to cater to tourists, although the inhabitants are friendly and helpful. Meals, refreshments and limited supplies can be purchased in Punta Abreojos, La Bocana, Bahía Asunción and Bahía Tortugas. Gasoline, sometimes siphoned from drums, is relatively expensive, and unleaded *magna sin* is not always available. Overnight accommodations, where they exist, are extremely modest, but fine primitive campsites can be found throughout the peninsula (wood, however, is scarce).

From Highway 1, the traveler can enter the Vizcaíno Peninsula at Vizcaíno Junction (44.8 miles southeast of the Guerrero Negro turnoff) or at an unsigned junction 15 miles west of San Ignacio. The following route descriptions are organized as a loop beginning at Vizcaíno (Fundolegal); each segment of the loop is outlined in a separate subsection. Most of the mileages, driving times and route descriptions are based on an expedition made in 1992 by an Auto Club research team; readers should keep in mind that conditions can change.

Vizcaíno to Rancho San José de Castro
(72 mi., 116 km.; 5 hrs.)

This route onto the Vizcaíno Peninsula has a raised surface most of the way.

It is a durable graded route, but is rather rough. Signs appear at most important junctions. Rancho San José de Castro is used here as a convenient route dividing point. The highway continues westward to Bahía Tortugas and is the lifeline between Highway 1 and that port. (The Bahía Tortugas description follows.) After Vizcaíno there is no fuel available until Bahía Tortugas, 103 miles away; Ejido Díaz Ordaz is the last chance for food or supplies of any kind.

Begin by taking the Vizcaíno turnoff from Highway 1 and following the paved road past the irrigated fields, orchards and vineyards of Ejido Díaz Ordaz (see *Mexico Highway 1*). The pavement ends after 20 miles, and the graded road continues west across scrub-covered desert. After passing a group of small ranches the road goes through an area of salt flats.

At mileage 44.9 is a junction (signed) with another graded dirt road that heads southwest to join the coastal road 6.4 miles south of Bahía Asunción. At mileage 39.4 a dirt road, which belongs to the salt company and is frequently closed, leads northeast to Scammon's Lagoon and Guerrero Negro. West of this junction the new road begins to climb into low foothills. Elephant trees and cacti grow here, and the bay is occasionally visible to the right. Shortly, the road ascends into mountains, sometimes slicing abruptly through ridges, other times following natural gaps in the hills.

At mileage 70.6, the road reaches the hard-to-find Malarrimo Beach turnoff; it is on the right-hand side about .5 mile east of the San José de Castro sign. After another .5 mile, a dirt road on the left leads 1.3 miles south to Rancho San José de Castro, and connects to the older dirt road leading south to Bahía Asunción.

Rancho San José de Castro, a cattle ranch with a large spring, is also a residence for magnesite miners. There are no facilities for tourists, but cold drinks are sold and the friendly ranchers provide information and directions.

Rancho San José de Castro to Bahía Tortugas
(31 mi., 50 km.; 2 hrs.)

West of the junction of the road to San José de Castro, the new road—bumpy in places—passes Rancho San Miguel, where cold refreshments are sold. At mileage 6.8 a dirt road veers off to the left 8.2 miles to Puerto Nuevo, a small fishing village.

Tom Dell

Abalone fishermen at Bahía Tortugas set out under the first light of dawn. The catch is processed locally and then flown to Ensenada for canning.

At this point the new road heads through the mountains, sometimes cutting through them, other times following ridge contours. The scenery is fairly desolate on this stretch. At mileage 31.3 the new road drops out of the mountains and enters Bahía Tortugas.

With a population of more than 3000, Bahía Tortugas is the metropolis of the Vizcaíno Peninsula. The town, with its rows of pastel-colored dwellings, sits beneath barren hills on the north side of an almost circular bay, which is one of the finest natural harbors on Baja California's Pacific coast. Bahía Tortugas makes its living from the sea. A large cannery processes abalone, shrimp and other marine products, many of which are trucked or flown to Ensenada. There is no fresh water in the area, and the town's supply must be brought in by ship or truck, or distilled from sea water in a small desalinization plant. Facilities include numerous stores and cafes, telegraph, radio communications, a medical center, an attractive church, rustic accommodations, a paved airstrip and a gasoline station. Prices are relatively high as all supplies must be hauled in over long distances. The town has an orderly progressive appearance and is a welcome stop for travelers. From Bahía Tortugas a dirt road runs 16.5 miles to Punta Eugenia at the western tip of the Vizcaíno Peninsula.

Rancho San José de Castro to Malarrimo Beach
(27 mi., 44 km.; 2:30 hrs.)

The rough road to Malarrimo Beach takes off northward from the Vizcaíno Junction-Bahía Tortugas route, about .5 mile east of the Rancho San José de Castro sign. After winding through narrow steep-walled arroyos for several miles, it climbs onto barren but colorful mesas, then makes a steep rugged descent into a wide canyon, which it follows to the shore of the Pacific Ocean. This road is subject to periodic closures because of rock slides, washouts and other hazards.

Because of its position on the north-facing side of the Vizcaíno Peninsula, Malarrimo Beach is struck head-on by the prevailing currents of the North Pacific. As a result, it has been the dumping place for flotsam and jetsam from thousands of miles away, including giant redwood logs, World War II food tins, Japanese fishing floats, timbers from sunken vessels and trash thrown overboard from ships. Stories of cases of Scotch and other valuable items being found here are probably true, but Malarrimo has been pretty thoroughly picked over. Still, the careful beachcomber can make some interesting discoveries. The beach itself is very windy, and the best campsites are just inland near the mouth of the canyon. Driftwood for fires is abundant. Motorists should be cautious of quicksand in some areas along the beach.

Rancho San José de Castro to Bahía Asunción
(35 mi., 56 km.; 1:45 hrs.)

The graded road to Bahía Asunción branches south from the Vizcaíno Junction-Bahía Tortugas route .5 mile west of the Malarrimo Beach turnoff; follow the signed road to the left 1.3 miles to San José de Castro, bear left, go 4.3 miles, then turn right (south) onto the dirt road to Bahía Asunción. The road climbs into a range of dark brown mountains, vegetated with cholla, pitahaya and garambullo cacti, along with agave, spiny shrubs and elephant trees. After crossing a saddle, the road descends onto a wide, sloping plain; the ocean is visible in the distance to the west. The road enters a shallow arroyo and follows the sandy bottom for 1.5 miles, then winds upward to a gap between a flat-topped volcanic butte and a range of barren hills. Later the road traverses low, chalk-colored hills, then runs southeast along the base of a volcanic mesa. It rounds the south end of the mesa and emerges onto a sparsely vegetated coastal plain. After dropping into a sandy arroyo, the road turns south and reaches Bahía Asunción at mileage 37.5.

Bahía Asunción is a windblown town of 1500 situated on a low peninsula opposite rocky Isla Asunción. Like Bahía Tortugas, Bahía Asunción is supported by the abalone and lobster trade and has a cannery that ships its products by truck to Ensenada and other towns. Facilities include rustic accommodations, gasoline (*nova* only), cafes, a pharmacy, small stores, a health center, a tiny movie theater, telephone and radio communications, a military camp and an airstrip. A graded road leaves town from behind the health center and runs 7.9 miles northwest along the coast to San Roque, a fishing village.

Bahía Asunción to Punta Abreojos
(59 mi., 93 km.; 2 hrs.)

This is one of the easier legs of the loop trip around the Vizcaíno Peninsula. Although the road has a few sandy stretches, there are no steep grades and the surface is regularly graded. After leaving Bahía Asunción, the road parallels the curve of the shoreline along the edge of an arid coastal lowland, running about .5 mile inland from the beach most of the way. Several dirt roads provide access to the shore, which is littered with a

variety of shells. Primitive campsites can be found all along the beach, but the wind is constant and wood is scarce. Shore fishing is excellent. At mileage 3.9 is a junction with the graded road that leads north to the Vizcaíno Junction-Rancho San José de Castro road. Eighteen miles from Bahía Asunción the road passes a small shrine, then reaches the junction with a dirt road to Punta Prieta, a fishing village. At mileage 21.7, a road branches right to San Hipólito, another fishing village.

To the north is Cerro Mesa, with its unusual magenta and green rock strata. The road continues to follow the coastline to La Bocana, reached by a turnoff at mileage 47.7. This cannery town of 800 has stores, cafes, a clinic, gasoline and mechanical assistance. Beyond La Bocana the road veers inland and skirts a shallow inlet. The surface from here to Punta Abreojos is smooth hard-packed dirt, which permits speeds of up to 50 mph and is a natural airstrip. South of La Bocana, at mileage 10.9, the road enters Punta Abreojos.

Punta Abreojos has another fishing cooperative with a cannery that sends abalone and lobster to the markets of the north. It sits on a sandy spit between the ocean and a salt marsh. Facilities in this village of 700 include a store, a cafe, gasoline drums, a telegraph office, radio communications and two lighthouses. Just north of Punta Abreojos is an airstrip.

Punta Abreojos to Highway 1
(53 mi., 85 km.; 2 hrs.)

This is a long drive over barren, empty land on a wide, graded road. A carefully driven passenger car can make the trip without difficulty, but because some of the road has a jarring washboard surface, travel can be uncomfortable. Leaving Punta Abreojos the route passes an airstrip, then swings north across level, barren desert. At mileage 6.1 is a signed junction with a road leading 3.1 miles to Campo René, where rustic cabañas and windy campsites can be found on the beach. After skirting the southern flank of flat-topped Cabo Santa Clara Mesa, the road bears northeast across rolling, cactus-covered terrain. Visible to the west is a group of volcanic peaks rising from the desert. Approaching Highway 1 the road enters a "forest" of cardón cacti. To the south, some distance away, Laguna San Ignacio is visible. Highway 1 is reached at mileage 53, 15 miles west of San Ignacio.

Highway 1 to San Francisco de la Sierra
(23 mi., 37 km.; 1:30 hrs.)

High mesas and deep canyons, a settlement inhabited by traditional ranchers, and trails that lead to Indian cave paintings are features of this isolated route. The road, partly graded with some rough sections, is suitable only for sturdy high-clearance vehicles.

At 27.6 miles northwest of San Ignacio the route turns off Highway 1. After heading northeast over six miles of level desert, displaying cardón, yucca válida and ocotillo, the road makes a sharp, winding ascent onto a mesa. Southeast of the mesa a vast lonesome canyon may be viewed. Climbing more mesas and passing occasional ranches, the road comes to an abrupt descent at about 22 miles. The village of San Francisco is visible across the canyon. Winding down, then upward, the road reaches the village after 1.5 miles. The high country has barrel cactus, agave, occa-

sional cirios and closely spaced brush. Temperatures are cooler; the climate has more rainfall and is classified as semiarid.

San Francisco de la Sierra (elevation 4500 feet) and vicinity are inhabited by Californios, descendants of Spanish ranchers who settled the interior highlands in the 1700s. Raising mules, horses and goats, they have to the present remained rather isolated from the mainstream of Mexican culture. The village has a school, church and small store; meals are available upon request. Mule trails lead from the village to cave paintings made by Indians several hundred years ago. The drawings are protected by the federal government and visitors must be accompanied by ranchers who are authorized guides. Pack trips to the paintings require three or four days. One small cave is located near the village, but even it requires a guide and a small fee is charged.

Highway 1 to San José de Magdalena
(9 mi., 15 km.; 0:30 hr.)

The short side trip to the picturesque old village of San José de Magdalena can be made in a standard passenger car. The road becomes rough past the village, however, and is only suitable for vehicles with high ground clearance. From a well-marked junction 17.5 miles south of Santa Rosalía on Highway 1, the graded dirt road branches west and traverses a sparsely vegetated plain for 3.5 miles. It then enters a range of barren foothills and negotiates a series of short, steep grades before dropping into a palm-lined canyon. After following the edge of the canyon past several ranches and an interesting cemetery, the road crosses a streambed and arrives in San José de Magdalena. This is an attractive oasis village with groves of stately palms, many colorful flower gardens and thatched-palm dwellings interspersed with concrete-block houses. Farming sustains the local economy; crops include dates, citrus fruits and several varieties of vegetables. San José de Magdalena dates back to Baja California's Spanish colonial days when it was a visiting station of the Mulegé mission. Evidence of the village's history can be seen in the old stone walls running along the valley floor and in the ruins of a chapel built by the Dominicans in 1774. The Mission Guadalupe ruins can be reached by horseback from Rancho San Isidro, 10 miles southeast of San José de Magdalena.

▬
Highway 1 to Ciudad Insurgentes via La Purísima
(118 mi., 190 km.; 5 hrs.)

Because of their isolation, the Purísima and Comondú oases preserve a sense of an earlier era. A new graded-dirt road across the ruggedly scenic Sierra de la Giganta now leads from Highway 1 to the oasis villages of San Isidro and La Purísima. Wide and well-graded most of the way, the road is suitable for high-clearance vehicles.

The junction with the new road is 47 miles south of Mulegé (or 37 miles north of Loreto) on Highway 1. The road winds through a series of narrow canyons, walled by steep volcanic bluffs. Vegetation is thick and consists of cardón, pitahaya, three varieties of cholla, palo adán, mesquite and dense underbrush. At mileage 11.3 is a junction: to the left is the road to San José de Comondú and San Miguel de Comondú; to the right is a seldom-used portion of the old La Purísima/San Isidro road. Proceed straight ahead. A mile beyond the junction, the road tops a low ridge via a rocky grade, then descends into a long, winding valley. The route meanders in and out of the valley, occasionally crossing sparsely vegetated hills of volcanic boulders, until at mileage 30.7 it

John Austerman

SIDE ROUTES

After traversing many miles of rough mountain and desert terrain, the motorist comes to this viewpoint overlooking the Valle de la Purísima.

R. Clark Hunter

Oasis palms in Valle de la Purísima, backed by a butte and steep canyon walls.

reaches the rim of the La Purísima Valley. After dropping 700 feet to the valley floor via a series of steep switchbacks, the road becomes a palm-lined avenue with a stone aqueduct alongside. It passes orchards and cultivated fields before arriving in San Isidro at mileage 35.2. San Isidro, a community of 600 inhabitants, has a cafe, limited supplies, a telegraph, a clinic and a rustic motel. Three miles farther down the valley is La Purísima.

The oasis village of La Purísima sits amid groves of palms in the bottom of a deep valley that is walled in by high cliffs and surrounded by rugged, barren desert. Thanks to an irrigation system fed by spring water, the valley is intensively farmed and yields a variety of crops, including dates, mangos, grapes, citrus fruits, corn, beans and tomatoes. The town itself, with a population of about 700, has a well-worn look. La Purísima began in 1730, when a Jesuit mission was moved herefrom a site several miles

away. The native Indian population was decimated by disease, and the mission was abandoned in 1822; only stone ruins remain. The present village dates from the late 19th century, when the fertile valley was resettled by Mexican farmers—ancestors of today's friendly residents of La Purísima. Modest accommodations can be found here, along with gasoline, meals, limited supplies, a post office and a municipal office.

Leaving La Purísima the road continues down the valley for another 3.5 miles to a junction. The right fork is a graded road running northward for 120 miles to San Ignacio; the route to Ciudad Insurgentes bears left here and climbs out of the valley onto a high mesa. Paved most of the way, it then heads southward, winding among barren rounded hills. Thirteen miles from the junction is a signed road to the fishing village of Las Barrancas, site of a joint German/Mexican solar energy project. At mileage 76.8 from Highway 1 (or 34.8 miles from La Purísima), the road arrives at Ejido Pancho Villa—a dusty, windblown farming cooperative. Here the Comondú road angles in from the left, and a road to Poza Grande, another farming community, veers off to the right; proceed straight ahead for Ciudad Insurgentes. The road continues to run in a straight line through open desert punctuated by irrigated fields. Here on the Santo Domingo (Magdalena) Plain, farmers utilize water drawn from deep wells to transform a sandy desert into productive fields of wheat and other crops. About 22 miles past Ejido Pancho Villa is the junction with a 1.5-mile side road to Santo Domingo, a farming community with a store, a cafe and gasoline. Two miles farther is the junction with the road coming in from Loreto and Mission San Javier.

Southward 15 miles farther lies the large farm market town of Ciudad Insurgentes. From Insurgentes a paved road leads 24 miles west to the fishing port of Puerto López Mateos.

Highway 1 to Ciudad Insurgentes via Comondú
(103 mi., 165 km.; 5 hrs.)

For the first 11.3 miles the route to Comondú is shared with the San Isidro/La Purísima road. Except for these first few miles, which are wide and graded, the road is narrow and winding with numerous steep, rocky grades. The trip to Comondú can be made with sturdy, high-clearance vehicles; however, the southern approach from Ciudad Insurgentes offers a much better road.

The unmarked junction with Highway 1 is 47 miles south of Mulegé and 37 miles north of Loreto. From the junction the road cuts a straight westward

swath across open desert for five miles, then begins a gradual ascent through a steep-walled canyon. At mileage 11.3 is an unsigned, four-way intersection. Straight ahead is San Isidro and La Purísima; to the right is an abandoned road. For Comondú, turn left. The road now winds upward over grades of up to 15 percent to the summit of the Sierra de la Giganta. It then crosses a plateau, climbs another summit and descends through a rocky arroyo. After traversing low hills for several miles the road comes to the edge of a deep canyon. Nestled far below in a forest of date palms is Comondú. Just ahead is a junction near a roadside cemetery. Straight on lies a new graded road to San Isidro and La Purísima. To the left the road drops sharply via a series of steep switchbacks to the valley floor, reaching San José de Comondú at mileage 36.

Comondú is really two villages: San José de Comondú and, two miles farther west, San Miguel de Comondú. The combined population of these twin oasis villages is about 600. Although the surrounding volcanic mesas are nearly devoid of vegetation, the floor of the valley is a seven-mile-long strip of green. Sufficient water from nearby springs nourishes crops of figs, grapes, dates, sugarcane and vegetables. In San José de Comondú, just left of the point where the road enters the village, is the site of a Jesuit mission moved here in 1737; one stone building still stands. The original bells, which date from 1708, hang from a standard alongside the church. San José also has a grocery store and a clinic. San Miguel has a worn look with many deserted buildings, but possesses an aura of historic charm. It has a general store that also sells gasoline (*nova* only). Meals may be ordered at a private home. Leaving Comondú a graded road winds down the canyon, which gradually opens up onto a wide, sparsely vegetated coastal plain. The road is wide, well-graded and easy to follow. About 25 miles beyond Comondú (or 61 miles from Highway 1) the road arrives at Ejido Pancho Villa, where it joins the La Purísima/Ciudad Insurgentes route.

Loreto to Mission San Javier

(23 mi., 37 km.; 2 hrs.)

The trip from Loreto to Mission San Javier is one of Baja California's most rewarding side routes. In addition to one of North America's most beautiful Spanish missions, it offers superlative

John Austerman

Mission San Javier, a beautifully preserved example of the Jesuit missions, still serves as a parish church for local residents. The drive to the mission is one of Baja's most rewarding side trips.

mountain and canyon scenery. An Auto Club team in 1992 found the road in fairly good condition, graded with a few rough spots. Sturdy high-clearance vehicles should be used. The mission can also be reached from the Pacific side of the peninsula, but this approach is considerably longer and has many rocky arroyo crossings.

From a signed junction 1.1 mile south of the Loreto turnoff, the road leads westward from Highway 1 through low rounded hills for about six miles. It then begins a gradual winding climb into the rugged Sierra de la Giganta, following the steep wall of a deep arroyo. At mileage 9.5 there is a rocky section. The old road is visible meandering along the palm-studded floor of the canyon. A mile farther the road swings to the left, offering travelers an excellent view of the gaping canyon below and the blue Gulf of California in the distance. Rancho Las Parras, 12.2 miles from Highway 1, has a small stone chapel and groves of citrus and olive trees. Six miles beyond the rancho is a junction with a rough road to Comondú, 25.8 miles to the north. The road then gently winds for 4.4 miles through a narrow canyon to San Javier. The vegetation changes from desert to steppe (semiarid) because of the increased elevation. Local agriculture involves raising goats and cattle and growing olives, oranges and mangos.

Mission San Javier sits in the bottom of a deep valley beneath towering walls of dark gray stone. Surrounding the mission is the village of San Javier, which has a small store, cafe, telephone and a divided parkway instead of the

Tom Dell

Much of the agricultural bounty of the Santo Domingo Valley is shipped via San Carlos, located 36 miles west of Ciudad Constitución via a paved highway.

usual plaza. The impressive mission is of a Moorish style that is dramatic in its simplicity; its stonework and ornamentation are considered outstanding. This was the second of Baja California's Jesuit missions, founded in 1699 but not completed until 1758. That a church of this size could be built in such a rugged, remote region and survive in such a fine state of preservation to the present day is truly remarkable.

Beyond the mission, the road continues to head southwest down the canyon, fording several arroyos and passing several small ranches. The canyon gradually widens into a broad valley, and irrigated farms appear along the road. Finally, 43.8 miles beyond San Javier, the road reaches the junction with the La Purísima/Ciudad Insurgentes route. This section takes almost three hours to traverse. From this point it is 15.5 miles to the junction with Highway 1 in Ciudad Insurgentes.

Ciudad Constitución to San Carlos

(36 mi., 58 km.; 0:45 hr.)

The paved route to San Carlos (Mexico Highway 22) leaves Highway 1 in the northern part of Ciudad Constitución. After running alongside irrigated fields for seven miles it traverses gently undulating desert terrain, which is heavily vegetated with cardón, cholla, pitahaya and dense brush. After reaching the mangrove-edged shore of Bahía Magdalena, Highway 22 crosses a bridge and enters San Carlos, located on an irregular peninsula in the bay.

San Carlos (also known as Puerto San Carlos) is a port built to handle shipments of wheat, garbanzo and cotton grown in the Santo Domingo Valley. The port also has a commercial fishing fleet and packing plant (tuna and sardines). With a population of about 6000, it has developed some limited facilities for tourists, including several restaurants and cafes, three motels, a rustic campground, a public beach, several markets, a clinic and a Pemex station (*nova* and diesel). Visitors find recreation in fishing, boating and whale watching.

At a junction 6 miles west of Highway 1 on the San Carlos road is a paved road to Villa Benito Juárez. From there a dirt road leads northwest for 28 miles to Puerto López Mateos. In this port, population 4000, whale-watching trips are offered in the winter. By taking this road and then traveling eastward from Puerto López Mateos to Ciudad Insurgentes, the motorist can make a loop trip through this interesting desert area.

Highway 1 to Mission San Luis Gonzaga
(26 mi., 42 km.; 2 hrs.)

When an Auto Club research team drove to the picturesque settlement of San Luis Gonzaga in November 1987, they found this route to be in generally good condition; however, a sturdy, high-clearance vehicle is needed. From Highway 1, at a point 2.2 miles south of Villa Morelos (10 miles south of Ciudad Constitución), turn east on the road marked Presa Ihuagil. After a mile, cultivated fields give way to native desert covered with cardón and a variety of brush. After 15 miles of flat terrain is the junction with a road leading west to Ciudad Constitución. Just beyond this is a dam, Presa Ihuagil, whose reservoir is only partially filled.

Take the right fork and follow the road along the top of the dam, then curve sharply to the right. The road on the second leg of the trip is rougher than

on the first part, as it winds its way southeast over gently rolling land toward San Luis. Abundant vegetation includes cardón and cholla cacti. Several forks off the main road can cause confusion, and the route crosses several stream beds that can be troublesome during or after the occasional rains. For the last five miles ranches and grazing cattle are numerous. At mileage 23.7 is a roadside shrine.

Except for a modern school, the village of San Luis Gonzaga could be a museum piece from the past. The stone mission, founded in 1737, is still in use and has a colorful well-kept interior. The mission and a companion building formerly used for living quarters face on a large square. Also facing the square are two other stone buildings—an abandoned store and a former public building that now serves as a kind of dormitory. Adjacent are several farm houses. Cattle ranching and date palms support the inhabitants.

Santa Rita to Puerto Chale
(15 mi., 24 km.; 0:30 hr.)

This route, for the most part, is wide and graded. The road leaves the main highway just north of the village of Santa Rita and descends gently through barren countryside, passes the tiny hamlet of El Médano, then crosses an arroyo. Puerto Chale is a fishing village on mangrove-edged Bahía Almejas. The village has a market and a church. There are no tourist facilities, but fishing is excellent. Snook are said to lurk among the mangroves during winter, scallops are caught and the waters are good for diving.

La Paz to Pichilingue and Beaches to the North

(17 mi., 29 km.; 1 hr.)

The easy drive to Pichilingue and the beaches to the north make an enjoyable half-day excursion from La Paz. The paved road to Pichilingue (Mexico Highway 11) is a northward continuation of Paseo Alvaro Obregón—La Paz's bay-front thoroughfare. The road hugs the shore of Bahía de La Paz, offering fine views of cactus-covered hills, mangrove thickets and the clear, incredibly blue waters of the bay. Playa Coromuel, an attractive beach that is popular with La Paz residents, is 2.6 miles from Avenida 5 de Mayo, the last major street of the city. About a mile farther north are La Concha Beach Resort and El Caimancito, which has a public beach, a restaurant and the official governor's mansion. At Pichilingue, 9 miles from La Paz, is the government-built ferry terminal used by the La Paz-Mazatlán and La Paz-Topolobampo ferries (see Transportation section in the *Appendix*). In addition to the ferry port facilities, Pichilingue has a commercial fishing fleet, warehouses and cafes.

The road has recently been paved to the beaches beyond Pichilingue. Just after the ferry terminal is Playa Pichilingue, another popular beach. A short distance farther north the road cuts inland, then a paved spur reaches the shore of Puerto Balandra, a lovely inlet that makes a good spot for a picnic. A trail leads up a hill to a viewpoint above the inlet. Past Puerto Balandra the road runs another mile to Playa Tecolote, an attractive *playa pública,* where pavement ends. A good dirt road lined with scenic desert plants turns east and follows the shoreline to a gravel mine and Playa Cachimba, eight miles northeast of Pichilingue. Surf fishing is reportedly good here. Visible offshore is 14-mile-long Isla Espíritu Santo, a destination for kayakers and wildlife observers.

La Paz to San Juan de Los Planes

(29 mi., 45 km; 1:30 hrs.)

An excellent all-day excursion from La Paz, the side trip to Los Planes offers travelers a chance to visit a fast-growing agricultural region and to explore beautiful beaches that are seldom seen by tourists. After leaving Highway 1 at a well-marked junction on the southern outskirts of La Paz, a paved road signed "BCS 286" runs between rolling hills for nine miles, then climbs onto the northern shoulder of the Sierra de la Laguna. At mileage 11.9 is Rancho La Huerta, a long-established cattle ranch with a brick chapel, a small cemetery and a cafe. Beyond La Huerta the road passes turnoffs to several more ranches as it winds through countryside covered with cardón, cholla, pitahaya, copalquin (a small deciduous tree) and heavy underbrush. At mileage 15.9 the road reaches a summit; visible ahead are the cultivated fields of Los Planes, the blue expanse of Bahía de la Ventana, and barren mountainous Isla Cerralvo. From the summit the road makes a long, steady descent onto a level coastal plain, where it comes to a junction at mileage 23.7. To the left a good graded road leads seven miles to El Sargento and La Ventana, fishing and ranching villages on the western shore of lovely Bahía de la Ventana. Continue straight ahead for Los Planes. At mileage 25.8 is an intersection with a new road on the right leading 14.8 miles to the village of San Antonio on Highway 1.

The route continues 3.2 miles farther to San Juan de Los Planes (or Los Planes, as it is commonly called), the center of a rapidly developing farming region. Water from deep wells irrigates fields of cotton, corn, chiles, tomatoes and beans. Los Planes is a friendly town of about 1000 with a cafe, three stores, telephone service, and a health center. The pavement continues past the center of town for a few miles en route to Ensenada de los Muertos (Deadman Bay), 13.4 miles to the northeast. Here is found a beautiful, curving bay with a small fish camp. Fine primitive campsites can be found here; fishing is excellent, and swimming is good. Punta Arena de la Ventana, directly opposite Isla Cerralvo on the eastern shore of Bahía de la Ventana, can be reached by backtracking two miles toward Los Planes, then turning right on a signed dirt road. This road leads past a cattle ranch, an airstrip and a group of salt-evaporating ponds to the isolated Hotel Las Arenas (closed at present) on the shore of the bay. North of the hotel is a lighthouse.

Highway 1 to La Ribera
(7 mi., 11 km.; 0:15 hr.),

Cabo Pulmo
(23 mi., 37 km.; 0:45 hr.), **and**

San José del Cabo
(80 mi., 129 km.; 4:30 hrs.)

With the longest seacoast extension of any side route in Baja California, this road follows along the East Cape (Cabo del Este). From a junction 11.6 miles south of Los Barriles on Highway 1 a paved road leads eastward past fields of hay and corn for 7.2 miles to La Ribera, a farming community of about 2000 with stores, a cafe, a trailer park and a Pemex station. From La Ribera a graded dirt road crosses rolling scrub-covered countryside for 4.8 miles to the Hotel Punta Colorada, situated atop a low bluff

above a lovely beach. A little to the west a new paved road turns southeast, takes a more inland route over 10.5 miles of hilly terrain and reaches the gulf coast near La Abundancia, where it joins a graded dirt road that parallels the scenic shoreline to Cabo Pulmo. This village is a collection of thatched huts, two small seafood restaurants and a launch ramp on a picturesque tropical beach. Fishing and diving are said to be excellent here; offshore is a pretty coral reef.

The road south of Cabo Pulmo is wide and fairly good. It is passable for low-clearance vehicles, but a washboard surface requires sturdy autos. Fine open campsites are abundant along this section of coastline. Five miles past Cabo Pulmo is Los Frailes, a village named for the adjacent jagged promontory that forms the easternmost point of the Baja California peninsula. The village has vacation homes, trailers and a hotel. At mileage 55, beyond a wide sandy wash near Rancho Vinorama, is a junction with a graded road leading 24 miles southwest over the coastal foothills to Highway 1.

Ahead, the road continues to follow the coast past miles of beautiful beaches and a landscape that contains pitahaya and elephant trees. Three miles beyond the junction is a massive wild fig tree next to the road. Six miles later the rusting hulk of a large vessel may be seen by walking down to the water's edge. Several miles farther the road swings inland, passes through densely vegetated terrain and climbs between two cone-shaped peaks to a low ridge that offers the first glimpse of San José del Cabo. Along the last few miles are new vacation homes at Laguna Hills and the fishing village of La Playa. After crossing many roads on the outskirts of San José del Cabo, the road enters the center of town at mileage 80.0.■

Recreation

T he very soul of Baja is in enjoying the rugged outdoors. The pristine beaches lend themselves to swimming, surfing and beachcombing. Ocean waters offer prime sportfishing opportunities. The peninsula's rugged highways and trails challenge the off-road wanderer. Hikers enjoy exploring the deserts and mountains.

Little exists in the way of formalized recreational activities commonly found in the United States, although major resorts offer some planned activities. The availability of recreational supplies and items are limited throughout all but a few areas of Baja California, so travelers are advised to bring those items with them from home.

GOLF

Considering the nature of recreation in Baja California, a surprising number of golf courses exist, most of them located in the major cities or operated by resort hotels. In addition to the courses listed below, duffers might take a swing at Rancho Tecate Resort, near Tecate, which has a small semi-private course, or at Cábo Real Golf Course and Hotel Palmilla Golf Club, both of which are in the Los Cabos region. Cabo Real is a public 18-hole course and Palmilla is a private 18-hole club.

Information for the following listings was provided by the courses to the Automobile Club of Southern California for publication. The semi-private courses may have restrictions on public play ranging from members and guests only to liberal reciprocal agreements with members of other courses; please contact the course directly for details. Reservations are advised at most courses.

Bajamar

Bajamar Country Club
21 miles north of Ensenada, off highway 1D at Bajamar resort development. Phone (619) 232-4653, 01152 (66) 20-3305.
This is a semi-private 18-hole course. Par 72, 5972 yards, open daily. Fees include mandatory golf cart: Monday through Friday $45; Saturday and Sunday $55. Facilities include clubhouse, locker room, golf shop, driving range; tennis, swimming; restaurant, cocktails.

Cabo San Lucas

Cabo del Sol Golf Club
5 miles northeast of Cabo San Lucas off Highway 1. Phone

01152 (114) 3-3149; (800) 637-2226.

This is a public 18-hole course. Par 72, 7050 yards, open daily. Fees include mandatory golf cart: October to May, $115; June to September, $85. Facilities include golf pro, golf shop and rental clubs.

Cabo San Lucas Country Club
On east edge of Cabo San Lucas, just north of Highway 1 (Boulevard Lázaro Cárdenas). Phone 01152 (114) 3-1922; (800) 854-2314.
This is a semi-private 18-hole course. Par 72, 7100 yards, open daily. Fees include mandatory golf cart: November to May, $75; June to October, $50. Facilities include golf shop and driving range.

Ensenada

Baja Country Club
9 miles south of Ensenada via Highway 1, then 1 mile east. Phone 01152 (617) 3-0303.
This is a semi-private 18-hole course. Par 72, 6820 yards, 119 slope, open daily. Fee includes mandatory golf cart: $34. Facilities include caddies, locker room, electric carts, professional, golf shop, rental clubs, driving range; coffee shop and cocktails.

Loreto

Campo de Golf Loreto
In Nopaló, just south of the Loreto Inn. Phone 01152 (113) 3-0788.
This is a public 18-hole course. Par 72, 6400 yards, open daily. Fee $20. Facilities include electric carts, golf pro, golf shop, rental clubs; coffee shop.

Mexicali

Club Deportivo Campestre de Mexicali
West of Highway 5 on the southern

outskirts of the city. Phone 01152 (65) 61-7130 or 61-7170.
This is a semi-private 18-hole course. Par 72, 6516 yards. Open Tuesday through Sunday. Fees include mandatory golf cart: October through April, $32; May through September, $20. Facilities include clubhouse, locker room, golf pro, golf shop, driving range, rental clubs; swimming pool, tennis courts, playgrounds; restaurant, cocktail lounge.

Rosarito

Real del Mar Golf Club
7 miles north of town center off Highway 1D (toll highway). Phone 01152 (66) 13-3401.
This is a semi-private 18-hole course. Par 72, 6400 yards, open daily. Fees include mandatory golf cart: Monday through Friday $43; Saturday and Sunday $49. Facilities include golf pro, clubhouse, golf shop, driving range; tennis; snack bar.

San José del Cabo

Campo de Golf San José (formerly Los Cabos)
Off Boulevard Mijares, situated among the condominiums and hotels in the resort area. Phone 01152 (114) 2-0905.
This is a public 9-hole course. Par 35, 2879 yards, open daily. Fees are $16 for 9 holes, $30 for 18 holes. Facilities include golf pro, clubhouse, locker room, golf shop, electric carts, pull carts, rental clubs; snack bar.

Tijuana

Club Social y Deportivo Campestre (Tijuana Country Club)
3 miles east of downtown Tijuana via Boulevard Agua Caliente. Phone 01152 (66) 81-7855 or 81-7863.

This is a semi-private 18-hole course. Par 72, 6200 yards, open daily. Fees: $22 weekdays, $27 weekends. Facilities include clubhouse, caddies, electric carts, golf pro, golf shop, rental clubs, driving range; snack bar.

HUNTING

Most of the hunting on the peninsula is in the north, in the state of Baja California. Several varieties of rabbits populate the region. Ducks are found in the lagoons and marshes along both coasts; black brant are plentiful in San Quintín Bay; quail, pheasant and dove are found throughout the state. Although mule deer and desert bighorn sheep inhabit some areas in Baja California, they are scarce, and special permits are required to hunt them. Hunting seasons vary according to species, but most open seasons occur between September and the end of February.

Hunting in Baja California requires a special-purpose visa, a consular certificate, a Military Gun Permit, a hunting permit and during the hunt the presence of a licensed outfitter's assistant. In addition to the above, when hunting for mule deer or desert bighorn sheep, a contract with a licensed Mexican organizer must be purchased. It is advisable to contact an American organization that specializes in hunting in Mexico to obtain the documents and to make arrangements with a Mexican contract organizer.

Weapons are forbidden in Mexico unless they are brought into the country during hunting seasons for the express purpose of hunting. Only two sporting firearms and 50 rounds of ammunition for each are permitted. Military and .22 caliber rimfire weapons and all pistols are prohibited. Bow and arrow hunting requires a special permit.

Standard Licensing Procedure

1. Consular Certificate

This document is issued by all Mexican Consulates. Applicants must present a letter of good conduct from their local police department or sheriff's office vouching for their moral character, plus two color, front-view passport-size photographs. The consular certificate is not a hunting permit—it is merely an authorization for the hunter to enter Mexico in this capacity, and is also required when applying for a Military Gun Permit. It will contain a description of each firearm, including kind, make, serial number, caliber or gauge and number of cartridges. The hunter needs a consular certificate for each state within Baja California.

2. Hunting Permits (Licenses)

Hunters must purchase permits for each Mexican state in which they intend to hunt and for each bird or animal they intend to hunt. Hunting permits are issued in the names of individual hunters and are not transferable. Each permit is only valid for the current season and in the state for which it was issued.

All the paperwork necessary for hunting in Baja California may be handled by the Southern California organization listed below. They also furnish information on hunting conditions and government regulations (which are subject to change). Depending on the types of mammals or birds hunted, the total cost of all the permits ranges from about $350 to $500. For information about the specific services offered, contact the Mexican Hunting Association, 6840 El Salvador St., Long Beach, CA 90815; (310) 430-3256, FAX (310) 430-9584.

RECREATION

WATER RECREATION
Boating

Anyone planning to operate a private boat in Mexican waters, regardless of size or construction, must first obtain a Mexican Boat Permit issued by the Mexico Department of Fisheries. Permits are sold on a yearly basis and are valid for 12 months from the date of issue. Fees for permits are based on the length of the craft: under 23 feet, $24.75; 23 feet to 29 feet 11 inches, $49.50; 30 feet and over, $74.25. (These fees are subject to change; contact the Department of Fisheries office for current fees.)

Applications for Mexican Boat Permits are available at the Mexico Department of Fisheries in San Diego. Completed applications should be sub-mitted to the Mexico Department of Fisheries at 2550 5th Avenue, Suite 101, San Diego, CA 92103-6622; (619) 233-6956. The office is open Monday through Friday 8 a.m. to 2 p.m.

Boat permit applications must include a copy of the boat's registration document. The boat registration document has to be shown before applying for a boat permit. Fees must be paid by cashier's check or money order for the exact amount due to Oficina Recaudadora de Pesca (personal checks are not accepted). For mail orders, include a stamped return envelope.

Fishing

The Gulf of California is widely considered to offer the world's finest fishing. Virtually every popular saltwater species—including marlin, sailfish, roosterfish, cabrilla, dolphinfish (mahi-mahi), sierra, yellowtail, sea bass, wahoo and bonito—can be found here. Favorite Gulf fishing areas are Bahia de los Angeles, Cabo San Lucas, the East Cape, La Paz, Loreto, Mulegé with nearby Bahía Concepción and San Felipe. On the Pacific Ocean side, Ensenada calls itself the "yellowtail capital of the world" and San Quintín Bay offers a variety of species.

Licenses

Any nonresident alien must possess a valid Mexican Sportfishing License before fishing in Mexican waters. This license covers all types of fishing and is valid anywhere in Mexico. Everyone aboard private boats in Mexican waters must have a fishing license regardless of age and whether or not they are fishing. Licenses for people fishing on commercial sportfishing boats are normally provided by the boat operators. A fishing license is also officially required for underwater fishing and free diving.

Fishing licenses are issued for periods of one week, one month and one year, effective at 12:01 a.m. on the starting date specified on the license application. Fees for licenses are $15.05 for one week, $22.80 for one month and $30.10 for one year. (These fees are subject to change; contact the Department of Fisheries office for current fees.) Mexican fishing licenses are not transferable, and each license must include the person's full legal name, home address and telephone number.

Applications for Mexican Sportfishing Licenses can be obtained at the Mexico Department of Fisheries office in San Diego. Completed applications should be submitted to the Mexico Department of Fisheries at 2550 5th Avenue, Suite 101, San Diego, CA 92103-6622; (619) 233-6956. The office is open Monday through Friday 8 a.m. to 2 p.m.

FISHING QUALITY PROFILE

Fish	Pacific				Gulf							
	Ensenada	San Quintin	Bahia Tortugas	Cabo San Lucas	San Felipe	Puertecitos	San Luis Gonzaga	Bahia de L.A.	Mulege	Loreto	La Paz	Las Cruces to Punta Palmilla
Albacore	6-10	6-10	6-10									6-10
Barracuda	4-10	4-10	6-10									
Black marlin		4-10										
Black sea bass											8-11	
Bluefin tuna			6-10									
Corvina					3-9	5-8	3-9	2-6	5-10	4-10	6-10	4-10
Crevalle											1-10	4-10
Grouper	6-9	6-9				4-10	4-10	4-10	4-10	5-7	4-10	4-10
Marlin				2-7		4-10	4-10	6-9	5-7	5-6	5-7	4-6
Needlefish											5-9	5-8
Rockfish	10-4	10-4										
Roosterfish						6-9	6-9	11-2		10-3	4-10	7-9
Sailfish				6-9				5-6	5-7	6-7	6-11	4-11
Sea bass									5-10			
Seatrout					4-10				5-10			
Sierra					5-9	6-10				10-4	10-6	4-7
Skipjack				5-9							5-7	5-7
Snapper									4-10	4-10	4-10	4-10
Snook				6-9				5-10				
Swordfish				6-9								
Tuna				5-9								
Wahoo				6-9						1-3	4-12	6-10
White sea bass	4-10	4-10	4-10		11-4	11-3						
Yellowfin Tuna											4-12	4-5
Yellowtail	4-10	4-10	4-10	4-5							12-5	4-5

This chart indicates *best fishing* months, not legal seasons. Numbers refer to months in sequence; 6-10 is June through October

Applications must be accompanied by a cashier's check or money order for the exact amount due, payable to Oficina Recaudadora de Pesca (personal checks are not accepted). For mail orders, include a stamped return envelope.

The Mexico Department of Fisheries also has offices in Mexico (Oficina de Pesca), but it is advisable to obtain fishing licenses before crossing the border.

Daily Bag Limits and Other Regulations

Each fisherman is permitted to catch up to 10 fish per day, with no more than five fish of the same species. In addition, anglers are subject to the following limits: no more than one billfish (marlin, sailfish or swordfish) and two tarpon or halibut. In brackish waters anglers are permitted to take up to 20 perch and 20 carp per day. Once the permitted limit has been bagged, all further catches must be released.

Except when skin or scuba diving, fish must be taken by angling with a hand-held line or a line attached to a rod. The use of nets (except handling nets), traps, poisons or explosives is prohibited. Skin and scuba divers may only fish with hand-held spears or band-powered spear guns. It is illegal to sell, trade or exchange the fish caught. Fish can be eviscerated and filleted, but a patch of skin must be left to permit identification. The taking of abalone, lobster, shrimp, pismo clams, cabrilla, totuava, oysters and sea turtles is prohibited by Mexican law. Anyone wishing to purchase any of these species to take into the United States must first obtain a form from the Mexican Government Fish Commission; only the Oficinas de Pesca located within Mexico provide this form. All purchases of these species must be made at designated public markets or fishing cooperatives.

U. S. Customs Regulations

Sportfishers may bring into the United States only fish for personal consumption. Shellfish, except for lobster and shrimp, are prohibited. The number of fish must not exceed the Mexican bag limit. Fish transported across the border can be eviscerated but must be identifiable; usually the head, tail or a patch of skin left intact will suffice. Anyone bringing fish into the United States will be asked by Customs officials to present a valid Mexican fishing license or a Mexico Department of Fisheries form covering the purchase of the fish. For more information, contact the United States Fish and Wildlife Law Enforcement Agency at (619) 661-3130.

Sites for Fishing and Water Sports

Bahía de los Angeles—The bay, which is protected by 45-mile-long Isla Angel de la Guarda, offers a fine sheltered anchorage for boats. Sportfishing is excellent; anglers will find yellowtail, roosterfish, sea bass, corbina and other popular game fish in the waters around the nearby islands, and marlin are occasionally hooked in the deeper waters farther offshore. Fishing trips can be arranged, and there are several launch ramps for private boats.

Cabo San Lucas—Sportfishing is the top attraction for many visitors. Located at the convergence of the warm waters of the Gulf of California and the cooler Pacific waters, Cabo San Lucas offers excellent fishing throughout the year. Favorite species are marlin, sailfish, swordfish, tuna and wahoo. Sportfishing cruisers usually cost $285 to $385 per day; skiffs (*pangas*) cost about $160 per day. Popular excursions are a trip by glass-bottom boat around the tip of the peninsula. Arrangements for fishing and boat trips may be made in many hotels or at the docks in the harbor. The waters are also good for scuba diving and snorkeling. A full-service dive shop is located across from Plaza Las Glorias.

Ensenada—Sportfishing for yellowtail, as well as for barracuda, bonito and albacore, is excellent during the summer season (April to November). Bottom-feeding species, such as whitefish and sea bass, are caught throughout the year. Arrangements for sportfishing trips can be made at the sportfishing piers off Boulevard Lázaro Cárdenas and at some shops on Avenida López Mateos. Rates for charter fishing cruisers vary depending on size of craft and number of passengers; rates start at about $550 per day. Open-party boats start at $35 per person. In addition, surf fishing is good along the sandy beaches and rocky shorelines both north and south of the city.

Skin diving is good all year, especially around Punta Banda. Surfers like the rocky beach near San Miguel village, a few miles north of Ensenada.

La Paz—Every popular saltwater species is found in the waters off La Paz—including marlin, sailfish, roosterfish, cabrilla, dolphinfish (mahimahi), sierra, yellowtail, sea bass, wahoo and bonito. Fishing is good all year, but March through October is the best season for big-game species. Cruisers, which rent for about $250 to $350 per day, are available through many hotels; the price usually includes captain, crew and license. Shiffs cost $180 per day for two persons.

The best beaches lie to the north of the city along Highway 11, the road to Pichilingue. Sailboating, sailboarding scuba diving are all popular.

San José del Cabo—Skiffs (*pangas*) for fishing are available at Pueblo La Playa, a seaside village 1.5 miles southeast of San José via a graded dirt road. Prices, including captain, are $150 for 6 hours. Splendid sandy beaches line the hotel row just south of San José. Swimming in the gulf is not recommended due to dropoff and currents, but all the hotels have pools. Many local tour operators offer excursions in the Los Cabos region by land and sea.

Loreto—Famous for roosterfish, Loreto's offshore waters hold virtually every major game species that inhabits the Gulf of California, including marlin, sailfish, sierra, yellowtail and grouper. Because fishing is good in the hot season, Loreto attracts as many visitors in summer as the rest of the year. Boat trips may be arranged to Isla Coronado for clam digging and observing large numbers of sea lions and pelicans. Scuba diving is also popular.

Mulegé—Sportfishing in the Gulf of California and in nearby Bahía Concepción is excellent, and fishing trips can be arranged at any of Mulegé's hotels. Fishing is best from May to October. Scuba diving is also very good; a full-service dive shop is located in town on Calle Francisco Madero, the main street. The beach, two miles northeast of town, can be reached by following an extension of Calle Madero, a good dirt road, along the river.

San Felipe—The gulf waters yield white sea bass, cabrilla, corbina, dorado, sierra, yellowtail and various other species. Sportfishing rates vary, with skiffs (*pangas*) ranging from $30 to $45 per person per day (for 1 to 5 passengers); six-day open party trips on large boats are about $600 per

RECREATION

person. Boats are available from several dealers along Paseo de Cortez, the central waterfront drive. Another popular sport is sailboating.

San Quintín—The waters of Bahía de San Quintín offer a seasonal paradise for sportsmen. Black brant (a type of goose) migrate to the area each winter and are popular game. Fishing is excellent; although fish are comparable in size and species to those found in Southern California waters, the bay offers both an abundance of fish and a relative lack of anglers. The daily costs for fishing boats (with guide) are about $150 for skiffs (*pangas*) and $225 to $335 for cruisers. Good surf fishing and clam digging enhance the appeal of the beaches along the shore of the outer bay. The quiet waters of the inner bay provide a fine, protected anchorage for small boats.■

Appendix

The information included in this chapter is provided solely as a service to our readers, and no endorsement of any service by the Automobile Club of Southern California is implied or intended. Because the schedules of most operators change frequently, detailed listings and fares are given only for ferry service. If you plan a bus trip to Baja California, contact the bus company or companies for a list of departures; air schedules and fares can be obtained either from the individual carriers or at any Auto Club Travel Agency office.

TRANSPORTATION
Air Service

Since flight schedules change on a frequent basis, they are not listed in this publication. Carriers listed below operate either within Baja California or between California and Baja California. Current schedules and fares can be obtained from the airlines' ticket offices or any Auto Club Travel Agency office. The Auto Club is not responsible for discontinuance of any flight or service.

Aero California operates daily flights from Los Angeles to Loreto, La Paz and Los Cabos Airport (San José del Cabo), and from Tijuana to La Paz. (310) 322-2644; (800) 237-6225.

Aeromexico operates daily flights from Los Angeles to La Paz; it also flies from Tijuana to La Paz. (800) 237-6639.

Air L.A. flies daily from Los Angeles to Tijuana. (310) 215-8234; (800) 933-5952.

Alaska Airlines flies daily from Los Angeles and San Diego to Los Cabos. (800) 426-0333.

Mexicana Airlines has flights on Tuesday and Friday through Sunday from Los Angeles to Los Cabos. (310) 646-7321; (800) 646-7321.

Bus Service
Domestic

The Central de Autobuses (Central Bus Terminal) is located in the La Mesa district on Boulevard Lázaro Cárdenas at Boulevard Alamar in eastern Tijuana. Information can be obtained by calling the terminal at 01152 (66) 21-2911 or 21-2982. Two companies, **Autotransportes de Baja California (ABC) and Tres Estrellas de Oro,** offer regular passenger service in Baja California between

Tijuana, Ensenada, San Felipe and Mexicali. From Mexicali there are connections for Mexico City and the interior. The same two lines also run from Tijuana to Baja California Sur. The trip to La Paz lasts about 24 hours and the fare is about $56 one way. The phone for Tres Estrellas de Oro is 01152 (66) 84-1407.

The old bus terminal located in downtown Tijuana at Calle Comercio and Avenida Madero serves some small local companies. Passengers arriving here by Greyhound bus can obtain inexpensive transportation on one of these small local buses to any business section of Tijuana.

International

Greyhound Lines offers frequent departures from downtown terminals in both Los Angeles and San Diego to Tijuana. Some buses let off passengers in Tijuana at the old downtown terminal; others go to the Central Bus Terminal (for addresses see the preceding description under "Domestic"). Fares to Tijuana from Los Angeles are $13 one way, $26 round trip. From San Diego the fares are $4 one way, $7 round trip. Fares to Calexico from Los Angeles are $19 one way, $36 round trip. In Southern California call (800) 231-2222; in Los Angeles (213) 629-8402; in San Diego call (619) 239-3266.

Five Star Tours provides service from San Diego to Tijuana. Six buses leave daily from the San Diego's Amtrak Depot at Broadway at Kettner Boulevard and go to the Mexicoach Terminal near the Jai Alai stadium on Avenida Revolución between calles 6 and 7. Round-trip fare is $8. Five Star Tours also provides bullfight trips. Phone (619) 232-5049.

Mexicoach runs many buses daily from the trolley station in San Ysidro

to the Mexicoach Terminal in Tijuana. Round-trip tickets are $2.

San Diego Trolley provides daily rail service between downtown San Diego and the international border at San Ysidro. Trolleys operate from 5 a.m. to 1 a.m., with 15-minute service most of the time; maximum one-way fare is $1.75. (619) 233-3004.

Car Rentals

A few American rental agencies allow customers to drive their vehicles into Mexico; others may arrange rentals with affiliated companies in Mexico. Check with individual companies for their policies. Car rental agencies are located in the larger cities and at the airports in Baja California. Auto rentals are much more expensive in Mexico than in the United States.

Ferry Service and Schedules

The ferry system, a vital transportation link between Baja California and Mexico's mainland, carries both vehicles and passengers. Formerly owned and operated by the Mexican government, the ferry system was sold in 1989 to a private Mexican company, Grupo Sematur. Rates under the new owner have increased substantially, but service has improved. In the past, motorists often had difficulty obtaining reservations.

If you plan to ship your vehicle to the mainland, you must obtain a car permit. Permits are available at ferry ports, but it is simpler to obtain them at border crossings. **Note: applicants for car permits must present the original current registration or a notarized bill of sale for each vehicle; copies and temporary papers are not accepted.** (See *Tourist Regulations and Travel Tips*, Automobile Requirements.)

Ferry reservations may be made by telephone from the United States or within Mexico, but some knowledge of Spanish is necessary. Most travelers prefer to make reservations in person at the ferry offices. Reservations should be made at least a week in advance, and a month in advance during holiday periods, although some people report getting a reservation on short notice.

Pets are permitted on the ferries when accompanied by the appropriate health certificates which have been visaed by a Mexican Consul (see *Tourist Regulations and Travel Tips*).

In La Paz the ferry ticket office is on Guillermo Prieto at Cinco de Mayo, two blocks southeast of Plaza Constitución. It is open Monday through Friday from 7 a.m. to 1 p.m. and 4 to 6 p.m., Saturday and Sunday from 8 a.m. to 1 p.m.; phone 01152 (112) 5-3833 or 5-4666. The ferry terminal is located at Pichilingue, the deepwater port for La Paz, 10 miles north of the city. Ferry information may also be obtained at the State Tourism Office; 01152 (112) 2-5939. In Santa Rosalía the ferry office is located in the terminal building on Highway 1 just south of the main entrance into the city; 01152 (115) 2-0013 or 2-0014. The Cabo San Lucas to Puerto Vallarta ferry is no longer operating. Within Mexico, ferry information may be obtained by calling the toll-free number 91 (800) 696-96.

Each ferry contains a telephone, cafeteria and medical assistance.

La Paz-Mazatlán—Ferries depart from both ports Sunday through Friday at 3 p.m. (Saturday sailings during holiday periods). Sailing time is about 19 hours.

La Paz-Topolobampo (Los Mochis)—Ferries depart from La Paz Wednesday through Monday at 8 p.m. They leave Topolobampo on Monday through Saturday at 9 a.m. Sailing time is about nine hours.

Santa Rosalía-Guaymas—Ferries depart from Santa Rosalía on Wednesday and Sunday at 8 a.m. They leave

FERRY RATES (shown in dollars)

ROUTE	PASSENGER CLASS				VEHICLE TYPE				
	Salon (Padded seats)	Tourist (Roomette with washbasin and bunks for four persons)	Cabin (Beds and bath for two persons)	Special Cabin (Beds, lounge and bath for two persons)	Car, Small Truck, and Van up to 16.4 feet (5 meters)	16.5 to 21.3 feet (5 to 6.5 meters)	Car or Truck with Trailer up to 29.5 feet (9 meters)	29.5 to 55.8 feet (9 to 17 meters)	Motor-home over 16.4 feet (5 meters)
La Paz-Mazatlán	18	37	55	73	134	175	242	457	228
La Paz-Topolo-bampo	12	(not included on this route)			82	106	148	278	140
Santa Rosalia-Guaymas	12	24	(not included on this route)		94	124	170	321	161

Guaymas on Tuesday and Friday at 8 a.m. Sailing time is about eight hours.

Tours

As a result of the increasing popularity of Baja California as a tourist destination, many tour operators offer organized tours of the peninsula. These include cruises, air tours, bus tours and even a four-wheel-drive tour. The Automobile Club of Southern California's Travel Agency can handle bookings on most tours; call or visit any Travel Agency office for details.

SPEAKING SPANISH

This section lists some of the Spanish phrases and sentences which are most useful to visitors in Baja California. A basic knowledge of the language may be helpful. Many of the Baja Californianos who deal with tourists speak English; if they don't, they're glad to help you along with your attempts at their language. Spanish is not difficult to pronounce. A study of the following pronunciation rules will be sufficient to make yourself understood.

Pronunciation

The pronunciation of the Spanish language presents few difficulties. The spelling is almost phonetic; nearly every letter has one sound which it retains at all times.

Vowels

A pronounced as in *father*.
E pronounced as in *bed*.
I pronounced as in *pizza*.
O pronounced as in *hold*.
U pronounced as in *junior*.

Diphthongs

Spanish diphthongs are pronounced as very swift elisions of the component vowels equally stressed.

ue as in **weh**   *fuente*
au as in English **ouch**   *gaucho*

Consonants

Consonants do not differ materially from the English. The few differences can be summarized as follows:

C is pronounced with a soft sound before *e* and *i*. Otherwise it has a *k* sound.
cinco   SEEN-ko

G is like a strong English h, when it precedes *e* and *i*. In all other cases it is like English *g* in go.
gente   HEN-te

H always silent.

J pronounced like a strong English *h*.

LL pronounced like the English *y*.
caballo   kah-BAH-yo

Ñ combination of n and y.
niño   NEEN-yo

Qu pronounced like *k*.

Z is always pronounced like the English s.

Accent or Stress

1. When a word ends in a vowel, n or s, the stress falls on the next to the last syllable.
hombre   OM-bre
hablan   AH-blan
estos   ES-tos

2. When the word ends in a consonant other than n or s, the stress falls on the last syllable.
hablar   ah-BLAR

3. In some cases an accent mark will be found over a vowel. This does not change the pronunciation of that vowel, but indicates that the stress falls

on that syllable.

gramática	gra-MAH-ti-ca
corazón	cor-a-SOWN

Words and Phrases

Note: Nouns in Spanish are either masculine or feminine, and there are two words meaning "the": *el* is used before masculine nouns, *la* before feminine nouns. The plural of *el* is *los*, of *la* is *las*. After words given on these pages the gender is indicated by (m.) for masculine, (f.) for feminine. For instance, say *el hotel* and *los hoteles; la posada* and *las posadas*. The word *"usted"* meaning *"you,"* is usually abbreviated Ud. or Vd. An adjective also agrees in gender with the noun it modifies. For example, *el hombre pequeño*—the small man; *la camisa roja*—the red shirt. In most cases, the adjective follows the noun.

Language

Do you understand English?
¿Entiende Ud. el inglés?
I do not speak Spanish.
No hablo español.
Yes, sir; no, madam.
Si, señor; no, señora.
Very little
Muy poco; (or) poquito
I do not understand.
No entiendo.
Do you understand me?
¿Me entiende Ud.?
Please speak slowly.
Por favor hable despacio.
I wish to speak with an interpreter.
Quisiera hablar con un intérprete.
What are you saying?
¿Qué dice?

Polite Phrases

Good morning./**Buenos días.**
Good afternoon./**Buenas tardes.**
Good night./**Buenas noches.**
Goodbye./**Adiós; hasta la vista.**
Thank you./**Gracias.**
Yes, very good./**Sí; muy bueno.**
Please/**Por favor**
Excuse me./**Perdóneme.**
I am very sorry./**Lo siento mucho.**

To Explain Your Needs

I need; we need.
Necesito; necesitamos.
I would like to telephone.
Quisiera telefonear.
I am hungry; we are hungry.
Tengo hambre; tenemos hambre.
I am thirsty; we are thirsty.
Tengo sed; tenemos sed.
I am cold; we are cold.
Tengo frío; tenemos frío.
I am warm; we are warm.
Tengo calor; tenemos calor.
I am tired; we are tired.
Estoy cansado (a); estamos cansados.
I am sick; we are sick.
Estoy enfermo (a); estamos enfermos.
The child is sick; tired.
El niño (la niña) está enfermo (a); cansado (a).

Directions

north/**norte**	south/**sur**
east/**este**	west/**oeste**

(Note: In some addresses, east is **oriente**, abbreviated **Ote.**; west is **poniente**, abbreviated **Pte.**)

Numerals

1	uno	16	diez y seis
2	dos	17	diez y siete
3	tres	18	diez y ocho
4	cuatro	19	diez y nueve
5	cinco	20	veinte
6	seis	21	veinte y uno
7	siete	30	treinta
8	ocho	40	cuarenta

9	nueve	50	cincuenta
10	diez	60	sesenta
11	once	70	setenta
12	doce	80	ochenta
13	trece	90	noventa
14	catorce	100	ciento
15	quince	200	doscientos

Days and Time

Sunday/**domingo**
Monday/**lunes**
Tuesday/**martes**
Wednesday/**miércoles**
Thursday/**jueves**
Friday/**viernes**
Saturday/**sábado**
today/**hoy**
tomorrow/**mañana**
yesterday/**ayer**
morning/**la mañana**
noon/**el mediodía**
afternoon/**la tarde**
tonight/**esta noche**
night/**la noche**
last night/**anoche**
midnight/**la medianoche**

What time is it?
¿Qué hora es?
It is one o'clock.
Es la una.
It is ten minutes past two.
Son las dos y diez.
It is a quarter past three.
Son las tres y cuarto.
It is a quarter of five.
Es un cuarto para las cinco.
It is 25 minutes of six.
Son veintecinco para las seis.
It is half past four.
Son las cuatro y media.

Useful Adjectives

bad/**malo**
beautiful/**hermoso**
cheap/**barato**
clean/**limpio**
cold/**frío**
difficult/**difícil**
dirty/**sucio**
early/**temprano**
easy/**fácil**
expensive/**caro**
fast/**rápido**
good/**bueno**
high/**alto**
hot/**caliente**
kind/**benévolo, bondadoso**
large/**grande**
low/**bajo**
late/**tarde**
long/**largo**
polite/**cortés**
sharp/**agudo**
short/**corto**
slow/**lento**
small/**pequeño**
ugly/**feo**
unkind/**despiadado, duro**

Colors

white/**blanco**
pink/**rosa**
black/**negro**
blue; dark blue/**azul; azul obscuro**
gray/**gris**
green; light green/**verde; verde claro**
brown/**café**
purple/**morado**
red/**rojo; colorado**
yellow/**amarillo**

At the Border

passport
pasaporte
tourist card
tarjeta de turista
age
edad
marital status
estado civil
single
soltero (m.); soltera (f.)

married
casado (m.); casada (f.)
widowed
viudo (m.); viuda (f.)
divorced
divorciado (m.); divorciada (f.)
profession; occupation
profesión; ocupación
vaccination card
certificado de vacuna
driver's license
licencia de manejar
car owner's title (registration)
título de propiedad (registración)
year of car
modelo (o año)
make (Ford, Mazda, etc.)
marca
license plate and state
placa y estado
chassis and motor number
número de chasis y motor
number of doors
número de puertas
number of cylinders
número de cilindros
number of passengers
número de pasajeros

On the Road

kilometer/**kilómetro (m.)**
highway/**carretera (f.)**
road/**camino (m.)**
street/**calle (f.)**
avenue/**avenida (f.)**
boulevard/**bulevar (m.)**
block/**cuadra (f.)**
corner/**esquina (f.)**
left side/**lado izquierdo (m.)**
right side/**lado derecho (m.)**

Show me the road to...
Enséñeme el camino a...
How far is...?
¿Qué tan lejos está...?
Can we get to...before dark?
¿Podemos llegar a ...antes del anochecer?
Is this road dangerous?
¿Es peligroso este camino?
Is that road in good condition?
¿Está en buen estado aquel camino?
Is it paved or is it a dirt road?
¿Está pavimentado o es de tierra?
Go straight ahead.
Siga adelante.
Turn to the right; left.
Vuelta a la derecha; izquierda.
What city, town, is this?
¿Qué ciudad, pueblo, es éste?
Where does this road lead?
¿A dónde conduce este camino?

In Case of Car Trouble

I want to ask you a favor.
Quiero pedirle un favor.
I need a tow truck.
Necesito una grua.
My car has broken down.
Se me ha descompuesto el carro.
My lights don't work.
Mis faros no funcionan.
The starter does not work.
El arranque no funciona.
I have run out of gasoline.
Se me acabó la gasolina.
Is there a gasoline station near here?
¿Hay una estación de gasolina cerca de aquí?
Is there a garage near here?
¿Hay un garage cerca?
Please send someone to repair my car.
Por favor mande a alguien a componer mi carro.
May I go with you to get a mechanic?
¿Puedo ir con usted a conseguir un mecánico?
Have you a rope to tow my car?
¿Tiene una soga para remolcar mi carro?

Do you want to help me push the car to one side of the road?

¿Quiere ayudarme a empujar el carro a un lado del camino?

Do you want to help me change a tire?

¿Quiere ayudarme a cambiar una llanta?

Do you want to be my witness?

¿Quiere ser mi testigo?

Arriving in Town

Is English spoken here?

¿Se habla inglés aquí?

Where is the center of town?

¿Dónde está el centro de la ciudad?

Where is X Street, X Square, the X Hotel?

¿Dónde está la Calle X, la Plaza X, el Hotel X?

May I park here?

¿Puedo estacionarme aquí?

Please direct me to the nearest post office.

Por favor diríjame a la oficina de correos mas cercana.

Where can I find a policeman, a hairdresser, a doctor, a drug store?

¿Dónde puedo hallar un policía, una estética, un médico, una farmacía?

Where is the police station, the chamber of commerce?

¿Dónde está la comisaría, la cámara de comercio?

Where can I find road maps, post cards, American papers?

¿Dónde se pueden hallar mapas de caminos, tarjetas postales, periódicos norteamericanos?

Please direct me to the railroad station, the bus station.

Por favor diríjame a la estación del ferrocarril, al terminal del autobús.

How often does the bus go by?

¿Que tan seguido pasa el autobús (camión)?

Does the bus stop here?

¿Para aquí el autobús?

Could you recommend a good restaurant; a good small hotel; a first class hotel?

¿Puede Ud. recomendar un buen restaurante; un buen hotel pequeño; un hotel de primera clase?

I wish to telephone, to telegraph, to cable.

Quiero telefonear, telegrafiar, cablegrafiar.

I wish to change some money.

Quiero cambiar dinero.

What is the rate of exchange?

Cuál es el tipo de cambio?

I want to cash a check.

Quiero cambiar un cheque.

At the Hotel

hotel/**hotel (m.)**
inn/**posada (f.)**
apartments/**apartamentos (m.)**
room/**cuarto (m.)**
furnished room/**cuarto amueblado**
bedroom/**recámara(f.)**
pillow/**almohada (f.)**
blanket/**cobija (f.), manta (f.)**
air conditioning/**aire acondicionado**
kitchen/**cocina (f.)**
bathroom/**cuarto de baño (m.)**
towel/**toalla (f.)**
wash cloth/**toalla chica (f.)**
soap/**jabón (m.)**
dining room/**comedor (m.)**
ice water/**agua con hielo (m.)**
hot water/**agua caliente (m.)**
elevator/**elevador (m.)**
stairway/**escalera (f.)**
key/**llave (f.)**
office/**oficina (f.)**
manager/**gerente (m.)**
maid/**camarista (f.)**

office employee/**empleado de oficina (m.)**
bellboy/**bellboy (m.)**
porter/**mozo de servicios (m.)**
guest/**huésped (m.)**

I want a single room, with bath.
Deseo un cuarto sencillo, con baño.
I want a room for two; with twin beds.
Deseo un cuarto para dos; con camas gemelas.
I want two connecting rooms.
Deseo dos cuartos comunicados.
A front room; a back room.
Un cuarto al frente; al fondo.
A quiet room.
Un cuarto tranquilo.
On the lower floor; upper floor.
En el piso bajo; piso alto.
Will you have the baggage brought up? ...down?
¿Quiere Ud. hacer subir ...bajar el equipaje?
We are leaving tomorrow.
Partimos mañana.
We are staying several days ...just tonight.
Nos quedaremos aquí unos pocos días...solamente esta noche.
What is the price (rate)?
¿Cuál es el precio (la tarifa)?
What is the minimum rate?
¿Cuál es el precio mínimo?
Do you accept checks in payment?
Acepta Ud. cheques en pago?
I want my bill, please.
Quiero la cuenta, por favor.
Have you hot running water?
¿Hay agua corriente y caliente?
The shower doesn't work.
La regadera no funciona.
Is there a garage?
¿Hay garage?

Where is the ladies' room, men's room?
¿Dónde está el baño (lavabo) de damas, de caballeros?
Where is the barber shop?
¿Dónde hay una peluquería?
Please send these clothes to the laundry.
Hágame el favor de mandar esta ropa a la lavandería.
Please clean and press this suit.
Hágame el favor de limpiar y planchar este traje.
I want it today; tomorrow.
Lo quiero hoy; mañana.
Please call me at six o'clock.
Hágame el favor de llamarme a las seis.
Please forward my correspondence to this address.
Por favor reexpida mi correspondencia a esta dirección.
Do you want to prepare a lunch for us to carry with us?
¿Quiere Ud. prepararnos un almuerzo para llevárnoslo?

At the Garage

How much is gasoline per liter?
¿Cuánto cuesta el litro de gasolina?
Fill up the gasoline tank; the radiator.
Llene el tanque de gasolina; el radiador.
Give me five, ten, fifteen, twenty liters.
Deme cinco, diez, quince, veinte litros.
Check the oil; change the oil.
Vea el aceite; cambie el aceite.
Please lubricate the car; wash the car.
Favor de lubricar el carro; lavar el carro.
Please tighten the brakes; adjust the brakes.
Favor de apretar los frenos; ajustar los frenos.

Please tune the engine; change the sparkplugs.

Favor de poner al punto (afinar) el motor; cambiar las bujías.

My tire has a puncture. Can you repair the tube?

¿Mi llanta tiene un agujero. Puede reparar la cámara?

The tire is flat.

La llanta está desinflada.

The horn is not working.

La bocina no funciona.

Put water in the battery.

Ponga agua en la batería.

The battery needs charging.

La batería necesita carga.

Please put another bulb in this headlamp.

Favor de reemplazar el foco de este faro.

The gasoline tank is leaking.

El tanque de gasolina está goteando.

The gas line is clogged.

La tubería de gasolina está tapada.

The engine heats.

El motor se calienta.

The exhaust is choked.

Está obstruido el tubo de escape.

The steering gear is out of order.

La dirección está descompuesta.

The radiator leaks.

El radiador gotea.

The clutch slips.

El embrague resbala.

There is a short circuit.

Hay un cortocircuito.

The windshield wiper does not work.

El limpiavidrios del parabrisa no funciona.

The taillight does not work.

El faro trasero no funciona.

Please clean the windshield.

Favor de limpiar el parabrisa.

When will the repairs be finished?

¿Cuándo terminará la reparación?

How much do I owe you?

¿Cuánto le debo?

At the Restaurant

Please bring me the menu.

Favor de traerme el menú.

I like my meat rare (well done).

Quiero la carne tierna (bien cocida).

Please bring me the check.

Favor de traerme la cuenta.

breakfast/**desayuno (m.)**
lunch/**almuerzo (m.)**
dinner/**comida (f.)**
supper/**cena (f.)**
knife/**cuchillo (m.)**
fork/**tenedor (m.)**
spoon/**cuchara (f.)**
cup/**taza (f.)**
glass/**vaso (f.)**
napkin/**servilleta (f.)**
bill/**cuenta (f.)**
tip/**propina (f.)**

Bread

bread/**pan (m.)**
crackers/**galletas (f.)**
toast/**pan tostado (m.)**

Fruit

apple/**manzana (f.)**
avocado/**aguacate (m.)**
banana/**plátano (m.)**
dates/**dátiles (m.)**
figs/**higos (m.)**
fruit/**fruta (f.)**
guava/**guayaba (f.)**
lemon/**limón (m.)**
lime/**lima (f.)**
nuts/**nueces (f.)**
olives/**aceitunas (f.)**
orange/**naranja (f).**
peach/**durazno (m.)**

pineapple/**piña (f.)**
strawberries/**fresas (f.)**

Vegetables

beans/**frijoles (m.)**
beets/**betabeles (f.)**
cabbage/**repollo (m.); col (f.)**
corn/**maíz (m.)**
lettuce/**lechuga (f.)**
onion/**cebolla (f.)**
peas/**chícharos (m.)**
potatoes/**papas (f.)**
rice/**arroz (m.)**
string beans/**tejotes (m.)**
sweet potatoes/**camotes (m.)**
tomatoes/**tomates (m.)**
vegetables/**legumbres (f.)**

Meat, Pork, Poultry, Eggs, Fish

sausage/**chorizo (m.)**
meat/**carne (f.)**
beef/**carne de res (f.)**
beefsteak/**biftec (m.) filete (m.)**
veal/**ternera (f.)**
lamb/**carne de carnero**
lamb chops/**chuletas de carnero**
roast/**asado (m.)**
pork/**carne de puerco**
ham/**jamón (m.)**
bacon/**tocino (m.)**
chicken/**pollo (m.)**
egg/**huevo (m.)**
fried/**frito**
soft-boiled/**tibio**
hard-boiled/**cocidos duro**
scrambled/**revueltos**
duck/**pato (m.)**
turkey/**guajolote (m.); pavo (m.)**
abalone/**abulón (m.)**
clam/**almeja (f.)**
fish/**pescado (m.)**
scallops/**callos (m.)**
shrimp/**camarónes (m.)**
lobster/**langosta (f.)**

Beverages, Liquors

beer/**cerveza (f.)**
brandy/**aguardiente (m.)**
champagne/**vino de champaña (m.)**
cocktail/**coctel (m.)**
coffee/**café (m.)**
with cream/**con leche**
without cream/**sin leche**
gin/**ginebra (f.)**
milk/**leche (f.)**
rum/**ron (m.)**
tea/**té (m.)**
water/**agua (m.)**
whiskey/**whiskey (m.)**
wine/**vino (m.)**

Desserts

cake/**pastel (m.)**
candies/**confites; dulces (f.)**
custard/**flan (f.)**
ice cream/**helado (m.)**

Other Foods

butter/**mantequilla (f.)**
cheese/**queso (m.)**
flour/**harina (f.)**
honey/**miel de abejas (f.)**
pepper/**pimienta (f.)**
salad/**ensalada (f.)**
salt/**sal (f.)**
sauce/**salsa (f.)**
soup/**sopa (f.), caldo (m.)**
sugar/**azúcar (m.)**

Miscellaneous Glossary

communal farm/**ejido**
unleaded (gasoline)/**magna sin**
assembly plants/**maquiladoras**
public beaches/**playas públicas**

SUGGESTED SUPPLY LISTS

The items included in the following lists will help make a trip to Baja California safe and enjoyable. Two lists

Bill Cory

During the 1973 research trip, Auto Club personnel check out equipment and vehicles at Rancho Santa Inés. (Auto Club Historical Photo)

are shown: the first, for all trips, lists items that should be taken on any trip down the peninsula; the second, for backcountry travel, is more extensive and necessary only for those planning extended off-road and camping trips. Travelers should use their own discretion in deciding which items to include. It is better, however, to take along too much than too little, if there is room in the vehicle. All items on the first list should also be included in preparation for backcountry trips.

All Trips

For vehicles ...

Air filters
Brake fluid
Flares
Fuses (check amperage)

Motor oil
Power steering fluid
Tools
Water (5 gal. for radiator)
Window cleaner

For people ...

Can opener
Canteen
Dark glasses
Drinking water and cups
First aid kit
Flashlight and batteries
Insect repellent
Keys (extra, for car)
Paper towels
Salt tablets
Skin lotion
Sunburn cream

Sun shade
Toilet tissue
Trash bags

Backcountry Trips

For vehicles ...

Alternator brushes
Baling wire
Battery cables
Bolts and nuts (assorted sizes)
Chamois (for straining gasoline)
Duct tape
Electric fuel pump
Electric tape
Fittings (gas lines)
Fire extinguisher
Gaskets (head, fuel pump)
Gasoline cans (two, 5-gal.)
Gasoline filter (in-line)
Grease
Hammer (heavy)
Hoses and clamps (radiator)
Hydraulic jack (small sand-support
  board)
Ignition coil(s)
Ignition module
Lug wrench
Radiator sealant
Spare tires (extra)
Spark plugs
Tire inflator
Tow rope
Tube repair kit
Universal joints
Valve cores
Water cans (two, 5-gal.)
Wire (10-gauge electrical)
Wire connectors

For people and camps ...

Blankets
Camp cook set
Camp knives

Chairs (folding)
Cleanser
Compass
Cots
Crowbar
Detergent (liquid)
Dishes
Eating utensils
First aid kit (large)
Flashlight (large)
Fly swatter
Fuel (stove and lantern)
Funnels (small and large)
Gloves (leather)
Grate (for cooking)
Hatchet
Lantern (extra mantles)
Matches (wooden)
Netting (mosquito)
Notebook
Pail or bucket
Pens and pencils
Portable toilet
Radio (portable, short-wave or CB)
Rags
Rope (small)
Scrub brush
Shovels (folding)
Signal mirror
Sleeping bags
Snake bite kit(s)
Soap (freshwater and saltwater)
Stove
Table (folding)
Tarpaulins
Tent
Toilet paper
Towels (bath, face)
Trash bags (large and small)
Wash cloths
Water purification tablets ■

Lodging and Restaurants

Lodging and Restaurants lists hotels, motels, and resorts in Baja California operating as of November 15, 1994. Properties are listed alphabetically under the nearest town, with lodging facilities first and restaurants second. The location is given from the center of town or from the nearest major highway.

Accommodations in Baja California are diverse, ranging from small motels to luxurious seaside resorts. Many of the peninsula's resorts and certain hotels in major cities have all the services and facilities normally associated with first-class hotels in the United States. Tourists in Baja California should remember, however, that no matter where they are staying, they are in a foreign country, and there may be a different, more relaxed approach to service and housekeeping. If travelers keep this in mind, their visits will be more enjoyable.

The lodging and restaurant properties listed in these pages have been inspected at least once in the past year by a trained representative of the Automobile Club of Southern California. In surprise inspections, each property was found to meet AAA's extensive and detailed requirements for approval. These requirements are reflective of current industry standards and the expecta-

tions of the traveling public. Less than two-thirds of the lodging establishments open for business are listed in AAA publications.

Many listings include AAA's esteemed "Diamond" rating, reflecting the overall quality of the establishment. Many factors are considered in the process of determining the Diamond rating. In lodging properties, the facility is first "classified" according to its physical design—is it a motel, a hotel, a resort, an apartment, etc. Since the various types of lodging establishments offer differing amenities and facilities, rating criteria are specific for each classification. For example, a motel, which typically offers a room with convenient parking and little if any recreational or public facilities, is rated using criteria designed only for motel-type establishments—it is not compared to a hotel with its extensive public and meeting areas, or to a resort with its wide range of recreational facilities and programs. The diamonds do, however, represent standard levels of quality in all types of establishments.

This book also lists accommodations which are not AAA-rated, but nearly attain AAA standards. In these cases, the ♦ symbol will be missing from the listing. Wherever the inclusion of non-rated hotels, motels and resorts occurs, they are listed as a courtesy and convenience to readers. No endorsement is implied or intended.

The number of lodgings listed in this chapter is limited in the following towns: Ciudad Constitución, Loreto, Mulegé, Santa Rosalía and Tecate. Information about hotels and motels in these towns may be obtained at state tourism offices throughout the peninsula and in the tourist newspaper *The Baja Sun.* These sources also mention other hotels in the larger cities of Baja California. The names of some additional hotels and motels are also mentioned in the highway route logs of this book.

There is no charge for a property to be listed in AAA publications. Many lodgings and restaurants, however, choose to purchase display advertising. These display ads sometimes provide additional information about popular features of the establishment.

Nearly all lodging and restaurant facilities accept credit cards as forms of payment for services rendered. The following symbols are used to identify the specific cards accepted by each property.

AE	American Express
CB	Carte Blanche
DI	Diner's Club International
MC	MasterCard
VI	VISA

Facilities accommodating handicapped travelers are largely unavailable in Baja California. The Automobile Club recommends contacting the lodging establishment directly should a traveler have special needs.

LODGING

The following accommodations classifications appear in this book.

Bed & Breakfast—Usually a small establishment emphasizing personal attention. Individually decorated guest rooms provide an at-home feeling and may lack some amenities such as TVs, phones, etc. Usually owner-operated with a common room or parlor where guests and owners can interact during evening and breakfast hours. May have shared bathrooms. A continental or full hot breakfast is included in the room rate.

Complex—A combination of two or more kinds of lodgings.

Cottage—Individual bungalow, cabin or villa, usually containing one rental unit equipped for housekeeping. May have a separate living room and bedroom(s). Parking is usually at each unit.

Country Inn—Similar in definition to a bed and breakfast. Offers a dining room reflecting the ambience of the inn. At a minimum, breakfast and dinner are served.

Hotel—A multi-story building usually including a coffee shop, dining room, lounge, room service, convenience shops, valet, laundry and full banquet/meeting facilities. Parking may be limited.

Lodge—Typically two or more stories with all facilities in one building. Located in vacation, ski, fishing areas, etc. Usually has food and beverage service. Adequate on-premises parking.

Motel—Usually one or two stories; food service, if any, consists of a limited facility or snack bar. Often has a pool or playground. Ample parking, usually at the guest room door.

Motor Inn—Usually two or three stories, but may be a high-rise. Generally

LODGING AND RESTAURANTS

has recreation facilities, food service and ample parking. May have limited banquet/meeting facilities.

Apartment—Usually four or more stories with at least half the units equipped for housekeeping. Often in a vacation destination area. Units typically provide a full kitchen, living room and one or more bedrooms, but may be studio-type rooms with kitchen equipment in an alcove. May require minimum stay and/or offer discounts for longer stays. This classification may also modify any of the other lodging types.

Condominium—A destination property located in a resort area. Guest units consist of a bedroom, living room and kitchen. Kitchens are separate from bedrooms and are equipped with a stove, oven or microwave, refrigerator, cooking utensils and table settings for the maximum number of people occupying the unit. Linens and maid service are provided at least twice weekly. This classification may also modify any of the other lodging types.

Historic—Accommodations in restored, pre-1930 structures, reflecting the ambience of yesteryear and the surrounding region. Rooms may lack some modern amenities and have shared baths. Usually owner-operated and provides food service. Parking is usually available. This classification may also modify any of the other lodging types.

Resort—May be a destination unto itself. Has a vacation atmosphere offering extensive recreational facilities for such specific interests as golf, tennis, fishing, etc. Rates may include meals under American or Modified American plans. This classification may also modify any of the other lodging types.

Suite—Units have one or more bedrooms and a living room, which may or may not be closed off from the bedrooms. This classification may also modify any of the other lodging types.

A property's diamond rating is not based on the room rate or any one specific aspect of its facilities or operations. Many factors are considered in calculating the rating, and certain minimum standards must be met in all inspection categories. If a property fails approval in just one category, it is not listed in Club publications. The inspection categories include housekeeping, maintenance, service, furnishings and decor. Guest comments received by AAA may also be reviewed in a property's approval/rating process.

These criteria apply to all properties listed in this publication:

- Clean and well-maintained facilities
- Hospitable staff
- Adequate parking
- A well-kept appearance
- Good quality bedding and comfortable beds with adequate illumination
- Good locks on all doors and windows
- Comfortable furnishings and decor
- Smoke detectors
- Adequate towels and supplies
- At least one comfortable easy chair with adequate illumination
- A desk or other writing surface with adequate illumination

Lodging ratings range from one to five diamonds and are defined below:

♦—Good but unpretentious. Establishments are functional. Clean and comfortable rooms must meet the basic needs of privacy and cleanliness.

♦♦—Shows noticeable enhancements in decor and/or quality of furnishings over those at the one-diamond level. May be recently constructed or an older property. Targets the needs of a budget-oriented traveler.

♦♦♦—Offers a degree of sophistication with additional amenities, services and facilities. There is a marked upgrade in services and comfort.

♦♦♦♦—Excellent properties displaying high levels of service and hospitality and offering a wide variety of amenities and upscale facilities, inside the room, on the grounds and in the common areas.

♦♦♦♦♦—Renowned for an exceptionally high degree of service, striking and luxurious facilities and many extra amenities. Guest services are executed and presented in a flawless manner. Guests are pampered by a very professional, attentive staff. The property's facilities and operations set standards in hospitality and service.

Room rates shown in the listings are provided by each establishment's management for publication by the Automobile Club of Southern California. During special events or holiday periods rates may exceed those published and special discounts or savings programs may not be honored. High-season rates are always shown; off-season rates are listed if they are substantially lower than the rest of the year. Rates are for typical rooms, not special units, and do not include taxes or service charges. A 10-percent sales tax is imposed on all hotel, restaurant and nightclub bills. Some establishments, particularly in the Los Cabos region, add a service charge of 10 to 20 percent to room bills; it is typically a gratuity fee used in lieu of tipping, but this may not always be the case. Upon check in, be sure to understand what additional charges, if any, will be added to the bill.

Some hotels quote prices in pesos, others in dollars. All prices listed in this book are given in dollar equivalents. All establishments accept dollars; however, you can sometimes get a better price by paying in pesos. When making reservations, be sure to have a clear understanding of the price you will pay.

In addition to the dates for which the rates are valid, each rate line lists the prices quoted for one person (abbreviated 1P) and for two persons (2P); the two-person rate may be for either one or two beds. Figures following these abbreviations are the price(s) for the specified room and occupants. Most rates listed are European plan, which means that no meals are included in the rate. Some lodgings' rates include breakfast [BP] or continental breakfast [CP]. At a few properties you will find the American Plan [AP] which includes three meals, or a Modified American Plan [MAP] which offers two meals, usually breakfast and dinner. Most establishments also provide a per-person rate applicable to the third or more individuals staying in the same room or unit; this rate is added to the two-person rate listed in the rate line.

Many properties welcome children in the same room with their parents at no additional charge; individual listings indicate if there is an age limit. There may be charges for additional equipment, such as roll-aways or cribs.

All baths have a combination tub and shower bath unless noted otherwise. Since nearly all establishments have air conditioning, telephones and color TV, only the absence of any of these items is noted in the listing. Check-in time is shown only if it is after 3 p.m.; check-out time is shown only if it is before 10 a.m. Service charges are not shown unless they are $1 or more, or at least five percent of the room rate.

LODGING AND RESTAURANTS

If the pet acceptance policy varies within the establishment, no mention of pets is made. A heated pool is heated when it is reasonable to expect use of a pool. Outdoor pools may not open in winter.

Reservations are always advisable in resort areas and may be the only way to assure obtaining the type of accommodations you want. Deposits are almost always required. Should your plans change and you need to cancel your reservation, be aware of the amount of notice required to receive a refund of your deposit. Be sure to confirm the price of your accommodations at the time your reservations are made. Always request a written confirmation from the hotel, motel or resort. Due to the slowness of Baja California mail service, all correspondence should be sent at least six weeks in advance. In the hotel mailing addresses, *BC* is the abbreviation for the state of Baja California and *BCS* stands for the state of Baja California Sur.

Fire warning and protection equipment are indicated by the symbols Ⓓ (all guest rooms have smoke detectors) and Ⓢ (all guest rooms have sprinklers). Some properties have reserved rooms for non-smokers; look for the ⊘ symbol in the listing and be sure to request a smoke-free room both when you make a reservation and upon registration.

RESTAURANTS

Restaurants listed in this publication have been found to be consistently good dining establishments. In metropolitan areas, where many restaurants are above average, we select some of those known for the superiority of their food, service and atmosphere and also those offering a selection of quality food at moderate prices (including some cafeterias and family restaurants). In smaller communities the restaurants considered to be the best in the area may be listed.

The type of cuisine featured at a restaurant is used as a means of classification for restaurants. You will find listings for Steakhouses and Continental cuisine as well as a range of ethnic foods, such as Chinese, Japanese, Italian and yes, American. Special menu types, such as early bird, a la carte, children's or Sunday brunch, are also listed. We have tried to indicate something about each restaurant's atmosphere and appropriate attire. The availability of alcoholic beverages is shown, as well as entertainment and dancing.

Price ranges for an average, complete meal without alcoholic beverage are indicated by each $ symbol representing 10-dollar increments in the price range. Taxes and tips are not included.

Restaurant ratings are applied to two categories of operational style—full-service eating establishments, and self-service, family-dining operations such as cafeterias or buffets.

◆—Good but unpretentious dishes. Table settings are usually simple and may include paper placemats and napkins. Alcoholic beverage service, if any, may be limited to beer and wine. Usually informal with an atmosphere conducive to family dining.

◆◆—More extensive menus representing more complex food preparation and, usually, a wider variety of alcoholic beverages. The atmosphere is appealing and suitable for either family or adult dining. Service may be casual, but host or hostess seating can be expected. Table settings may include tablecloths and cloth napkins.

♦♦♦—Extensive or specialized menus and a more complex cuisine preparation requiring a professional chef contribute to either a formal dining experience or a special family meal. Cloth table linens, above-average quality table settings, a skilled service staff and an inviting decor should all be provided. Generally, the wine list includes representatives of the best domestic and foreign wine-producing regions.

♦♦♦♦—An appealing ambience is often enhanced by fresh flowers and fine furnishings. The overall sophistication and formal atmosphere visually create a dining experience more for adults than for families. A wine steward presents an extensive list of the best wines. Smartly attired, highly skilled staff is capable of describing how any dish is prepared. Elegant silverware, china and correct glassware are typical. The menu includes creative dishes prepared from fresh ingredients by a chef who frequently has international training. Eye-appealing desserts are offered at tableside.

♦♦♦♦♦—A world-class operation with even more luxury and sophistication than four-diamond restaurants. A proportionally large staff, expert in preparing tableside delicacies, provides flawless service. Tables are set with impeccable linens, silver and crystal glassware.

Buena Vista

Hotel Buena Vista Beach Resort
(formerly Spa Buena Vista)
♦♦ *Resort*

On shore of Bahía de Palmas, ¼ mile east of Highway 1. Phone (619) 425-1551, FAX 425-1832; (800) 752-3555. U.S. reservations agent: 16211 E Whittier Bl, Whittier, CA 90603.
All year   1P $65   2P $80
$15 per extra person. Resort on hillside overlooking the sea. 60 units. Shower baths; no phones, no TV. 2 pools, whirlpools, beach, scuba diving, tennis, horseback riding. Fishing trips arranged in cruisers and pangas. Meal plans available. 10% service charge. 30-day cancellation notice. Dining room open 6 a.m. to 9 p.m.; cocktails, bar. DI, MC, VI. ☐D

Cabo San Lucas

Lodging

Hotel Cabo San Lucas
♦♦♦ *Resort Complex*
On Chileno Bay, 11 miles east of Cabo San Lucas on Highway 1. Phone (213) 852-0824; (800) 733-2226. U.S. reservations agent: PO Box 48088, Los Angeles, CA 90048.
All year   1P $80-$180   2P $80-$180
$25 per extra person. Suites $145 to $180; 2- to 7-bedroom villas $265 to $1000. Holiday rates higher. Meal plans available. Hotel overlooking Gulf of California. Distinctive Colonial styling. 130 units. Cable TV, private balconies; some shower baths, fireplaces; some refrigerators. Pool, beach, scuba diving, snorkeling, sailboating, sailboarding, tennis, nature trails, horseback riding. Yacht anchorage. Fishing trips arranged. No pets. Dining room and terrace

(reservations only) open 6:30 to 10 a.m., noon to 2:30 and 7 to 10:30 p.m.; cocktails, bar, entertainment. 15% service charge. 14-day cancellation notice, 30 days for holiday periods. AE, MC, VI. **(See ad on back cover.)**

Club Cabo   *Motel*
3 miles east of town center; turn east off Highway 1 on road to Club Cascadas. Mailing address: Apdo Postal 463, Cabo San Lucas, BCS, Mexico. Phone 01152 (114) 3-3348.
All year   1P $35-$40   2P $40-$60
$5-$10 per extra person. 5 units. Motel-type rooms in RV park. Shower baths; 3 rooms with air conditioning, 4 with kitchen; no phones.

Hotel Finisterra   ♦♦♦ *Resort Complex*
Located on rugged promontory at southernmost tip of Baja California peninsula. Mailing address: Hotel Finisterra, Cabo San Lucas, BCS, Mexico. Phone 01152 (114) 3-0000, 3-0192; (714) 476-5555; (800) 347-2252.
All year   1P $90-$130   2P $99-$130
$10-$15 per extra person. Spectacular view of Land's End, the Gulf of California and the Pacific Ocean. 197 units. Cable TV, movies, radios, private balconies; some shower baths, efficiencies; 6 luxury suites with fireplace. 2 pools, whirlpools, beach, scuba diving, snorkeling, tennis, horseback riding. Fishing trips arranged. Dining room open 6:30 a.m. to 9:30 p.m.; cocktails, lounge, entertainment. 15% service charge. 7-day cancellation notice, 30 days for holiday periods. AE, MC, VI. ⊘ **(See ad page 185.)**

Hotel Hacienda   ♦♦♦ *Resort Complex*
South of Highway 1 on Cabo San Lucas Bay. Mailing address: Apdo Postal 34, Cabo San Lucas, BCS 23410, Mexico. Phone 01152 (114) 3-0122; (213) 852-0824; (800) 733-2226. U.S. reservations agent: PO Box 48088, Los Angeles, CA 90048.
All year   1P $99-$189   2P $99-$189
$25 per extra person. Townhouses $195 to $279 for up to 4 persons. Resort hotel overlooking the bay. 112 units. Cable TV, movies, shower baths, private balconies or patios; some air conditioning. Pool, beach, tennis, sailing, sailboarding, scuba diving, snorkeling, horseback riding. Yacht anchorage. Hunting; fishing trips arranged on various sized cruisers. 15% service charge. 14-day cancellation notice, 30 days for holidays. Dining room open 6:30 to 11 a.m., noon to 3 and 7 to 10 p.m.; cocktails, poolside bar; entertainment, snack bar. AE, MC, VI. **(See ad on back cover.)**

Marina Fiesta Resort Hotel   ♦♦♦ *Condominium Hotel*
Resort condo hotel on east side of the marina at Marina Lotes. Mailing address: Marina Lote 37, Cabo San Lucas, BCS, Mexico. Phone 01152 (114) 3-2856; (800) 332-2252. U.S. reservations: 9051-C Siempre Viva Rd, Suite 40-478, San Diego, CA 92173.
4/16-12/23   1P $110-$300   2P $110-$300
12/24-4/15   1P $125-$350   2P $125-$350
$30 per extra person in suites. 5- to 7-stories. 1-and 2-bedroom suites $240 to $375; penthouse suite $400. 115 units. Cable TV, movies, refrigerators, kitchens and utensils; some shower baths. Pool, whirlpools, exercise room, boat ramp, marina. No pets. Restaurant open 6 a.m. to 10 p.m.; cocktails. 2-day cancellation notice. AE, MC, VI. **(See ad page 186.)**

Hotel Plaza Las Glorias   *Hotel*

Part of a large complex that includes condominiums and a shopping center, between Bl Marina and the harbor. Mailing address: Bl Marina s/n Lotes 9 y 10, Cabo San Lucas, BCS 23410, Mexico. Phone 01152 (114) 3-1220; reservations (800) 342-2644.

All year   1P $80-$130   2P $90-$155

$15 per extra person. 287 units. Cable TV, some refrigerators. Pool, fishing. 2 restaurants, open 7 a.m. to 11 p.m.; cocktails.

Pueblo Bonito Resort   ♦♦♦ *Resort Hotel*

3 blocks south of Highway 1 on El Médano. Mailing address: Apdo Postal 460, Cabo San Lucas, BCS, Mexico. Phone 01152 (114) 3-2900; FAX 3-1995; (800) 262-4500.

4/7-12/21   1P $145-$180   2P $145-$180
12/22-4/6   1P $185-$225   2P $185-$225

$30 per extra person. New beach-front hotel on Cabo San Lucas Bay. 141 units. Cable TV, movies, efficiencies. Pool, exercise room, beach, scuba diving, snorkeling, boating. Fishing trips arranged. No pets. 10% service charge. 2 restaurants, open 7 a.m. to 10 p.m.

In the route descriptions, towns that contain stores and facilities useful to the traveler are show in heavy black print.

Siesta Suites Hotel ♦♦ *Suite Hotel*
Downtown near the marina on Calle E Zapata at Hidalgo. Mailing address: Apdo Postal 310, Cabo San Lucas, BCS, Mexico. Phone 01152 (114) 3-2773; phone & FAX (909) 945-5940. U.S. reservations: 8966 Citation Ct, Alta Loma, CA 91737.

All year 1P $41-$50 2P $41-$50

$10 per extra person. 15 units. Shower baths, kitchens with utensils; some air conditioning, some radios; no TV, no phones. Pool. Fishing trips arranged. No pets. 15-day cancellation notice.

Solmar Suites Resort ♦♦ *Resort Complex*
Resort located on the southernmost tip of the peninsula. Phone 01152 (114) 3-0022; (310) 459-9861; (800) 344-3349. U.S. reservations: PO Box 383, Pacific Palisades, CA 90272.

All year 1P $130-$180 2P $130-$180

$22-$26 per extra person. 90 units. Most rooms face the Pacific Ocean. Cable TV, movies, private balconies. 3 pools, whirlpools, beach, diving, snorkeling, tennis. Fishing trips on cruisers. MAP and AP plans available. 10% service charge. 7-day cancellation notice. Restaurant open 6:30 a.m. to 10 p.m.; cocktails, entertainment, poolside bar. AE, MC, VI.

Restaurants

Carlos 'n Charlie's ♦♦ *Mexican*
On Bl Marina 20. Varied menu. Phone 01152 (114) 3-1280.
$9 to $20. Open noon to midnight. Cocktails. AE, CB, DI, MC, VI.

Da Giorgio ♦♦♦ *Italian*
3 miles northeast of town center, then ½ mile south, adjacent to Misiones del Cabo. No phone.
$10 to $18. Open 8 a.m. to 11 p.m. Open-air, palapa-covered structure with view of Land's End. Seafood and pasta. Cocktails, bar. AE, MC, VI.

Peacocks/Pavo Real Restaurant ♦♦ *Continental*
Two blocks southeast of Highway 1 on Paseo del Pescador. Phone 01152 (114) 3-1858.
$18 to $28. Open 6 to 11 p.m. European cuisine. Cocktails, bar.

Ristorante Galeón Italiano ♦♦ *Italian*
½ mile south of town center on Bl Marina across from the wharf. Phone 01152 (114) 3-0443.
$10 to $20. Open 4 to 11 p.m. View of the bay and the town. Pasta, veal and seafood. Cocktails, bar. MC, VI.

Romeo y Julieta Ristorante ♦♦ *Italian*
¼ mile south of town center at entrance to Pedregal condominium district. Phone 01152 (114) 3-0225.
$8 to $18. Open 4 to 11 p.m. Quaint hacienda atmosphere. Pasta, pizza and seafood. Cocktails. MC, VI.

Salsitas   ♦ *Mexican*
At the marina in Plaza Bonita shopping center. Phone 01152 (114) 3-1740.
$9 to $17. Open 7 a.m. to 11 p.m. Indoor and outdoor seating with variety of
Mexican dishes. Cocktails. AE, MC, VI.

Villa Alfonso's Restaurante   ♦♦♦ *Nouvelle Mexican*
Between Bl Lázaro Cárdenas and the bay on El Médano. Phone 01152 (114)
3-0739.
$21-$30. Open 6 to 10:30 p.m. Mexican Colonial house with dining room and
patio features international nouvelle cuisine. Cocktails. MC, VI.

Cataviña

Hotel La Pinta   *Motor Inn*
On Highway 1, 1 mile north of Rancho Santa Inés. Mailing address: Apdo
Postal 179, San Quintín, BC, Mexico. Phone (619) 422-6900; (800) 336-
5454. U.S. reservations agent: Mexico Resorts International, 740 Bay Bl,
Suite 105, Chula Vista, CA 91910.
All year   1P $60   2P $65
$10 per extra person; maximum 4 persons per room. Suite $125. Spanish-style
hotel in scenic rock-strewn area. 28 units. Cable TV, shower baths; no phones.
No electricity 2 to 4 p.m. Pool, recreation room, playground. Dining room open
7 a.m. to 10:30 p.m.; cocktails, bar. 3-day cancellation notice. MC, VI. **(See ad
page 191.)**

Ensenada

Lodging

Casa del Sol Motel   ♦ *Motel*
At avs López Mateos and Blancarte. Mailing address: Apdo Postal 557, En-
senada, BC 22800, Mexico. Phone 01152 (617) 8-1570; (800) 528-1234.
All year   1P $48-$53   2P $58-$68
$8 per extra person. 48 units. Cable TV, shower baths; some air conditioning,
some kitchens. Pool. Small pets. 3-day cancellation notice. Restaurant, bar, gift
shop adjacent. AE, MC, VI.

El Cid Motor Hotel   *Motor Inn*
At Av López Mateos 993. Mailing address: Apdo Postal 1431, Ensenada, BC
22800, Mexico. Phone 01152 (617) 8-2401; FAX 8-3671. U.S. reservations:
PO Box 786, Chula Vista, CA 91910.
All year   1P $52   2P $72
Motor inn with attractive Spanish styling. 52 units. Suites available. Air conditioning, cable TV, radios; some shower baths, some private balconies. Pool. No
pets. Fishing trips arranged. No pets. 3-day cancellation notice. Dining room
and coffee shop open 7:30 a.m. to 10:30 p.m.; cocktails, lounge. **(See ad page
189.)**

Ensenada Travelodge ♦♦ *Motor Inn*
At Av Blancarte 130, near Av López Mateos. Mailing address: Av Blancarte
130, Ensenada, BC, Mexico. Phone 01152 (617) 8-1601; (800) 578-7878.
All year   1P $70   2P $75-$90
$8 per extra person. Family rates available. Suites available. 52 units. Cable TV,
movies, radios, shower baths. Heated pool, whirlpool. No pets. 7-day cancellation notice. Restaurant open 7:30 a.m. to 11 p.m. Cocktails, bar. AE, MC, VI.
Ⓓ ⊘ **(See ad below.)**

Estero Beach Resort Hotel ♦♦ *Resort Complex*

8 miles south of city center via Highway 1 and graded side road. Mailing address: Apdo Postal 86, Ensenada, BC, Mexico. Phone 01152 (617) 6-6230.

| 5/1-9/10 | 1P ... | 2P $48-$82 |
| 9/11-4/30 | 1P ... | 2P $28-$72 |

$6 per extra person. Suites $110-$180. Beach-front resort complex on attractive grounds. 115 units. Cable TV, many private patios or balconies; some shower baths. Beach, tennis, recreation room, archaeological museum, gift shop, boat ramp, boat rentals, water skiing, fishing, horseback riding. No pets. 3-day cancellation notice. Restaurant open 8 a.m. to 10 p.m.; cocktails. MC, VI. ∅

Hotel La Pinta *Motor Inn*

At Av Floresta and Bl Bucaneros. Mailing address: Apdo Postal 929, Ensenada, BC 22800, Mexico. Phone 01152 (617) 6-2601. U.S. reservations agent: Mexico Resorts International, 740 Bay Bl, Suite 105, Chula Vista, CA 91901. (800) 336-5454; (619) 422-6900.

| Fri-Sat | 1P $60 | 2P $65 |
| Sun-Thu | 1P $40 | 2P $45 |

$10 per extra person. 52 units. Cable TV, shower baths. Pool. No pets. 3-day cancellation notice. Restaurant open 7:30 a.m. to 10 p.m. MC, VI. **(See ad page 191.)**

Hotel Misión Santa Isabel *Hotel*

At Bl Lázaro Cárdenas and Av Castillo. Mailing address: Apdo Postal 76, Ensenada, BC 22800, Mexico. Phone 01152 (617) 8-3616; (619) 259-6260. US reservations agent: 1085 Woodside Wy, Del Mar, CA 92014.

| All year | 1P $60 | 2P $65 |

$10 per extra person. Suites $82-$88. Charming colonial-style hotel. 58 units. Cable TV, shower baths. Facilities for meetings, pool. 3-day cancellation notice. Restaurant open 7 a.m. to 11 p.m.; cocktails, bar.

Hotel Santo Tomás *Motel*

On Bl Lázaro Cárdenas (Costero) at Av Miramar. Mailing address: Bl Lázaro Cárdenas 609, Ensenada, BC, México. Phone 01152 (617) 8-1503; (800) 528-1234.

| Fri-Sat | 1P $54 | 2P $58 |
| Sun-Thu | 1P $50 | 2P $54 |

$4 per extra person. 3-story motel. 80 units. Cable TV, shower baths. No pets. 3-day cancellation notice.

Restaurants

Casino Royal Restaurant ♦♦♦ *French*

Southeast of main hotel row at Bl Las Dunas 118, near Bl Lázaro Cárdenas. Phone 01152 (617) 7-1480.

$11 to $20. Open noon to midnight. Elegantly decorated mansion style building. Cocktails. MC, VI.

El Rey Sol Restaurant ♦♦♦ *French*

½ mile south of town center on Av López Mateos at Av Blancarte. Phone 01152 (617) 8-1733.

$9 to $22. Open 7:30 a.m. to 11 p.m. French and Mexican cuisine. Cocktails, bar. AE, MC, VI. **(See ad page 189.)**

Now You Can Travel Baja Without Changing Hotels.

Take advantage of La Pinta's "Baja Travel Pass" coupon book for $119.50 per person double occupancy (plus tax). You'll enjoy La Pinta's regular low rates along with free breakfast daily.

Your Travel Pass book includes: 4 nights' accommodations at any of six locations and full breakfast daily. Plus these special bonuses:

- $5 food and beverage bonus (per person/per night) available at our Ensenada and Loreto locations.

- Coupon for two jumbo margaritas at any location.

- 50% Discount coupon off your next visit to our Ensenada location (not good in conjunction with "Travel Pass").

Passbook coupons may be used at one location for 4 nights or in any desired combination of 4 different locations. Stays need not be consecutive.

Why carry cash when you can pre-pay your trip and save money too!

LODGING AND RESTAURANTS
Ensenada

Enrique's Restaurant ♦ *Mexican*
On Highway 1-D, 1½ miles north of town center. Phone 01152 (617) 8-2461.
$4 to $16. Open 8 a.m. to 11:30 p.m. Closed January 1, May 1, September 16, December 25. Mexican food, steaks and seafood. Cocktails. MC, VI.

Haliotis ♦♦ *Seafood*
On Calle Delante (Agustín Sanginés) 179, ½ mile east of Highway 1. Phone 01152 (617) 6-3720.
$6 to $15. Open Wednesday through Monday 1 to 11 p.m. Seafood, chicken and beef. Beer and wine. MC, VI.

La Cueva de los Tigres ♦ *Seafood*
2½ miles south of town center on Mexico Highway 1, then ½ mile west on gravel road. Phone 01152 (617) 8-2653.
$7 to $25. Open 11 a.m. to midnight. Closed January 1, March 20, May 1, September 16, December 25. Attractive beachfront restaurant features seafood, steaks and Mexican cuisine. Cocktails, lounge. MC, VI.

▬ ˙
Guerrero Negro

Lodging

Hotel El Morro *Motel*
1 mile west of Highway 1 on east edge of town. Mailing address: Apdo Postal 144, Guerrero Negro, BCS 23940, Mexico. Phone 01152 (115) 7-0414.
All year   1P $26   2P $27-$31
$4 per extra person. Modest motel. 32 units. Fans (no air conditioning), shower baths; no phones. Restaurant open noon to 10 p.m.; bar.

Hotel La Pinta *Motor Inn*
On Highway 1 at the 28th parallel. Mailing address: Guerrero Negro, BCS 23940, Mexico. US reservations agent: Mexico Resorts International, 740 Bay Bl, Suite 105, Chula Vista, CA 91910. Phone 01152 (115) 7-1300; (619) 422-6900; (800) 336-5454.
All year   1P $60   2P $65
$10 per extra person. 4-person maximum per room. Single-story hotel near Paralelo 28 monument. 27 units. Shower baths, 2-bed rooms; no air conditioning, no phones. No pets. 3-day cancellation notice. Dining room open 7 a.m. to 10:30 p.m.; cocktails, bar. Trailer park adjacent. **(See ad page 191.)**

Restaurant

Malarrimo Restaurant ♦ *Seafood*
1 mile west of Highway 1 on east edge of town. Phone 01152 (115) 7-0250.
$6 to $14. Open 7:30 a.m. to 10:30 p.m. Seafood and Mexican specialties; bar; museum, tourist information. Cocktails.

La Paz

Lodging

Cabañas de los Arcos ♦♦ *Motel*
Opposite the malecón, at Alvaro Obregón and Rosales. Mailing address: Apdo Postal 112, La Paz, BCS 23000, Mexico. Phone 01152 (112) 2-2744, FAX 5-4313; (714) 476-5555, FAX 476-5560. Reservations: 18552 MacArthur Bl, Irvine, CA 92715.
All year 1P $72 2P $75
$10 per extra person. Four-story hotel wing and 16 bungalows in tropical garden setting. 52 units. Cable TV, movies, radios, shower baths. Pool. Fishing trips arranged. No pets. 7-day cancellation notice. Restaurant and bar at Hotel Los Arcos, ½ block away. AE, MC, VI.

Casa La Paceña Guest House *Cottage*
On Bravo two blocks from La Paz Bay. Mailing Address: Apdo Postal 158, La Paz, BCS 23000, Mexico. Phone 01152 (112) 5-2748.
11/15-6/15 1P $30 2P $35
$5 per extra person. Open 11/15 to 6/15. 3 units. Radios, shower baths, bay view, TV in common room; no phones. Pets. 5-day cancellation notice.

Hotel Los Arcos ♦♦ *Hotel*
Opposite the malecón, facing La Paz Bay, at Alvaro Obregón and Allende. Mailing address: Apdo Postal 112, La Paz, BCS, Mexico. Phone 01152 (112) 2-2744, FAX 5-4313; (714) 476-5555, FAX 476-5560. Reservations: 18552 MacArthur Bl, Irvine, CA 92715.
All year 1P $72 2P $75
$10 per extra person. Suite $85. Colonial-style hotel. 130 units. Cable TV, movies, radios, shower baths. Pool, sauna. Fishing trips arranged. No pets. 7-day cancellation notice. Coffee shop open 7 a.m. to 10 p.m.; dining room open noon to 11 p.m. (see listing); cocktails, bar. AE, MC, VI. **(See ad page 185.)**

Hotel Mediterrane *Lodge*
On Allende ½ block from Bl Alvaro Obregón. Mailing address: Allende 36-B, La Paz, BCS 23000, Mexico. Phone & FAX 01152 (112) 5-1195.
10/1-8/31 1P $30-$40 2P $30-$40
$5 per extra person. Open 10/1-8/31. Mexican/European style villa. 5 units. Radios, shower baths; some air conditioning; no phones. Fishing trips arranged. Restaurant adjacent. 5-day cancellation notice.

Restaurants

Caballo Blanco de la Paz ♦♦ *Mexican*
1½ miles southwest of town center at Abasolo (Highway 1) and Jalisco. Phone 01152 (112) 5-5952.
$8 to $18. Open noon to midnight. Hacienda style setting. Mexican cuisine featuring steak and seafood. Cocktails.

El Molino Steak House ♦ *Steak & Seafood*
At the marina on Bahía de la Paz, Legaspy and Topete. Phone 01152 (112) 2-6191.

$9 to $19. Open noon to midnight. Palapa setting features steak, seafood and poultry; cocktails, bar. MC, VI.

El Taste   ♦♦ *Mexican*
½ mile southwest of town center on Paseo Alvaro Obregón at Juárez. Phone 01152 (112) 2-8121.
$9 to $18. Open 8 a.m. to midnight. Overlooks the malecón and the bay. Mexican cuisine including beef and seafood. Cocktails. MC, VI.

La Paz - Lapa de Carlos 'n Charlies   ♦ *Mexican*
On Alvaro Obregón at 16 de Septiembre. Phone 01152 (112) 2-6025.
$9 to $20. Open Wednesday through Monday, noon to 11 p.m. Palapa and patio dining on waterfront. Mexican cuisine, including steaks and seafood. Cocktails. MC, VI.

La Pazta   ♦♦ *Italian*
On Allende ½ block from Bl Alvaro Obregón, near Hotel Mediterrane. Phone 01152 (112) 5-1195.
$9 to $15. Open 1 to 10 p.m., closed Tuesdays. Trattoria featuring fresh pasta made to order and Swiss dishes and fondues. AE, MC, VI.

Restaurant Bermejo   ♦♦ *Mexican*
In the Hotel Los Arcos. Phone 01152 (112) 2-2744.
$15 to $25. Open noon to 11 p.m. Attractive dining room with view of bay. Cocktails, bar. Seafood, steak and Mexican dishes. AE, MC, VI.

▬
Loreto

Lodging

Hotel La Pinta   *Motor Inn*
On beach, 1 mile north of town plaza. Mailing address: Apdo Postal 28, Loreto, BCS, Mexico. Phone 01152 (113) 5-0025; (619) 422-6900; (800) 336-5454. U.S. reservations agent: 740 Bay Bl, Suite 105, Chula Vista,CA 91910.

| All year | 1P $48-$60 | 2P $50-$65 |

$12 per extra person; 4-person maximum per room. 49 units. Spacious rooms. Shower baths, private patios; some TVs, fireplaces; no phones. Pool, beach, tennis. Fishing trips and golf arranged. Pets. 3-day cancellation notice. Dining room open 7 a.m. to 10 p.m.; cocktails, bar. MC, VI. **(See ad page 191.)**

Hotel Mercure El Cortés   ♦♦ *Resort Hotel*
(formerly Loreto Inn)
At Nopoló, 8½ miles south via Highway 1 and paved road to beach. Mailing address: Apdo Postal 35, Loreto, BCS 23880, Mexico. Phone 01152 (113) 3-0700, FAX 3-0377; (800) 472-3394. U.S. reservations: 16211 E Whittier Bl, Whittier, CA 90603.

| 2/1-3/31 | 1P $70 | 2P $70 |
| 4/1-1/31 | 1P $70-$85 | 2P $70-$85 |

$15 per extra person. 4-person maximum per room. 8 suites, $110. Modern 3-story hotel on beach with attractive landscaping. 130 units. Most rooms have private patios. Cable TV, movies, shower baths. 2 pools, beach, tennis, golf. Fishing trips arranged, scuba diving, boating, sailboarding and horseback riding. No pets. 2 restaurants and coffee shop open 7 a.m. to 11 p.m.; cocktails, bar. AE, DI, MC, VI. **(See ad page 195.)**

Hotel Oasis
Motor Inn
On shore of Loreto Bay, ½ mile south of town plaza. Mailing address: Apdo Postal 17, Loreto, BCS 23880, Mexico Phone 01152 (113) 5-0112.

4/1-10/31 [AP]	1P $75	2P $100
11/1-3/31	1P $45	2P $55

$20 to $40 per extra person. Set in palm grove. 35 units. Spacious rooms. Shower baths, 2 double or 3 single beds; some patios. Pool, beach, tennis. Fishing trips arranged in cruisers and pangas. 30-day cancellation notice. Dining room open 4:30 to 11 a.m., 12:30 to 3 and 6:30 to 8:45 p.m.; cocktails, bar.

Restaurant

El Nido Steakhouse
◆◆ *Steak & Seafood*
At town entrance 1 mile east of Highway 1 on Salvatierra 154. Phone 01152 (113) 5-0284.
$9 to $17. Open noon to 11 p.m. Closed December 25. Ranch atmosphere. Cocktails. MC, VI.

Mexicali

Lodging

Holiday Inn ◆◆◆ *Motor Inn*
On Bl Benito Juárez, 5 miles southeast of border crossing. Mailing address: PO Box 5497, Calexico, CA 92231. Phone 01152 (65) 66-1300; (800) 465-4329.
All year   1P $79   2P $86
$10 per extra person. Suites $96 to $103 for 2 persons. Tastefully furnished motor hotel. 171 units. Cable TV, radios. Pool, 1 lighted tennis court. No pets. Facilities for meetings. Restaurant and coffee shop open 7 a.m. to 1 a.m.; cocktails, bar, entertainment. AE, MC, VI.

Holiday Inn Crowne Plaza ◆◆◆ *Hotel*
At Bl López Mateos and Av de los Héroes in Centro Cívico Comercial. Mailing address: Av de los Héroes 201, Mexicali, BC 21000, Mexico. Phone 01152 (65) 57-3600; (619) 470-3475.
All year   1P $110-$140   2P $110-$140
$20 per extra person. Family plan available. New high-rise hotel. 158 units. Cable TV, movies, radios. Pool. 3-day cancellation notice. 2 restaurants open 6:00 a.m. to 1 a.m.; cocktails, bar. AE, MC, VI. Ⓓ ⊘

Hotel Lucerna ◆◆ *Motor Inn*
At Bl Benito Juárez 2151, 5½ miles southeast of border crossing. Mailing addresses: Bl Benito Juárez 2151, Mexicali, BC 21270, Mexico; PO Box 2300, Calexico, CA 92231. Phone 01152 (65) 66-1000; (800) 582-3762.
All year   1P $70   2P $73
$12 per extra person. Suites $86 to $132. Beautifully landscaped grounds. 175 units. Cable TV, radios, refrigerators, some shower baths, some private balconies. Meeting rooms available. 2 pools, tennis. No pets. 1-day cancellation notice. 2 dining rooms (see listing) and coffee shop open 7 a.m. to 2 a.m.; cocktails, bar, nightclub, gift shop. AE, DI, MC, VI.

Restaurant

Rívoli ◆◆◆ *French*
At Bl Benito Juárez 2151 in the Hotel Lucerna. Phone 01152 (65) 66-1000.
$15 to $32. Open 7 p.m. to 1 a.m. Monday through Saturday. Varied menu. Cocktails. AE, DI, MC, VI.

Mulegé

Lodging

Hotel Hacienda *Historic Hotel*
In center of town at Francisco Madero across from town plaza. Mailing address: Francisco I. Madero 3, Mulegé, BCS, Mexico. Phone 01152 (115) 3-0021; (800) 464-8888.
All year   1P $25   2P $25

$5 per extra person. 16 units. Historic 2-story inn with landscaped interior patio. Shower baths; some air conditioning, some fans; no phones. Pool, rental mountain bikes. 3-day cancellation notice. Restaurant open 8 a.m. to 10 p.m.; cocktails, bar. Banquet with entertainment on Sunday.

Hotel Serenidad   *Motor Inn*
At mouth of river, 2½ miles south of town off Highway 1. Mailing address: Apdo Postal 9, Mulegé, BCS 23900, Mexico. Phone 01152 (115) 3-0530; FAX 3-0311.
All year   1P $40-$43   2P $50-$53
$9 per extra person. 2-bedroom cottages, $99. Ranch-style resort on shore of river. 50 units. Shower baths, 2-bed rooms; no phones. Pool. Fishing trips arranged in cruisers and skiffs. Airstrip; aviation gasoline available. Auto mechanic available. Gift shop. Dining room open 6:30 a.m. to 9:30 p.m.; cocktails, bar. Banquet with live music on Wednesday and Saturday.

Restaurant

Las Casitas   ♦ *Mexican*
In the hotel of the same name in center of town. Phone 01152 (115) 3-0019.
$6 to $16. Attractive patio setting. Mexican cuisine, specializing in beef and seafood. Features Friday evening fiesta buffet with mariachi band. Cocktails. Open 7:30 a.m. to 10 p.m.

Punta Chivato

Hotel Punta Chivato   *Hotel*
On Punta Chivato, 15 miles east of Highway 1 (turnoff 15 miles north of Mulegé). Mailing address: Apdo Postal 18, Mulegé, BCS, Mexico. Phone 01152 (115) 3-0188.
All year   1P $45-$55   2P $45-$55
$10 per extra person. Resort situated on a low bluff overlooking the gulf. 34 units. Shower baths, private patios; no phones. Pool, beach, scuba diving, fishing trips arranged in skiffs (pangas). 7-day cancellation notice. Airstrip (unicom on 122.8 for incoming aircraft). Gasoline and aviation fuel. Dining room open 6 a.m. to 9 p.m.; cocktails, bar.

Rosarito

Lodging

Brisas Del Mar Motel   *Motor Inn*
In center of town on Bl Benito Juárez 22. Mailing address: PO Box 1867, Chula Vista, CA 91912. Phone 01152 (611) 2-2547 (phone and FAX); (619) 685-1246; (800) 697-5223.
6/1-9/30 & Fri-Sat   1P $53-$63   2P $53-$63
10/1-5/31 Sun-Thu   1P $43-$63   2P $43-$63
Two-story motel. 66 units. Cable TV. Pool, playground. No pets. 3-day cancellation notice. Restaurant open 7 a.m. to 10:30 p.m; cocktails.

198

Calafia *Motel*
On Highway 1, 6½ miles south of town center. Mailing address: PO Box
433857, San Ysidro, CA 92143. Phone 01152 (661) 2-1581, FAX 2-1580;
(800) 225-2342.

3/1-9/30	1P ...	2P $36-$59
10/1-2/28	1P ...	2P $22-$49

$10 per extra person. 60 units. 1-, 2- and 3-bedroom mobile homes with
kitchens. Historic location on a bluff overlooking the ocean. Cable TV, shower
baths; no phones. Pool; museum. Restaurant; Mon-Thu 9 a.m. to 10 p.m., Fri-
Sun 8 a.m. to 11 p.m.; cocktails, bar; disco. 3-day cancellation notice. **(See ad
below.)**

Hotel Festival Plaza *Hotel*
In center of town on Bl Benito Juárez. Mailing address: Bl Benito Juárez E,
Rosarito, BC 22710. Phone 01152 (661) 2-2950 (phone and FAX); (800)
453-8606.

4/1-9/8	1P ...	2P $30-$65
9/9-3/31	1P ...	2P $25-$60

$10 per extra person. 8-story hotel. 1 block from beach; ocean-view rooms.
120 units. 13 villas. Cable TV, shower baths. Amusement park; whirlpool. Cafeteria, restaurant, bar; nightclubs. AE, MC, VI.

**In the route descriptions, towns that contain stores and
facilities useful to the traveler are show in heavy black print.**

Las Rocas Hotel and Suites   ♦♦♦ *Motor Inn*

6 miles south of town on Highway 1. Mailing address: PO Box 8851, Chula Vista, CA 92012. Phone 01152 (661) 2-2145, 2-2140; (800) 733-6394.
6/1-9/30 &

Fri-Sat 10/1-5/31	1P $70-$90	2P $70-$90
10/1-5/31	1P $60-$90	2P $60-$90

$8 per extra person. Suites $110-$150. New hotel on a bluff overlooking the ocean. 74 units. Cable TV; some refrigerators, microwaves, fireplaces, ocean-view balconies. Pool, whirlpool, tennis. No pets. 3-day cancellation notice. Restaurant open 7:30 a.m. to 10 p.m. Cocktails. AE, MC, VI. **(See ad below.)**

Residence Inn Marriott Real Del Mar   *Suite Hotel*

Off Highway 1D (toll road), 7 miles north of town center by Real del Mar Golf Club. Mailing address: Km 19.5, Tijuana, Baja California, Mexico. Phone 01152 (661) 3-3453; (800) 331-3131.

6/1-9/30 & Fri-Sat	1P $79-$149	2P $79-$169
10/1-5/31 Sun-Thu	1P $69-$109	2P $69-$139

$10 per extra person. New all-suite hotel overlooking the ocean. 62 units. Cable TV, VCPs. Pool, whirlpool, exercise room. Dining room open 11 a.m. to 10 p.m.; cocktails.

Rosarito Beach Hotel   *Resort Hotel*

In south part of town on Bl Benito Juárez, facing the Pacific Ocean. U.S. reservations agent: PO Box 430145, San Diego, CA 92143. Phone 01152 (661) 2-1106; (619) 498-8230; (800) 343-8582.
4/1-9/11 &

Fri-Sat 9/12-3/31	1P $59-$119	2P $59-$119
Sun-Thu 9/12-3/31	1P $39-$99	2P $39-$99

$10 per extra person. 280 units. Suites. Facilities for meetings. Cable TV, shower baths; some rooms with private balcony. 2 pools, 3 whirlpools, beach, sauna, gym, racquetball, basketball, tennis. No pets. 3-day cancellation notice. 2 restaurants open 7:30 a.m. to 10 p.m.; buffet with live music Friday and Saturday evenings; cocktails, 2 bars; gift shop. MC, VI. **(See ad page 200.)**

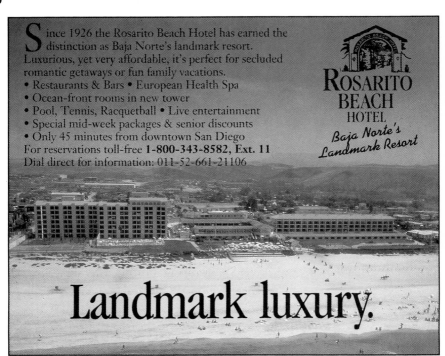
Restaurants

El Nido Steakhouse   ♦♦ *Steak & Seafood*
At Bl Benito Juárez 67. Phone 01152 (661) 2-1431.
$8 to $15. Open 8 a.m. to midnight. Closed September 16 and December 25. Ranch atmosphere. Cocktails.

Los Pelícanos   ♦♦ *Steak & Seafood*
On the beach at Calle Ebano 113. Phone 01152 (661) 2-1757.
$8 to $15. Open 8 a.m. to midnight. Closed September 16 and December 25. Cocktails. MC, VI.

▬
San Felipe

Lodging

Motel El Capitán   *Motor Inn*
On Av Mar de Cortez, corner of Manzanillo across from State Tourism office. Mailing address: PO Box 1916, Calexico, CA 92232. Phone 01152 (657) 7-1303.

Fri-Sat	1P $45	2P $45 (up to 4 persons)
Sun-Thu	1P $36	2P $36 (up to 4 persons)

$5 per extra person. 40 units. Shower baths; some color TVs, radios. Pool. Sailboat charters arranged. 3-day cancellation notice. Restaurant open 7 a.m. to 10 p.m., bar.

Experience the Sea of Cortez
At San Felipe's Best Resort

186 rooms and 31 suites with color TV via satellite,
air conditioning and telephones.
3 swimming pools, with swim-up bar.
Basketball court and 2 tennis courts.
Gift and curio shop.
Los Pelicanos Bar and La Terraza Restaurant.
Fishing and Sail boats nearby.
The best beach for swimming, sunbathing,
jogging or just plain walking.

Hotel **Las Misiones**
BEACH RESORT AND TENNIS COMPLEX
SAN FELIPE, BAJA CALIFORNIA

MEXICO RESORTS INTERNATIONAL
800-336-5454
Box 120637 • Chula Vista, CA 91912
4126 Bonita Rd., Bonita, CA 91902

Hotel Las Misiones ♦ *Motel*
1¼ miles south of town at Av Misión de Loreto 148. Phone 01152 (657) 7-
1281; (619) 472-6767; (800) 336-5454. U.S. reservations agent: 233 Paulin
Av, Box 7544, Calexico, CA 92231.
All year   1P $76   2P $76
$22 per extra person; special rates for children. 3-story hotel. 185 units. Cable
TV, movies; some rooms with private balcony, some efficiencies, some refriger-
ators. 2 pools, beach, tennis, meeting facilities. 3-day cancellation notice.
Restaurant and coffee shop open 7 to 11 a.m., 6 to 11 p.m.; cocktails, bar. AE,
MC, VI. **(See ad page 201.)**

Restaurants

El Nido Steakhouse ♦♦ *Steakhouse*
¼ mile south of town center on Av Mar de Cortez. No phone.
$9 to $18. Ranch atmosphere. Features steaks and seafood. Cocktails. Open
Thursday through Tuesday, 2 to 11 p.m.

▬ San Ignacio

Hotel La Pinta *Motor Inn*
1 mile west of Highway 1, on entrance highway leading to town plaza.
Mailing address: Apdo Postal 37, San Ignacio, BCS 23943, Mexico. Phone
01152 (115) 4-0300; (619) 422-6900; (800) 336-5454. U.S. reservations
agent: Mexico Resorts International, 740 Bay Bl, Suite 105, Chula Vista,
CA 91910.
All year   1P $60   2P $65
$10 per extra person; 4-person maximum per room. Spanish-style single-story
hotel set in palm grove with rooms facing interior patio. 28 units. Shower baths,
2-bed rooms; no phones. Pool, recreation room. 3-day cancellation notice. Dining room open 7 a.m. to 10:30 p.m.; cocktails, bar. MC, VI. **(See ad page
191.)**

▬ San José del Cabo

Lodging

Hotel Aguamarina *Hotel*
On beach 1½ miles west of town. Mailing address: Apdo Postal 53, San
José del Cabo, BCS, Mexico. Phone 01152 (114) 2-0110; (800) 897-5700.
4/2-12/19   1P $60   2P $60
12/20-4/1   1P $70   2P $70
$5-$10 per extra person. 99 units. Shower baths, some ocean-view rooms and
balconies. Pool, beach, fishing. 3-day cancellation notice. Dining room open 7
a.m. to 10:30 p.m.; cocktails.

Meliá Cabo Real ♦♦♦ *Resort Hotel*
On Highway 1, 7 miles west of town. Mailing address: Carretera a Cabo San
Lucas, Km. 19, San José del Cabo, BCS, Mexico. Phone 01152 (114) 3-
0967; (800) 336-3542.

| 4/20-12/19 | 1P $138 | 2P $138 |
| 12/20-4/19 | 1P $180 | 2P $180 |

$40 per extra person. Spacious ocean-front grounds. 309 units. Movies, VCPs. Pool, whirlpool, golf, tennis, scuba diving, snorkeling, fishing trips arranged.10% service charge. 3-day cancellation notice. 3 restaurants open 24 hours; cocktails. AE, MC, VI. [D]

Presidente Intercontinental Los Cabos ♦♦♦ *Resort Hotel*
On beach 1¼ miles west of town. Mailing address: Apdo Postal 2, San José del Cabo, BCS 23400, Mexico. Phone 01152 (114) 2-0211; FAX 2-0232; (800) 327-0206.

| 2/1-12/23 | 1P $120-$170 | 2P $120-$190 |
| 12/24-1/31 | 1P $145-$205 | 2P $145-$205 |

$20-$25 per extra person. 240 units. Suite available. Cable TV, movies, shower baths. Pool, tennis, scuba diving, snorkeling, boat rentals, fishing trips arranged. No pets. 10% service charge. 3-day cancellation notice. Dining room and coffee shop open 7 a.m. to 10:30 p.m.; cocktails, bar, disco. AE, CB, DI, MC, VI.

Tropicana Inn   *Motor Inn*
On Bl Mijares just south of town plaza. Mailing address: Bl Mijares 30, San José del Cabo, BCS 23400, Mexico. Phone 01152 (114) 2-1580, FAX 2-1590; FAX in USA (510) 939-2725.

| 5/1-12/20 | 1P $52 | 2P $52 |
| 12/21-4/30 | 1P $69 | 2P $69 |

$10 per extra person; children under 12 free. 2-story motel. 40 units. Attractive Mexican style. Cable TV, showers. Pool. No pets. 7-day cancellation notice. Restaurant open 8 a.m to 11 p.m.; cocktails. AE, MC, VI.

Restaurants

Da Giorgio Restaurant   ♦ *Italian*
5 miles west on Highway 1 near Hotel Palmilla on a hill overlooking the gulf. No phone.
$10 to $18. Open 3 to 11 p.m. Cocktails, bar. AE, MC, VI.

Damiana   ♦ *Mexican*
East side of town plaza at Boulevard Mijares No 8. Phone 01152 (114) 2-0499.
$9 to $20. Open 9 a.m. to 11 p.m. Patio and inside dining with Mexican and seafood cuisine. Cocktails, bar. MC, VI.

Ivan's European Restaurant   ♦ *Continental*
On Bl Mijares near town center; second floor overlooking town plaza. No phone.
$11 to $16. Open 7 a.m. to 11 p.m. Varied European cuisine. Cocktails.

Tropicana Bar & Grill   ♦ *Mexican*
On Bl Mijares just south of town plaza. Phone 01152 (114) 2-1580.
$10-$18. Open 8 a.m. to 11 p.m. Hacienda and patio dining featuring Mexican and European entrees. Cocktails. AE, MC, VI.

San Quintín

Motel Chávez
Motel

On Highway 1, 1½ miles north of the military camp. Mailing address: Apdo Postal 32, Valle de San Quintín, BC 22930, Mexico. Phone 01152 (616) 5-2005; (619) 479-3451. U.S. reservations agent: 2906 Morton Wy, San Diego, CA 92139.

All year   1P $21   2P $28

2-bed room for up to 4 persons, $28. 33 units. Fans, shower baths; no phones, no air conditioning. Restaurant open 7 a.m. to 10 p.m.; bar.

Hotel La Pinta
Motor Inn

2½ miles west of Highway 1 via paved road to outer San Quintín Bay. Mailing address: Apdo Postal 168, Valle de San Quintín, BC 22930, Mexico. Phone 01152 (616) 5-2878; (619) 422-6900; (800) 336-5454. U.S. reservations agent: Mexico Resorts International, 740 Bay Bl, Suite 105, Chula Vista, CA 91910.

All year   1P $60   2P $65

$10 per extra person; 4-person maximum per room. 56 units. Attractive Spanish-style, beach-side hotel. Movies, shower baths; some refrigerators, 2-bed rooms, balconies; no air conditioning. Beach, fishing, tennis. 3-day cancellation notice. Dining room open 7:00 a.m. to 10:30 p.m.; cocktails, bar. MC, VI. **(See ad page 191.)**

Old Mill Motel
Motor Inn

On eastern shore of inner San Quintín Bay, 4 miles west of Highway 1 via unpaved road. Mailing address: Apdo Postal 90, Valle de San Quintín, BC, Mexico. Phone (619) 428-2779; FAX 428-6269; (800) 479-7962. Reservations: 223 Via de San Ysidro, Suite 7, San Ysidro, CA 92173.

All year   1P $30-$60   2P $30-$60

$8 per extra person. Suites $80-$90. 28 units. Motel on site of old grist mill. Shower baths; some kitchenettes; no air conditioning, no TV, no phones. Beach, hunting, swimming, hiking; guide service available. Fishing trips arranged. 2-day cancellation notice. Gasoline and diesel. RV park, $15 per space. Restaurant open 6 a.m. to 9 p.m.; cocktails, bar. **(See ad below.)**

Rancho Sereno Bed and Breakfast ♦ *Bed & Breakfast*
1¼ miles south of the military camp, then 1½ miles west of Highway 1 on dirt road. Phone (909) 982-7087. U.S. reservations agent: 1442 Hildita Ct, Upland, CA 91786.
All year   (B) 1P $45-$55   (B) 2P $50-$60
$10 per extra person. 3 units. Ranch house on tree-shaded grounds. Electricity 8 a.m. to noon and 5 to 9 p.m. Shower baths; no air conditioning, no phones. Kitchen and recreation room with cable TV. Full breakfast served 8 to 10 a.m. Fishing trips arranged. Pets. 10-day cancellation notice. ⊘

▬ Santa Rosalía

Hotel El Morro *Motel*
On Highway 1, 1 mile south of Santa Rosalía ferry terminal. Mailing address: Apdo Postal 76, Santa Rosalía, BCS, Mexico. Phone 01152 (115) 2-0414.
All year   1P $25   2P $30
$5 per extra person; no charge for children under 6. 30 units. Suite available. Spanish-style hotel overlooking Gulf of California. Shower baths, 2-bed rooms, some private patios. Pool. No pets. 10-day cancellation notice. Dining room open Tuesday through Friday and Sunday 7:30 a.m. to 10 p.m., Saturday and Monday noon to 10 p.m.; cocktails, bar.

▬ Tijuana

Lodging

Grand Hotel Tijuana ♦♦♦ *Hotel*
(formerly Fiesta Americana)
At Bl Agua Caliente No 4500, ¼ mile east of Av Rodríguez adjacent to Tijuana Country Club. Mailing address: PO Box BC, Chula Vista, CA 92012. Phone 01152 (66) 81-7000; (800) 472-6385.
All year   1P $80   2P $80
$15 per extra person. 23-story hotel. 422 units. Suites available. Cable TV, radios. Heated pool, sauna, tennis. No pets. 3-day cancellation notice. 2 restaurants (see listing) and coffee shop, open 24 hours; cocktails, bar. AE, CB, DI, MC, VI. Ⓓ Ⓢ ⊘

Hotel Lucerna ♦♦ *Hotel*
At Paseo de los Héroes and Av Rodríguez in the Río Tijuana development. Mailing address: PO Box 437910, San Ysidro, CA 92143. Phone 01152 (66) 34-2000; (800) 582-3762.
All year   1P $66   2P $73-$81
$12 per extra person. Suites $82-$161. Modern 6-story hotel. 168 units. Cable TV, radios. Pool, tennis. No pets. 3-day cancellation notice. Restaurant (see listing) and coffee shop open 7 a.m. to 11 p.m.; cocktails, entertainment. AE, DI, MC, VI.

Hotel Real Del Río   *Hotel*

In Río Tijuana District, 2 blocks west of Av Rodríguez on Calle Velasco. Mailing address: Calle Velasco 409, Tijuana, BC, Mexico. Phone 01152 (66) 34-3100.

All year	1P $65	2P $67

2 suites, $105. 5-story hotel. 105 units. Cable TV. Restaurant open 7 a.m. to 10 pm.; cocktails, bar.

Restaurants

Boccaccio's   ♦♦ *Italian*

Near the Tijuana Country Club at Bl Agua Caliente 2500. Phone 01152 (66) 86-2266.

$10 to $28. Open 1 p.m. to midnight. Closed major holidays. Seafood, steaks and pasta. Cocktails. MC, VI.

Grand Bistrot Restaurante   ♦♦♦ *Continental*

At Bl Agua Caliente No 4500, ¼ mile east of Av Rodríguez in the Grand Hotel Tijuana. Phone 01152 (66) 81-7014.

$20 to $32. Open Monday through Saturday from 6 p.m. to midnight. Closed Sundays and major holidays. Elegant dining room features continental cuisine, prime rib a specialty. Cocktails. AE, CB, DI, MC, VI.

Rívoli   ♦♦♦ *French*

At Paseo de los Héroes and Av Rodríguez in the Hotel Lucerna. Phone 01152 (66) 84-2000.

$13-$29. Varied menu. Open 7 a.m. to 11 p.m. Closed major holidays. Cocktails. AE, MC, VI.

Tour de France   ♦♦♦ *French*

On Calle Gobernador Ibarra and Highway 1, across from Hotel Palacio Azteca. Phone 01152 (66) 81-7542.

$15 to $25. Open 1:30 to 10:30 p.m., Friday until 11:30 p.m. Several small dining rooms and patio. Cocktails. Closed Sunday.■

Campgrounds and Trailer Parks

For many visitors to Baja California, camping is an enjoyable and economical way to travel. In response to the need for information on campgrounds and trailer parks along the peninsula, and because it is generally inadvisable to camp in non-designated sites along major highways, the Auto Club has prepared these listings as a convenience to travelers.

CAMPING FACILITIES

Camping facilities in Baja California range from primitive sites with no amenities to fully developed recreational vehicle parks. Since the completion of the Transpeninsular Highway, many fully equipped private campgrounds and RV parks have been built for vacationers in popular resort areas. Their facilities generally approximate those of their U.S. counterparts; rates are somewhat lower. In addition, the Mexican government has built several trailer parks along Highway 1 as a convenience to travelers. Trailer parks and campgrounds are authorized to lease rental space for long-term parking so that repeat visitors are able to leave their trailers and motorhomes in Mexico between visits.

Despite the easy accessibility brought about by the Transpeninsular Highway, camping in Baja California requires careful preparation. Supplies are readily available only in the northern and southern areas of the peninsula; they are difficult to obtain in the sparsely populated mid-section of Baja California. Campers should therefore plan to be as self-sufficient as possible. Potable drinking water is scarce and should be carried, along with plenty of radiator water. Campers will also find it convenient to carry their own disposable trash bags. Travelers with recreational vehicles should bring extra fan belts, hoses and other parts, as well as tools. Tires, including spares, should be in good condition and regularly checked for air pressure. Since Highway 1 is generally narrow and without turnouts or solid shoulders, it is a good idea to carry flares in case of breakdown. For a complete list of what to take with you, see the Suggested Supply Lists in the *Appendix*.

Trash and waste from recreational vehicle disposal tanks should be disposed of only at designated locations. This makes collection easier and protects the scenic environment. Trash and litter of all kinds constitute an increasing problem in Baja California, particularly along the roads and on the beaches.

For more adventuresome (and self-sufficient) campers, the Mexican government has designated many spots along Baja California's scenic shoreline as *playas públicas* (public beaches). These primitive camping areas supposedly charge a small fee, usually $2 to $4 per night, but the fee is not always collected. Many have no facilities, but some have *palapas* (umbrella-shaped shelters built with dried palm fronds), trash cans and pit toilets. A few are operated by concessionaires; these generally have more facilities and charge a slightly higher fee. The most popular and accessible of the *playas públicas* are listed in this publication.

ABOUT THE LISTINGS

Each of the campgrounds and trailer parks listed in this section has been inspected by a representative of the Automobile Club of Southern California. Those which meet AAA standards are listed with the symbol ✓ before the name. All listings are as complete as possible, based on information available at our publication deadline. Considering Baja California's rapid rate of growth, however, travelers should keep in mind that changes may have occurred, particularly regarding rates and facilities.

Even at well-equipped trailer parks, facilities, maintenance and services may not be up to U.S. standards. Hookups occasionally aren't usable because of generator breakdowns; when this happens, the price is sometimes lowered. Many trailer parks lack telephones. Tap water is not suitable for drinking. Bathroom facilities are sometimes rustic and crowded. In addition, some of Baja California's campgrounds and trailer parks do not have English-speaking employees. Travelers should make use of a basic Spanish phrase book; some useful phrases and words are found in the Speaking Spanish section of the *Appendix*.

The Automobile Club of Southern California cannot guarantee the rates, services, maintenance or facilities of any campground or trailer park described in this publication.

Sites are listed alphabetically by city. The following abbreviations are used to denote hookups: **E**=electricity; **W**=water; **S**=sewer. All campgrounds and trailer parks are open all year unless otherwise noted.

In the mailing addresses of the following campgrounds, *BC* is the abbreviation for the state of Baja California and *BCS* stands for the state of Baja California Sur.

Bahía Concepción

Bahía El Coyote *(playa pública)*

17½ miles south of Mulegé off Highway 1; just after "Rcho El Coyote," turn at sign with beach symbol and go south ½ mile. No phone.
$3 to $4 per vehicle. On shore of the bay. Pit toilets, cabañas.

El Requesón *(playa pública)*

27 miles south via Highway 1 and unpaved road. No phone.
$3 per vehicle. Attractive location on sandspit that links beach with offshore island. Pit toilets, cabañas, palapas.

Playa Santispac *(playa pública)*
13½ miles south of Mulegé via Highway 1 and unpaved road. No phone.
$4 per vehicle. On beautiful Santispac Cove, part of Bahía Concepción. Flush toilets, showers, palapas, two cafes.

✓ Posada Concepción
15 miles south on Highway 1. Mailing address: Apdo Postal 14, Mulegé, BCS, Mexico. No phone.
$10 for 2 persons; $2 each additional person. Landscaped area overlooks the bay. 13 RV sites and area for tents. Hookups: EWS-13; electricity 10 a.m. to 10 p.m. Flush toilets, showers, spa, tennis, beach, skin diving, fishing trips arranged, boat ramp.

Bahía de los Angeles

Guillermo's Trailer Park
On the shore of the bay. Mailing address: Montes de Oca No 190, Fraccionamiento Buenaventura, Ensenada, BC, Mexico. No phone.
$6 for 2 persons, $1 each additional person. 40 RV sites. Hookups: EWS-15; electricity 7 to 11 a.m. and 5 to 9:30 p.m. Flush toilets, showers, beach, restaurant, bar, gift shop. Fishing trips arranged; boat ramp and boat rental. **(See ad below.)**

La Playa RV Park
On the shore of the bay. Mailing address: 509 Ross Dr, Escondido, CA 92029. Phone (619) 741-9583.
$10 for 2 persons, $3 each additional person. 30 RV sites, extensive area for tents. Hookups: E-30; disposal station. Electricity 7 a.m. to 9:30 p.m. Disposal station. Flush toilets, showers, fishing with guide, boat launch, ice, restaurant, bar.

Cabo San Lucas

Club Cabo
3 miles east of town center; turn east off Highway 1 on road to Club Cascadas. Mailing address: Apdo Postal 463, Cabo San Lucas, BCS, Mexico. Phone 01152 (114) 3-3348.

$10 to $15 ror 2 persons, $4 to $7 each additional person. RV park and motel rooms in open area. 8 RV sites, 4 RV or tent sites. E-12, WS-8. Flush toilets, showers.

El Arco Trailer Park

2 miles east of town on Highway 1. Mailing address: Km 5.5, Cabo San Lucas, BCS, Mexico. Phone 01152 (114) 3-1686.
$10 per site. Open area with view of Cabo San Lucas Bay. 85 RV or tent sites. EWS-65. Flush toilets, showers, laundry, pool, restaurant, bar.

El Faro Viejo Trailer Park

¾ mile northwest of town center near Highway 19, at Matamoros and Mijares. Mailing address: Apdo Postal 64, Cabo San Lucas, BCS 23410, Mexico. Phone 01152 (114) 3-4211.
$12 for 2 persons, $3 each additional person. Partly shaded area surrounded by wall. 19 RV or tent sites. Hookups: EWS-19. Flush toilets, showers, restaurant, bar.

✓ Vagabundos del Mar RV Park

1½ miles northeast of town center on Highway 1. Mailing address: Apdo Postal 197, Cabo San Lucas, BCS, Mexico. Phone 01152 (114) 3-0290.
$15 for 2 persons, $3 each additional person. 10-day cancellation notice. 95 RV sites. Hookups: EWS-95. Flush toilets, showers, laundry, pool.

✓ Villa Serena RV Park

4 miles east of town center on Highway 1, by Villa Serena Hotel. Mailing address: Apdo Postal 111, Cabo San Lucas, BCS, Mexico. Phone 01152 (114) 3-0509; (800) 932-5599.
$14 for 2 persons, $2 each additional person. 42 RV sites. Hookups: EWS-42. Flush toilets, showers, pool, whirlpool, gym, laundry, restaurant, bar. AE, MC, VI.

Ciudad Constitución

Campestre La Pila

1½ miles south of town center via Highway 1 and ½ mile west on unpaved road. Mailing address: Apdo Postal 261, Ciudad Constitución, BCS 23600, Mexico. Phone 01152 (113) 2-0562.
$8 for 2 persons; $2 each additional person. Open area bordered by irrigated farmland. 70 RV or tent sites. Hookups: E-32, disposal station. Flush toilets, showers, pool, picnic area, snack bar.

Colonia Guerrero

Mesón de Don Pepe

1 mile south via Highway 1. Mailing address: Apdo Postal 7, Colonia Guerrero, BC 22920, Mexico. Phone 01152 (616) 6-2216.
$6 to $8 for 2 persons; $2 each additional person; tents $4. Partly-shaded area adjacent to highway. 35 RV sites, 20 tent sites. Hookups: EWS-35. Flush toilets, showers, fishing, restaurant, bar; tourist information.

Posada Don Diego
1 mile south via Highway 1 and unpaved road, past first RV park. Mailing address: Apdo Postal 126, Colonia Guerrero, BC 22920, Mexico. Phone 01152 (616) 6-2181.
$9 for 2 persons; $1.50 each additional person. Pleasant area in rural setting. 80 RV or tent sites. Hookups: EW-80, S-60. Disposal station. Flush toilets, showers, laundry, ice, restaurant, bar, sports playfields.

—

El Pescadero

Los Cerritos RV Park
1½ miles south on Highway 19, then 1½ miles southwest via a dirt road. No phone.
$4 per vehicle. Wide beach on shore of the Pacific Ocean. 50 RV or tent sites. Flush toilets.

—

Ensenada

Campo Playa RV Park
1 mile southeast of downtown Ensenada, near intersection of Bl Lázaro Cárdenas and Calle Agustín Sanginés (Delante). Mailing address: Apdo Postal 21, Ensenada, BC, Mexico. Phone 01152 (617) 6-2918.
$10 for 2 persons, $2 each additional person. Fenced area near bay. 85 RV or tent sites. Hookups: E-60, WS-85. Flush toilets, showers, rec room.

✓ Estero Beach Trailer Park
8 miles south via Highway 1 and paved side road (signs posted at turnoff). Mailing address: Apdo Postal 86, Ensenada, BC, Mexico. Phone 01152 (617) 6-6225.
$12 to $16 for 2 persons; $3 each additional person. 3-day cancellation notice. Large seaside resort adjacent to Estero Beach Hotel. 58 RV sites, 50 tent sites. Hookups: EWS-58. Disposal station. Flush toilets, showers, private beach, boat launch, fishing, tennis, playground, clubhouse, restaurant, bar. MC, VI.

Playa Saldamando
On beach 10½ miles north via Highway 1 and steep, winding dirt road. Mailing address: 3965 College Av, San Diego, CA 92115. Phone (619) 286-4289.
$6 for 4 persons, $1 each additional person. 30 tent or RV sites. Disposal station. No hookups. Flush toilets, showers. No motorcycles.

San Miguel Village (Villa de San Miguel)
In El Sauzal, 8 miles north via Highway 1-D. On Bahía de Todos Santos, just south of toll gate. Mailing address: Apdo Postal 55, El Sauzal, BC 22760, Mexico. Phone 01152 (617) 4-6225.
$8 to $10 per vehicle. 30 RV sites, 100 tent sites. Hookups: EWS-30. Flush toilets, showers, beach, restaurant, bar, gift shop.

Guerrero Negro

Malarrimo Trailer Park
1 mile west of Highway 1 on east edge of town, next to Malarrimo Restaurant. Phone 01152 (115) 7-0250.
$8 for 2 persons, $2 each additional person. Open area. 22 RV sites. Hookups: EW-22. Flush toilets, showers, restaurant, bar. Whale-watching trips arranged, $30 per person.

La Paz

✓ Aquamarina RV Park
1½ miles southwest of city center, ½ mile off Highway 1 on Calle Nayarit. Mailing address: Apdo Postal 133, La Paz, BCS, Mexico. Phone 01152 (112) 2-3761.
$13 for 2 persons; $2 each additional person. Nicely landscaped area on the bay. 19 RV sites. EWS-19. Flush toilets, showers, laundry, pool, fishing trips, marina, boat ramp and storage. Fishing trips, boat trips and scuba diving arranged. MC, VI.

✓ Casa Blanca RV Park
3 miles southwest of town center on Highway 1, corner of Av Delfines. Mailing address: Apdo Postal 681, La Paz, BCS, Mexico 23000. Phone 01152 (112) 4-0009.
$13 for 2 persons; $2 each additional person. Partly shaded area surrounded by wall. 45 RV sites. Hookups: EWS-33. Flush toilets, showers, laundry, store, pool, tennis, rec room.

El Cardón Trailer Park
2½ miles southwest of city center on Highway 1. Mailing address: Apdo Postal 104, La Paz, BCS 23000, Mexico. Phone 01152 (112) 2-0078, FAX 2-1261.
$8 to $10 for 2 persons; $2 each additional person. 3-day cancellation notice. Shaded area surrounded by wall. 80 RV sites, 10 tent sites. Hookups: EWS-80. Flush toilets, showers, laundry, ice, pool, rec room, fishing trips.

✓ La Paz Trailer Park
2 miles southwest of city center off Highway 1, on Brecha California, in residential area. Mailing address: Apdo Postal 482, La Paz, BCS, Mexico. Phone 01152 (112) 2-8787.
$13 for 2 persons, $3 each additional person. 3-day cancellation notice. 48 RV sites, 5 tent sites. Hookups: EWS-48. Flush toilets, showers, laundry, pool, spa, groceries, tennis, rec room, bar. Fishing trips arranged, boat ramp nearby. AE, MC, VI.

Oasis Los Arípez Trailer Park
On La Paz bay, 9½ miles before central La Paz when approaching from the north, in the town of El Centenario, on Highway 1. Mailing address: Km 15 Transpeninsular Norte, La Paz, BCS, Mexico. No phone.

$10 for 2 persons; $2 each additional person. 7-day cancellation notice. 22 RV or tent sites. Hookups: EWS-29. Flush toilets, showers, laundry, beach, fishing, restaurant, bar.

La Salina

✓ Outdoor Resorts of Baja-Ensenada
On beach facing Pacific Ocean, 14 miles north of Ensenada off Highway 1-D. Mailing address: Apdo Postal 1492, La Salina, BC, Mexico. Phone 01152 (662) 0-1983.
$24 to $35 for 4 persons; $5 each additional person. 15-day cancellation notice. 134 RV sites. Hookups: EWS-134. Flush toilets, showers, pool, spa, tennis, laundry, groceries, restaurant, bar. MC, VI.

Loreto

✓ Loremar RV Park
½ mile south of town plaza on beach. Mailing address: Colonia Zaragoza, Loreto, BCS 23880, Mexico. Phone 01152 (113) 5-0711.
$11 for 2 persons, $2 each additional person; tent sites $8. 36 RV sites, 36 tent sites. Hookups: EWS-36. Flush toilets, showers, fishing, boat ramp, restaurant, bar.

Playa Juncalito *(playa pública)*
13 miles south of Loreto via Highway 1 and unpaved road. No phone.
$2 per vehicle. Attractive beach and view of mountains. No facilities.

Los Barriles

Martín Verdugo's Trailer Park
On beach of Bahía de Palmas, ½ mile east of Highway 1. Mailing address: Apdo Postal 17, Los Barriles, BCS 23501, Mexico. Phone 01152 (114) 1-0054.
$9 to $11 for 2 persons, $1 each additional person. Partially shaded area. 69 RV sites, 25 tent sites. Hookups: EWS-69. Flush toilets, showers, laundry, pool. Fishing trips arranged, boat launch. Restaurant and bar adjacent.

✓ Playa de Oro RV Resort
On beach of Bahía de Palmas, ½ mile east of Highway 1. Phone (818) 336-7494. Reservations: 3106 Capa Dr, Hacienda Heights, CA 91745.
$9 for 2 persons, $2 each additional person. 30-day cancellation notice. 54 RV sites, 2 tent sites. Hookups: EWS-54. Flush toilets, showers, boat ramp, laundry, ice, fishing, boating.

Mulegé

Hotel Serenidad Trailer Park
Near mouth of river, 2 miles southeast of town off Highway 1. Phone 01152 (115) 3-0530.
$10 for 2 persons; $2 each additional person. Partly shaded area next to the hotel. 15 RV or tent sites. Hookups: EWS-15. Disposal station. Flush toilets, showers, pool, tennis, boat ramp, restaurant, bar, rec room. Fishing trips arranged.

✓ The Orchard RV Park/Huerta Saucedo
½ mile south via Highway 1. Mailing address: Apdo Postal 24, Mulegé, BCS, Mexico. Phone 01152 (115) 3-0300.
$11 to $14 for 2 persons; $2 each additional person. Partly shaded area near river. 46 RV sites, 30 tent sites. Hookups: EWS-46. Disposal station. Flush toilets, showers, tennis, boat ramp, fishing.

✓ Villa María Isabel Trailer Park
1¼ miles south via Highway 1. Mailing address: Apdo Postal 5, Mulegé, BCS, Mexico. Phone 01152 (115) 3-0246.
$10 for 2 persons, $2 each additional person; tent site with palapa, $4 per person. Partly shaded area on river. 25 RV sites, 10 tent sites. Hookups: EWS-25. Disposal station. Flush toilets, showers, pool, laundry, bakery, recreation area, fishing, boat launch.

Puerto Escondido

✓ Tripui Resort RV Park
15 miles south via Highway 1 and paved side road, near Puerto Escondido. Mailing address: Apdo Postal 100, Loreto, BCS 23880, Mexico. Phone 01152 (113) 3-0818; FAX 3-0828.
$13 for 2 persons; $5 each additional person. 3-day cancellation notice. Landscaped grounds with large sites. 31 RV sites. Hookups: EWS-31. Flush toilets, showers, pool, groceries, gift shop, tennis, playground, restaurant, bar.

Punta Banda

La Jolla Beach Camp
8 miles west of Maneadero on BCN 23, on shore of Bahía de Todos Santos. Mailing address: Apdo Postal 102, Punta Banda, BC 22791, Mexico. No phone.
$6 for 2 persons; $2 each additional person. 120 RV sites, 80 tent sites. Hookups: E-20. Extension cords available. Disposal station. Flush toilets, showers, beach, boat launch, tennis, rec room, groceries, propane.

Villarino Camp
8 miles west of Maneadero on BCN 23, on shore of Bahía de Todos Santos. Mailing address: Apdo Postal 842, Ensenada, BC 22800, Mexico. Phone 01152 (667) 6-4246.
$10 for 2 persons; $4 each additional person. 100 RV or tent sites. Hookups: E-50, W-100, S-50. Flush toilets, showers, beach, boat ramp, groceries, cafe.

▬
Punta Chivato

Punta Chivato Campground
On Punta Chivato, 13 miles north of Mulegé via Highway 1, then 13½ miles east on graded dirt road. Phone 01152 (115) 3-0188.
$5 per vehicle. On the beach, open sites. 40 RV or tent sites; disposal station, no hookups. Pit toilets, cold showers. Groceries, gasoline. Fishing trips arranged in pangas. Office at Hotel Punta Chivato nearby.

▬
Rosarito

KOA Rosarito
7 miles north via Highway 1-D (San Antonio exit, east side of highway). Mailing address: PO Box 430513, San Ysidro, CA 92143. Phone 01152 (611) 3-3305.
$17 for 2 persons; $1 each additional person. 3-day cancellation notice. Grassy, partly-shaded sites on bluff overlooking ocean. 65 RV or tent sites. Hookups: EWS-65. Disposal station. Flush toilets, showers, laundry, playground, rec room, groceries, curio shop. Restaurant and bar nearby.

✓ Oasis Resort
On ocean beach 3 miles north off Highway 1-D, toll road (northbound, San Antonio exit; southbound, Oasis exit). Mailing address: PO Box 158, Imperial Beach, CA 91933. Phone 01152 (661) 3-3255; (800) 462-7472.
$30 to $35 for 2 persons. 7-day cancellation notice. 55 RV sites. Hookups: EWS-55. Flush toilets, showers, laundry, groceries, pool, sauna, whirlpool, tennis, playground, gym, restaurant, bar.

▬
San Felipe

Campo San Felipe Trailer Park
In town on the bay shore. Mailing address: 301 Av Mar de Cortez, San Felipe, BC 21850, Mexico. Phone 01152 (657) 7-1012.
$12 to $17 for 2 persons, $2 each additional person; tents $10. 34 RV or tent sites; 10 additional tent sites. Hookups: EWS-34. Flush toilets, showers, beach, billiard room, ice.

Club de Pesca Trailer Park

1 mile south of town center at end of Av Mar de Cortez. Mailing address: Apdo Postal 90, San Felipe, BC, Mexico. Phone 01152 (657) 7-1180.

$12 to $15 for 2 persons, $2 each additional person. Large landscaped park on gulf shore. 30 RV or tent sites; additional area on beach for large number of tents. Hookups: EW-30, disposal station. Flush toilets, showers, boat launch and storage, groceries.

Faro Beach Trailer Park

On Punta Estrella, 10 miles southeast of town via paved road. Mailing address: Apdo Postal 107, San Felipe, BC 21850, Mexico. No phone.

$25 per vehicle. Large, attractively landscaped park on terraced slope overlooking Gulf of California. 135 RV or tent sites. Hookups: EWS-135. Flush toilets, showers, pool, tennis, rec room, ice, bar.

La Jolla Trailer Park

½ mile west of town center at Manzanillo and Mar Bermejo in residential area. Mailing address: PO Box 978, El Centro CA 92244. Phone 01152 (657) 7-1222.

$15 for 2 persons, $2.50 each additional person. Sites with canopies. 55 RV or tent sites. Hookups: EWS-55. Flush toilets, showers, pool, spa, laundry, ice.

✓ Mar del Sol RV Park

1½ miles south of town center on Misión de Loreto, adjacent to Hotel Las Misiones. Phone 01152 (657) 7-1280; (619) 472-6767; in California (800) 336-5454. Reservations: 4126 Bonita Rd, Bonita, CA 91902.

$13 to $23 for 2 persons, $3 each additional person; children under 12 free. 3-day cancellation notice. Unshaded sites on attractive beach. 85 RV sites, 30 tent sites. Hookups: EWS-85. Flush toilets, showers, pool, whirlpool, boat launch, laundry, groceries. All hotel facilities open to campers. MC, VI.

Playa Bonita Trailer Park

1 mile north of town center via Av Mar de Cortez. Phone 01152 (657) 7-1215; (909) 595-4250. Reservations: 529 S Alvarado St, Los Angeles, CA 90057.

$17 per site. Picturesque area on beach with rocky hills behind. 29 RV or tent sites. Hookups: EWS-29. Flush toilets, showers. Fishing trips arranged.

Playa de Laura RV Park

In town at Av Mar de Cortez 333, San Felipe, BC, Mexico. Phone 01152 (657) 7-1128.

$13 to $18 for 2 persons, $2 each additional person. 45 RV sites, 10 tent sites. Hookups: EW-45, S-25.

Ruben's Trailer Park

1 mile north of town center via Av Mar de Cortez. Mailing address: Golfo de California 703, San Felipe, BC 21850, Mexico. Phone 01152 (657) 7-1091.

$12 to $15 for 2 persons, $2 each additional person. Picturesque area on gulf shore with rocky hills behind. 58 RV or tent sites. Hookups: EWS-58. Flush toilets, showers, beach, boat launch, fishing, laundry, restaurant, bar.

San Felipe Marina Resort RV Park
3 miles south of town on road to airport. Mailing address: 233 Paulin Av, Box 5366, Calexico, CA 92231. Phone 01152 (657) 7-1435.
$20 for four persons, $4 each additional person. 143 RV sites (motorhomes and trailers only). Hookups: EWS-143. Flush toilets, showers, laundry, restaurant, bar, rec room, pool, beach.

Vista del Mar RV Park
¾ mile north of town center on Av Mar de Cortez overlooking the bay. Mailing address: 233 Paulin Av, Box 5582, Calexico, CA 92231. Phone 01152 (657) 7-1252.
$12 for 2 persons, $3 each additional person. 21 RV or tent sites with shaded tables. Hookups: EWS-20. Flush toilets, showers.

▬
San Ignacio

La Candelaria Trailer Park
1 mile south of Highway 1 off entrance road to San Ignacio. Turn right just beyond Hotel La Pinta, then go ½ mile southwest over rough dirt road. No phone.
$3 per vehicle. Scenic area in a large grove of date palms. 30 RV or tent sites. Several palapas; no other facilities.

Trailer Park El Padrino
1 mile south of Highway 1 on entrance road to San Ignacio, just beyond Hotel La Pinta. Mailing address: Ctra Transpeninsular Km 0.5, San Ignacio, BCS 23930, Mexico. Phone 01152 (115) 4-0089.
$7 to $9 per space. 30 RV sites. Hookups: E-9, WS-20. Flush toilets, showers, restaurant, bar; tourist information.

▬
San José del Cabo

Brisa del Mar RV Resort
2 miles southwest of town center on Highway 1. Mailing address: Apdo Postal 45, San José del Cabo, BCS, Mexico. No phone.
$9 to $15 for 2 persons; $2 each additional person. Fenced area on beautiful beach facing Gulf of California. 112 RV or tent sites. Hookups: EW-40, S-80. Flush toilets, showers, pool, laundry, restaurant, bar.

▬
San Quintín

Enrique's/El Pabellón RV Park
9 miles south of Lázaro Cárdenas and 1 mile west of Highway 1 via dirt road. No phone.
$5 per vehicle. Open area with access to beach. 15 RV or tent sites; additional tent sites on beach. Hookups: W-27. Flush toilets, showers. Fishing trips arranged.

Santa Rosalía

✓ Las Palmas RV Park

2 miles south on Highway 1. Mailing address: Apdo Postal 123, Santa Rosalía, BCS, Mexico. Phone 01152 (115) 2-2270.
Rate for 2 persons: $10 RV, $6 tent; $1 each additional person. Grass sites. 30 RV or tent spaces. Hookups: E-5, W-30, S-21. Flush toilets, showers, laundry, restaurant, bar.

San Lucas Cove RV Park

9 miles south via Highway 1 and unpaved road. Mailing address: Apdo Postal 50, Santa Rosalía, BCS, Mexico. No phone.
$6 per vehicle. Open area adjacent to beach. 75 RV or tent sites. No hookups. Limited shower and toilet facilities. Disposal station, beach, fishing, boat ramp, restaurant.

Santo Tomás

El Palomar Trailer Park

North edge of the village on Highway 1 in olive tree-shaded area. Mailing address: Apdo Postal 595, Ensenada, BC, Mexico. Phone 01152 (617) 7-0650.
$10 for 2 persons; $2 each additional person. 50 RV sites and large area for tents. Hookups: EWS-25. Flush toilets, showers, pool, hunting, tennis, groceries, restaurant, bar, curio shop, gas station.

Todos Santos

El Molino Trailer Park

At southern end of town near Highway 19, behind Pemex station. Mailing address: Rangel y Villarino y Verduzco, Todos Santos, BCS 23300, Mexico. Phone 01152 (112) 5-0140.
$10 for 4 persons. 21 RV sites. Hookups: EWS-21. Flush toilets, showers, laundry.

San Pedrito RV Park

5 miles south on Highway 19 and 2 miles southwest via dirt road. Mailing address: Apdo Postal 15, Todos Santos, BCS, Mexico. Phone 01152 (112) 2-4520.
Rate for 2 persons: $13 RV, $3 tent; $2 each additional person. Open area on the shore of the Pacific. 71 RV or tent sites. Hookups: EWS-51. 8 cabañas. Flush toilets, showers, pool, laundry, recreation area, restaurant, bar.■

GET EVERYTHING FOR YOUR TRIP. FREE.

Maps, TourBooks® & Area Guides

Fee-Free American Express® Travelers Cheques

AIRLINE TICKETS

Complete Airline & Travel Reservations

Car Rental Reservations & Discounts

Hotel/Motel Reservations & Discounts

Dependable Emergency Road Service

Join the Auto Club of Southern California today and we'll give you everything you need for your trip. ✦ Free maps ✦ Free TourBooks®, CampBooks® and area guides ✦ Fee-free American Express® Travelers Cheques and ✦ Free Triptiks®, a personalized, mile-by-mile routing of your entire trip. And you'll love saving money with Member-only discounts on ✦ Tours and cruises ✦ Hotel/motel reservations ✦ Rental cars and ✦ Popular attractions across the country. All of these great travel benefits can be yours for a low annual membership fee. So why wait? Join AAA today and get everything for your trip. Free!

Call 1-800-882-5550, Ext. 145 (Outside So. CA: 1-800-AAA-HELP)

Associate memberships for your spouse and children are available for a nominal fee. Membership dues are subject to change without notice.

CAMPGROUNDS AND TRAILER PARKS

Geographical Index

The following is a complete listing of the place names that occur within this publication. Places with names printed in boldface type offer lodging or camping facilities; detailed listings for some of these names appear in the *Lodging & Restaurants* and *Campgrounds & Trailer Parks* chapters. A boldface page number denotes the primary reference of a particular place.

Index to Advertisers

For information about placing an advertisement in Automobile Club of Southern California publications, please contact:

Karen Clyne or Ginger Nichols
Publication Sales, H076
Automobile Club of Southern California
P.O. Box 2890
Los Angeles, CA 90099-4005
(213) 741-3571
FAX (213) 741-3489